THE POLITICS OF MUNIFICENCE
IN THE ROMAN EMPIRE

In the first two centuries AD, the eastern Roman provinces experienced a proliferation of elite public generosity unmatched in their previous or later history. In this study, Arjan Zuiderhoek attempts to answer the question why this should have been so. Focusing on Roman Asia Minor, he argues that the surge in elite public giving was not caused by the weak economic and financial position of the provincial cities, as has often been maintained, but by social and political developments and tensions within the Greek cities created by their integration into the Roman imperial system. As disparities of wealth and power within imperial polis society continued to widen, the exchange of gifts for honours between elite and non-elite citizens proved an excellent political mechanism for deflecting social tensions away from open conflicts towards communal celebrations of shared citizenship and the legitimation of power in the cities.

ARJAN ZUIDERHOEK is a lecturer in Ancient History at Ghent University.

GREEK CULTURE IN THE ROMAN WORLD

Editors
SUSAN E. ALCOCK, Brown University
JAŚ ELSNER, Corpus Christi College, Oxford
SIMON GOLDHILL, University of Cambridge

The Greek culture of the Roman Empire offers a rich field of study. Extraordinary insights can be gained into processes of multicultural contact and exchange, political and ideological conflict, and the creativity of a changing, polyglot empire. During this period, many fundamental elements of Western society were being set in place: from the rise of Christianity, to an influential system of education, to long-lived artistic canons. This series is the first to focus on the response of Greek culture to its Roman imperial setting as a significant phenomenon in its own right. To this end, it will publish original and innovative research in the art, archaeology, epigraphy, history, philosophy, religion, and literature of the empire, with an emphasis on Greek material.

Titles in series:

Athletics and Literature in the Roman Empire
Jason König

Describing Greece: Landscape and Literature in the Periegesis *of Pausanias*
William Hutton

Religious Identity in Late Antiquity: Greeks, Jews and Christians in Antioch
Isabella Sandwell

Hellenism in Byzantium: The Transformations of Greek Identity and the Reception of the Classical Tradition
Anthony Kaldellis

The Making of Roman India
Grant Parker

Philostratus
Edited by Ewen Bowie and Jaś Elsner

The Politics of Munificence in the Roman Empire: Citizens, Elites and Benefactors in Asia Minor
Arjan Zuiderhoek

THE POLITICS OF
MUNIFICENCE IN THE
ROMAN EMPIRE

Citizens, Elites and Benefactors in Asia Minor

ARJAN ZUIDERHOEK

CAMBRIDGE
UNIVERSITY PRESS

CAMBRIDGE
UNIVERSITY PRESS

University Printing House, Cambridge CB2 8BS, United Kingdom

One Liberty Plaza, 20th Floor, New York, NY 10006, USA

477 Williamstown Road, Port Melbourne, VIC 3207, Australia

314-321, 3rd Floor, Plot 3, Splendor Forum, Jasola District Centre, New Delhi - 110025, India

79 Anson Road, #06-04/06, Singapore 079906

Cambridge University Press is part of the University of Cambridge.

It furthers the University's mission by disseminating knowledge in the pursuit of education, learning and research at the highest international levels of excellence.

www.cambridge.org
Information on this title: www.cambridge.org/9781108994033

First published 2009
First paperback edition 2021

A catalogue record for this publication is available from the British Library

Library of Congress Cataloging in Publication data
Zuiderhoek, Arjan, 1976–
The politics of munificence in the Roman Empire : citizens, elites, and benefactors in Asia Minor / Arjan Zuiderhoek.
p. cm. – (Greek culture in the Roman world)
Includes bibliographical references and index.
ISBN 978-0-521-51930-4 (hbk. : alk. paper) 1. Greece – History – 146 B.C.–323 A.D. 2. Roman provinces – History. 3. Greece – Social conditions. 4. Roman provinces – Social conditions. 5. Elite (Social sciences) – Greece – History. 6. Social classes – Greece – History. 7. Benefactors – Greece – History 8. Gifts – Political aspects – Greece – History. 9. City and town life – Greece – History. 10. Rome – History – Empire, 30 B.C.–476 A.D. I. Title. II. Series.
DF240.Z85 2009
939'.2 – dc22 2008053773

ISBN 978-0-521-51930-4 Hardback
ISBN 978-1-108-99403-3 Paperback

For Irene

Contents

Maps, tables and figures

ix

Acknowledgements

I could not have written this book without the generosity of others. Onno van Nijf, who supervised the thesis on which the book is originally based, was and continues to be a source of inspiration and encouragement. Always ready to discuss and challenge my ideas, he frequently caused me to rethink large parts of the argument. It was he who introduced me to the fascinating world of the eastern Roman Empire, and who first taught me some Greek epigraphy, ten years ago on a sunny afternoon in Cambridge. I have not looked back since.

Wim Jongman has been a constant source of intellectual stimulus and support, both scholarly and practical, throughout the years, from my first undergraduate venturings into ancient history until this day. He read through, and meticulously corrected, the original thesis version of this book, and along the way provided me with some invaluable suggestions. The book is much the better for it.

Special thanks should also go to Ed van der Vliet. Over the years, I have profited greatly from his wide knowledge of matters ancient and anthropological, and from his ever-present and infectious enthusiasm for new ideas, however unorthodox or challenging. He too provided me with some priceless advice for the argument presented in this book.

Peter Garnsey was my mentor while I was in Cambridge, at first formally, when I was a student there, and later informally, when I returned as a Junior Research Fellow. Friendly and gentle, he allowed me the benefit of his great learning. In discussions, and as an external examiner to the original thesis, he provided me with a score of helpful suggestions. Without his encouragement, this book might perhaps not have been.

Many others provided help as well, by reading (portions of) the manuscript at various stages, by sending me comments, on the book or on work connected to it, or simply by discussing my ideas with me or helping me solve certain problems. In particular (but in no particular order) I would like to thank Luuk de Ligt, Harry Pleket, Ruurd Nauta,

Jan Willem Drijvers, Robin Osborne, Stephen Mitchell, Olivier Hekster, Rens Tacoma, Wytse Keulen, Chris Dickenson, Richard Alston, Bert Overbeek, Marlies Schipperheijn, Maaike Leemreize, Tjark Blokzijl, Taco Terpstra, Herman Paul, Vincent Tassenaar, Richard Johns, Djoeke van Netten, Vincent van Zuilen, Marcin Moskalewicz, Richard Paping, Richard Toye and the anonymous reader for Cambridge University Press.

My gratitude also goes to the institutions that made possible the writing of this book, the History Department at the University of Groningen, where I wrote a first draft as a graduate student, and in particular Homerton College, Cambridge, for awarding me a Junior Research Fellowship which allowed me largely to complete the book in its present form. An Assistant Professorship at Ghent University has now made it possible to add the finishing touches. In addition, I am grateful to Michael Sharp and particularly to Liz Noden at Cambridge University Press for their expert help and advice in guiding a first-time author towards publication, and to Iveta Adams for her meticulous copy-editing.

My greatest debt, however, I owe to my wife Irene, without whose love and support I could not even have begun my research. This book is for her.

Abbreviations

Abbreviations of names and works of Greek and Roman authors are according to the *Oxford Classical Dictionary*.

AM	*Mitteilungen des Deutschen Archäologischen Instituts. Athenische Abteilung*
Aphrodisias & Rome	J. M. Reynolds, *Aphrodisias and Rome: documents from the excavation of the theatre at Aphrodisias* (*JRS* Monographs 1; London: Society for the Promotion of Roman Studies, 1982)
BCH	*Bulletin de Correspondance Hellénique*
BE	*Bulletin Épigraphique* (in: *Revue des Études Grecques*)
CIG	*Corpus Inscriptionum Graecarum*
CIL	*Corpus Inscriptionum Latinarum*
de Hoz	M. P. de Hoz, *Die lydischen Kulte im Lichte der griechischen Inschriften* (Bonn: Habelt, 1999)
FE	*Forschungen in Ephesos*
I.Arykanda (*IK* 48)	S. Şahin, *Die Inschriften von Arykanda* (*IK* 48; Bonn: Habelt, 1994)
I.Assos (*IK* 4)	R. Merkelbach, *Die Inschriften von Assos* (*IK* 4; Bonn: Habelt, 1976)
IBM	*Greek inscriptions in the British Museum*
I.Ephesos (*IK* 11–17)	H. Wankel, R. Merkelbach *et al.*, *Die Inschriften von Ephesos* (*IK* 11–17; Bonn: Habelt, 1979–81)
IG	*Inscriptiones Graecae*
IGR	R. Cagnat, *Inscriptiones Graecae ad res Romanas pertinentes* (Paris: Leroux, 1911–27)

I.Histria	D. M. Pippidi, *Inscriptiones Scythiae Minoris Graecae et Latinae* I: *Inscriptiones Histriae et viciniae* (Bucharest: Romanian Academy, 1983)
IK	*Inschriften griechischer Städte aus Kleinasien*
I.Kibyra (*IK* 60)	Th. Corsten, *Die Inschriften von Kibyra* (*IK* 60; Bonn: Habelt, 2002)
I.Kyme (*IK* 5)	H. Engelmann, *Die Inschriften von Kyme* (*IK* 5; Bonn: Habelt, 1976)
I.Perge (*IK* 54)	S. Şahin, *Die Inschriften von Perge* (*IK* 54; Bonn: Habelt, 1999)
I.Priene	F. Hiller von Gaertringen, *Die Inschriften von Priene* (Berlin: Georg Reimer, 1906)
I.Selge (*IK* 37)	J. Nollé and F. Schindler, *Die Inschriften von Selge* (*IK* 37; Bonn: Habelt, 1991)
I.Side (*IK* 44)	J. Nollé, *Side im Altertum* II (*IK* 44; Bonn: Habelt, 2001)
I.Stratonikeia (*IK* 21–2)	M. Ç. Sahin, *Die Inschriften von Stratonikeia* (*IK* 21–2; Bonn: Habelt, 1981–90)
I.Tralleis (*IK* 36.1)	Fj. B. Poljakov, *Die Inschriften von Tralleis und Nysa* I: *Die Inschriften von Tralleis* (*IK* 36.1; Bonn: Habelt, 1989)
Jahresh. (*JÖAI*)	*Jahreshefte des Österreichischen Archäologischen Instituts*
Judeich	C. Humann, C. Cichorius, W. Judeich and F. Winter, *Altertümer von Hierapolis* (Berlin: Georg Reimer, 1898)
KP	J. Keil and A. von Premerstein, *Bericht über eine (zweite, dritte) Reise in Lydien*, in: *Denkschriften der Kaiserlichen Akademie der Wissenschaften in Wien (Phil. Hist. Klasse)* LIII.2, 1908 (I); LIV.2, 1911 (II); LVII.1, 1914 (III)
Lanck.	K. Lanckoronski, G. Niemann and E. Petersen, *Städte Pamphyliens und Pisidiens* (Vienna, 1890–2)
Laum II	B. Laum, *Stiftungen in der griechischen und römischen Antike. Ein Beitrag zur antiken Kulturgeschichte, zweiter Band: Urkunden* (Berlin: Teubner, 1914)

LW	Ph. Le Bas and W. H. Waddington, *Voyage archéologique en Grèce et en Asie Mineure* (Paris: Didot, 1870)
Malay, *Researches*	H. Malay, *Researches in Lydia, Mysia and Aiolis* (Ergänzungsbände zu den *Tituli Asiae Minoris* nr. 23; Vienna: Verlag der Österreichischen Akademie der Wissenschaften, 1999)
MAMA	*Monumenta Asiae Minoris Antiqua*
Mus. Iznik (Nikaia) (IK 9)	S. Şahin, *Katalog der antiken Inschriften des Museums von Iznik (Nikaia)* (IK 9; Bonn: Habelt, 1979)
OGIS	W. Dittenberger, *Orientis Graeci Inscriptiones Selectae* (Leipzig: Hirzel, 1903–5)
PAS	*Papers of the American School of Classical Studies at Athens*
P. Oxy.	*The Oxyrhynchus Papyri*
RE	A. Pauly and G. Wissowa (eds.) *Paulys Real-Encyclopädie der classischen Altertumswissenschaft* (Stuttgart: Metzler, 1894–1972)
RECAM III	S. Mitchell (with ass. of D. French and J. Greenhalgh), *Regional Epigraphic Catalogues of Asia Minor* III: N. P. Milner, *An epigraphical survey of the Kibyra-Olbasa region conducted by A. S. Hall* (British Institute of Archaeology at Ankara Monograph 24; Oxford: Oxbow, 1998)
REG	*Revue des Études Grecques*
Robert, *Ét. An.*	L. Robert, *Études Anatoliennes. Recherches sur les inscriptions grecques de l'Asie Mineure* (Paris: De Boccard, 1937)
R.Ph.	*Revue de Philologie*
SEG	*Supplementum Epigraphicum Graecum*
Syll.[3]	W. Dittenberger, *Sylloge inscriptionum Graecarum* (3rd edn; Leipzig: Hirzel, 1924)
TAM	*Tituli Asiae Minoris*

ADDITIONAL ABBREVIATIONS USED IN APPENDIX I

AE	*L'Année Épigraphique*
Heberdey (1923)	R. Heberdey, 'Gymnische und andere Agone in Termessus Pisidiae' in: W. H. Buckler and W. M. Calder (eds.) *Anatolian studies presented to Sir William Mitchell Ramsay* (Manchester University Press, 1923), 195–206
I. Adramytteion (IK 51)	J. Stauber, *Die Bucht von Adramytteion* II. *Inschriften, literarische Testimonia, Münzen* (*IK* 51; Bonn: Habelt, 1996)
I.Anazerbos (IK 56)	M. H. Sayar, *Die Inschriften von Anazerbos* (*IK* 56; Bonn: Habelt, 2000)
I.Erythrae u. Klazomenai (IK 1–2)	H. Engelman and R. Merkelbach, *Die Inschriften von Erythrae und Klazomenai* (*IK* 1–2; Bonn: Habelt, 1972–3)
I.Hadrianoi u. Hadrianeia (IK 33)	E. Schwertheim, *Die Inschriften von Hadrianoi und Hadrianeia* (*IK* 33; Bonn: Habelt, 1987)
I.Iasos (IK 28)	W. Blümel, *Die Inschriften von Iasos* (*IK* 28; Bonn: Habelt, 1985)
I.Ilion (IK 3)	P. Frisch, *Die Inschriften von Ilion* (*IK* 3; Bonn: Habelt, 1975)
I.Keramos (IK 30)	E. Varinlioglu, *Die Inschriften von Keramos* (*IK* 30; Bonn: Habelt, 1986)
I.Kios (IK 29)	Th. Corsten, *Die Inschriften von Kios* (*IK* 29; Bonn: Habelt, 1985)
I.Lampsakos (IK 6)	P. Frisch, *Die Inschriften von Lampsakos* (*IK* 6; Bonn: Habelt, 1978)
I.Laod. Lyk. (IK 49)	Th. Corsten, *Die Inschriften von Laodikeia am Lykos* (*IK* 49; Bonn: Habelt, 1997)
I.Magnesia	O. Kern, *Die Inschriften von Magnesia am Maeander* (Berlin: Spemann, 1900)
I.Magnesia am Sipylos (IK 8)	T. Ihnken, *Die Inschriften von Magnesia am Sipylos* (*IK* 8; Bonn: Habelt, 1978)
I.Mylasa (IK 34–5)	W. Blümel, *Die Inschriften von Mylasa* (*IK* 34–5; Bonn: Habelt, 1987–8)
I.Parion (IK 25)	P. Frisch, *Die Inschriften von Parion* (*IK* 25; Bonn: Habelt, 1983)
I.Prusa ad Olymp. (IK 39)	Th. Corsten, *Die Inschriften von Prusa ad Olympum* I (*IK* 39; Bonn: Habelt, 1991)

I.Prusias ad Hypium (*IK* 27)	W. Ameling, *Die Inschriften von Prusias ad Hypium* (*IK* 27; Bonn: Habelt, 1985)
I.Rhod. Per. (*IK* 38)	W. Blümel, *Die Inschriften der rhodischen Peraia* (*IK* 38; Bonn: Habelt, 1991)
I.Sestos (*IK* 19)	J. Krauss, *Die Inschriften von Sestos und der thrakischen Chersones* (*IK* 19; Bonn: Habelt, 1980)
I.Smyrna (*IK* 23–4)	G. Petzl, *Die Inschriften von Smyrna* (*IK* 23–4; Bonn: Habelt, 1982–90)
Milet	A. Rehm (with H. Dessau and P. Herrmann), *Inschriften von Milet* (Deutsches Archäologisches Institut; Berlin: De Gruyter, 1997)
Mon. Ant.	*Monumenti Antichi*
Robert, *Ét. Épigr.*	L. Robert, *Études épigraphiques et philologiques* (Paris: Champion, 1938)
Term. Stud.	R. Heberdey, *Termessische Studien* (Vienna and Leipzig: Hölder-Pichler-Tempsky, 1929)

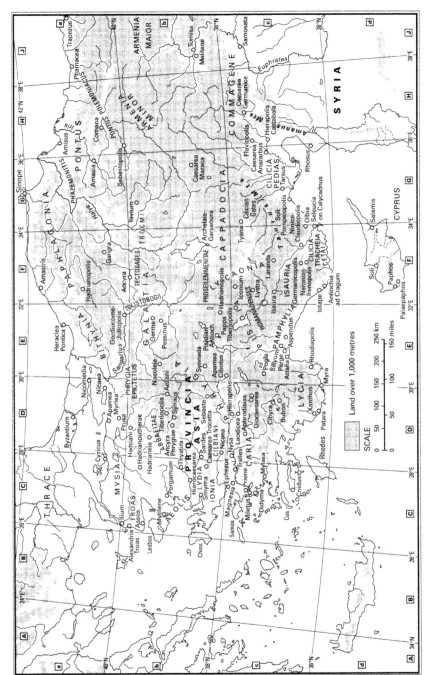

Roman Asia Minor

Introduction

This book concentrates on a central paradox of Roman social and political life under the Empire: how a society of such breathtaking inequality could produce an elite whose generosity towards their communities was, in terms of its sheer scope and extent, probably unique in the history of pre-industrial civilisations. The book focuses on Roman Asia Minor, an area particularly rich in cities, inscriptions and benefactors, but I wish to suggest tentatively that at least some of its conclusions could serve as working hypotheses for the study of euergetism in other regions of the Empire.

The boom in elite public giving visible in the cities of the Roman Empire from the later first century AD onwards was unprecedented. When it was over, in the early third century, it was never repeated on the same scale, although euergetism remained an element in civic politics during the later Empire. Historians have often sought to explain euergetism by interpreting it as the economic cornerstone of civic life. According to this (very common) interpretation, the private wealth of elite benefactors was instrumental in financing the public infrastructure of the Empire's cities, which themselves were unable to draw in sufficient revenues to pay for the necessary amenities from public money.[1] Other scholars have viewed euergetism as an ancient precursor to Christian charity and the modern welfare state.[2] According to yet another highly influential study, benefactors primarily gave to satisfy a psychological need to be generous, and to emphasise the social distance between themselves and their non-elite fellow citizens.[3] They did not, however, expect a return; their generosity was, in that sense, disinterested.

In this book, I argue that none of these interpretations stands entirely up to scrutiny, particularly because of their essential inability to provide a

---

[1] See Chapters 2 and 3 for references.
[2] In particular Hands (1968). For more detailed discussion see pp. 32–3.
[3] Veyne (1976). See pp. 113–14.

sufficient explanation for the unprecedented proliferation of munificence in the provincial cities during the early and high Empire. This remarkable boom in public giving should, I argue, at least in the eastern Roman provinces, be seen first and foremost as a political and ideological reaction of urban elites and their non-elite fellow citizens to certain social and political developments within civic society (primarily a growing concentration of wealth in the hands of local elites, and an increasing social and political oligarchisation/hierarchisation of civic life) generated by the integration of the cities into the Roman imperial system.

It is perhaps useful to state at the outset what this book is not. It is not a thorough empirical survey of euergetism as it existed in all its local and regional variations over the course of time across the whole of Asia Minor, nor is it an epigraphic study of the various types of documents that are our main source for the study of euergetism. Rather, the book is perhaps best described as a long, interpretative essay that aims to provide the broad outlines of an overall model for analysing the remarkable boom in public giving in the provincial urban societies of the early and high Empire. Roman Asia Minor is used as a first testing ground for some of the model's propositions. If the main elements of the model stand up to this test, and turn out to be of some use for the investigation of euergetism in other parts of the Empire, the book will have served its purpose.

CHAPTER I

Introducing euergetism: questions, definitions and data

The council (*boule*) and the people (*demos*) of Aphrodisias and the council of elders (*gerousia*) have set up in the midst of his public works this statue of Marcus Ulpius Carminius Claudianus, son of Carminius Claudianus high priest of (the League of) Asia who was grandfather and great-grandfather of (Roman) senators; honoured on many occasions by the emperors, he was husband of Flavia Apphia high priestess of Asia, mother and sister and grandmother of senators, devoted to her native city, (worthy) daughter of the city and of Flavius Athenagoras, imperial procurator who was father, grandfather and great-grandfather of senators; he himself was the son of a high priest of Asia, father of the senator Carminius Athenagoras, grandfather of the senators Carminii Athenagoras, Claudianus, Apphia and Liviana, treasurer of Asia, appointed curator of the city of Kyzikos as successor to consulars, high priest, treasurer, chief superintendent of temple fabric, and lifelong priest of the goddess Aphrodite, for whom he established an endowment to provide the priestly crown and votive offerings in perpetuity; for the city he established an endowment of 105,000 denarii to provide public works in perpetuity, out of which 10,000 denarii were paid for the seats of the theatre, and the reconstruction of this street on both sides from its beginning to its end, from its foundations to its wall coping, has felicitously been begun and will continue; in the gymnasium of Diogenes he built the anointing room with his personal funds and, together with his wife Apphia, he walled round the great hall and entrances and exits; he supplied at his own expense all the sculptures and statues in his public works; he also provided the white-marble pillars and arch together with their carvings and the columns with their tori and capitals; he established an endowment for the distribution of *honoraria* in perpetuity to the most illustrious city council and the most sacred council of elders; he often distributed many other donatives to the citizens, both those living in the city and those in the countryside; he often distributed other donatives to the whole city council and council of elders; he often made free gifts on every occasion, in keeping with the city's

wishes, to citizens and aliens alike; he installed numerous drains in
the swamps on the occasion of the channelling of the Timeless river;
he often and felicitously carried out embassies; he was all his life long
a devoted benefactor of his city.

He just recently contributed an additional 5,000 denarii for the
public work, making a total of 110,000 denarii.[1]

The honorific inscription for Carminius Claudianus, set up in Aphrodisias
some time around AD 170, offers a lively and detailed snapshot of the public generosity unceasingly displayed by the notables of Rome's provincial
cities during the early and high Empire. This phenomenon, christened
'euergetism' by modern ancient historians, after the Greek honorific title
euergetes (benefactor) that was often bestowed on publicly generous members of the civic elite, was so widespread, and is therefore so familiar to
scholars studying Roman provincial civic life and culture, that many tend
to take it rather for granted; indeed, given euergetism's sheer ubiquity in
the epigraphic record, and the fact that it ties in with so many other aspects
of civic life, it can sometimes be hard not to. Yet it is precisely the sheer
omnipresence of elite public generosity in Roman imperial cities, the fact
that it jumps out at us wherever we look, that is truly its most remarkable
feature, especially from a comparative perspective. Few societies in human
history have been quite so socially unequal as the Roman Empire. Most of
its wealth was controlled by a tiny elite of senators, knights and local town
councillors, all in all perhaps 5 per cent of the Empire's population.[2] The
gap between rich and poor was truly breathtaking. We can see this clearly
when we compare the minimum fortune legally required of a town councillor (*decurio/bouleutes*), 100,000 *sestertii*, with the subsistence budget of a
poor Roman: the curial census requirement would have sufficed to provide
for over 800 Romans at a level of bare subsistence for a year.[3] Within the
elite too, stratification was extremely steep: the minimum census requirement for a knight was HS 400,000, for a senator HS 1 (or 1.2) million.[4]
Yet senators often owned quite a lot more than that: the Younger Pliny's

[1] *CIG* 2782. Translation by Lewis (1974) 91–2, slightly adapted.
[2] See Jongman (2003) for some speculative quantification.
[3] Or for over forty Romans 'for ever', on the assumption of 5 per cent revenue per annum on
landed possessions, for which see Duncan-Jones (1982) 33. My estimate of the Roman annual
subsistence ration is based on the assumption that subsistence needs equal 250 kg wheat equivalent
per person/year. A wheat price of HS 3 per *modius* of 6.55 kg then puts the costs of one year's
subsistence at HS 115, or about 30 denarii. Annual subsistence need of 250 kg wheat equivalent: Clark
and Haswell (1970) 57ff. and 175; Hopkins (1980) 118 with note 51. Wheat price of HS 3 per *modius*:
Rostovtzeff, *RE s.v. frumentum*, 149; Hopkins (1980) 118–19; Duncan-Jones (1982) 51; Jongman (1991)
195 with note 2.
[4] Duncan-Jones (1982) 4.

fortune has been estimated at HS 20 million, and he is often considered a senator of middling wealth.[5]

And yet the Empire's elites, and in particular its local civic elites, displayed a public generosity unmatched by the upper classes of most other pre-industrial societies. Particularly during the period stretching from the late first into the early third centuries AD, elite gift giving flourished as never before or after in Roman society. Elite benefactors and their gifts are everywhere, all over our records, whether epigraphic or literary. We cannot escape them. This state of affairs begs a large question, and this book is an attempt to answer it: why was there such an unprecedented proliferation of elite public giving in the provincial cities of the Roman Empire during the late first, second and early third centuries AD? The question is all the more pertinent because by Roman imperial times euergetism already had a long history behind it, with origins in the early Hellenistic period, and some roots going much further back still, arguably to the liturgy system of Classical Athens, and the aristocratic gift-exchange of Homeric and Archaic Greece.[6] My answer is that the extreme popularity of civic euergetism during the early and high Empire resulted from the fact that the phenomenon was indispensable for the maintenance of social harmony and political stability in the Empire's provincial cities at a time when these communities experienced a growing accumulation of wealth and political power at the very top of the social hierarchy. To a large measure, the well-being and stable functioning of the Empire depended on the vitality of its cities, and their success in accomplishing the vital tasks of tax gathering, local administration and jurisdiction. Hence, from this perspective, euergetism's contribution to civic socio-political stability may well have been one of the keys to the survival and flourishing of the Roman imperial system as a whole during the first two centuries AD. The rise, and eventual fall, of the Roman Empire may have had as much to do with the (changing) behaviour of its local urban elites as with the level of depravity of its emperors, or the absence or presence of barbarian hordes waiting beyond its borders.

I will focus primarily on the public generosity displayed by the provincial elites of Roman Asia Minor during the early and high Empire. This area I shall use as a case study for the Empire more widely. In the chapters that follow, I shall first review some common arguments deployed by historians

---

[5] Duncan-Jones (1982) 17–32.

[6] On the Hellenistic origins of euergetism and the connections with archaic largesse and the Athenian system of liturgies see Veyne (1976) 186–228. On Hellenistic euergetism in general see e.g. Gauthier (1985); Quass (1993); Migeotte (1997).

to account for the centrality of euergetism in Roman imperial civic life, and argue why they are mostly unsatisfactory. After that, I will outline my own interpretation, which concentrates on the political and ideological side of munificence. First, however, we need to define our subject more closely (What precisely was euergetism?). Also the choice of Asia Minor and its local elites as the subject of a case study needs justification. Furthermore, to avoid confusion, we need clear definitions of the various collective social actors involved (Who precisely were the elite, or the demos?). Finally, I shall provide an overview of the data I have gathered on elite benefactions in Roman Asia Minor, primarily to elucidate the main chronological patterns in the evidence, so as to illustrate that the second century AD was indeed the era of euergetism's greatest proliferation in Asia Minor. These will be the subjects of the present chapter.

WHAT WAS EUERGETISM?

First some brief remarks on the historiography of the term itself. The term, or concept, 'euergetism' is a neologism, invented by modern ancient historians. It was first used in a work by A. Boulanger on Aelius Aristides and the sophists in Asia Minor and by H.-I. Marrou in his well-known study of Greek and Roman education. Its true fame came much later, however, with the seminal study of Paul Veyne.[7] The word derives, as we saw, from the Greek *euergetes*, or benefactor, an honorific title awarded to generous elite individuals, which we frequently encounter in inscriptions, and from the phrase *euergetein ten polin*, 'making a benefaction to the city'. In ancient Greek, *euergesia* was the term commonly used for a benefaction. The Latin *liberalitas* and the Greek *philotimia* cover much the same ground as the modern term euergetism, but both have wider connotations that make them less precise and therefore less suitable for analytical purposes. Hence, in this study I too shall employ the term (civic) euergetism or equivalents such as 'civic munificence' and 'elite public generosity'.

In my definition, euergetism was a form of gift-exchange between a rich citizen and his (occasionally her) city/community of fellow citizens, or groups within the citizenry. To make this definition more explicit, we can take the benefactions of Carminius Claudianus of Aphrodisias, listed in his honorific inscription quoted above, as our guide. The exchange between

---

[7] Boulanger (1923) 25; Marrou (1948); Veyne (1976), esp. 20 with note 7.

a benefactor and his/her community was commonly one of gifts for honours. Thus Carminius Claudianus provided endowments to Aphrodite for perpetual sacrifices, and to the city for public works. He financed reconstruction work on the theatre, made a major contribution to the Diogenes gymnasium and helped to restore and embellish the city's buildings and infrastructure in numerous ways. He gave distributions to the city council and the council of elders (*gerousia*), and to the citizens on a number of occasions, and even helped with the draining of swampland. As an influential member of the local and provincial elite of equestrian rank, with many individuals of senatorial rank in his immediate family, he was also well placed to act as ambassador to the emperor for his city, which he did on several occasions, apparently with good result. With these benefactions, especially his contributions to public buildings such as the theatre and gymnasium, and his distributions, Carminius Claudianus by and large moved in the mainstream of civic munificence in Roman Asia Minor.[8]

What did he get in return for all his generosity? Like virtually all public benefactors, he received a statue from the city, 'set up in the midst of his public works', with the long honorific inscription quoted above probably carved on its base. No doubt the act of setting up this statue with its inscription had been a public ceremony in itself, which involved a public honouring of the benefactor in the company of all his fellow citizens, and perhaps, as often happened on such occasions, the demos had even chanted in his praise (see Chapter 6 for a discussion of such honorific acclamations). Even though statues and honorific inscriptions were nearly universally awarded to civic benefactors, other honours are also known. Thus for example Q. Veranius Tlepolemos was honoured 'with a gold crown and a bronze portrait bust, with first- and second-degree honours and front seating for life at public spectacles' for his benefactions towards the city of Xanthos in Lycia around AD 150, while in AD 52/3 Eratophanes, son of Chareinos, was honoured by the Rhodians 'with a gold crown and statue as well as the dedication of a silver bust', and by the inhabitants of the city of Kys in Caria 'with the highest honours provided by the law' for his generosity towards both communities.[9] The honours, especially the inscriptions and public acclamations, were by no means empty rhetorical gestures. As we shall see in Chapter 6, these public honours were a vital ideological instrument for affirming the legitimacy of the existing

---

[8] See Chapter 5, pp. 76–7 and Fig. 5.1.
[9] For Tlepolemos see *IGR* III 628, for Eratophanes Smallwood (1967) 135, translation by Lewis (1974) 84–5.

socio-political order in the cities. They afforded the non-elite citizenry a means of expressing consent with the current division of power in society, while allowing the elite ample scope for self-representation as its 'natural' leading caste.

To be sure, Carminius Claudianus of Aphrodisias was not in all respects entirely representative of civic munificence in the Roman provinces. It is true that he by and large gave the things most other benefactors in Roman Asia Minor gave (see Chapter 5, Fig. 5.1), but he gave rather a lot. The combined value of his gifts was 110,000 denarii, or HS 440,000, that is, more than the minimum legal property requirement of a Roman knight (which Claudianus was), and over four times that of a city councillor, and this in one round of gifts![10] Generosity of this magnitude puts Claudianus more or less in the middle range between, on the one hand, donors like C. Vibius Salutaris of Ephesos, who donated a festival foundation to his city worth 21,500 denarii, and, on the other, truly magnificent benefactors such as Ti. Claudius Erymneus of Aspendus, who spent 2 million denarii on an aqueduct for his city, or Opramoas of Rhodiapolis in Lycia, Menodora from Sillyon in Pamphylia or Publia Plancia Aurelia Magniana Motoxaris of Selge, each of whom made donations to a value of about a million denarii.[11] As I will show in Chapter 2, however, elite benefactors able to make donations worth tens to hundreds of thousands of denarii or (far) more were comparatively rare, and they should not be seen as emblematic of civic munificence in general. Nor are the very long inscriptions that some of these extraordinary individuals received entirely representative of the type of honorific inscription that we most frequently encounter in the records of munificence. Far closer to what we typically come across is, for instance, the following (probably) second-century AD text from Hierokaisareia:

The council and people honoured Stratoneike daughter of Apollonides son of Protomachos, the priestess of Artemis, who behaved piously and generously [φιλοδόξως, implying that she made a contribution from her own money] during the festival of the goddess.[12]

---

[10] At 5 per cent annual return on landed property, this sum suggests that Carminius Claudianus must have owned property worth at least 2.2 million denarii, or HS 8.8 million, i.e. more than eight times the minimum senatorial census requirement. As this calculation is based on the patently absurd assumption that Claudianus spent his entire annual income on munificence, in reality he must have been considerably richer still.

[11] For Ti. Claudius Erymneus see *IGR* III 804, for Opramoas *IGR* III 739; *TAM* 578–9; Kokkinia (2000), with the comments of Coulton (1987) 172. For Menodora see Lanck. 1 nos. 58–61; *IGR* III 800–2 with van Bremen (1996) 109, for Motoxaris *I.Selge* (*IK* 37) 17 with van Bremen (1996) 100–3 and 109.

[12] For the text, translation and comments see Malay, *Researches* no. 51.

Or the following, early third-century, one from Smyrna:

To good fortune! The most famous city and metropolis, in beauty and greatness
the first in Asia, three times temple warden of the *Augusti* following the decrees of
the most holy Senate, and the pearl of Ionia, the city of Smyrna, his beloved fatherland, (honours) Iulius Menekles Diophantos, who as Asiarch shiningly donated
gladiatorial games with sharp swords (which lasted) for five days.[13]

Whether benefactors contributed just one column to a temple or financed
an entire gymnasium or large annual festival, what is important to remember is that they were involved in a strongly ideologically charged process
of exchange with their (non-elite) fellow citizens. A public benefaction,
together with the honours received in return for it, constituted a public,
political act, with very specific political and ideological aims and consequences. It is this interpretation of euergetism as a form of politics that I
shall try to defend in this study, because I believe that only such a definition provides us with a key to explaining the unprecedented proliferation
of public generosity in the Empire's provincial cities during the late first,
second, and early third centuries AD.

As will have become clear from the above, I do not deal in this book
with every form of gift-giving modern historians have from time to time
designated with the term euergetism. Instead I primarily focus on what
might be called *civic* euergetism, which should be taken to encompass every
instance when a member of the local or provincial elite used his (or her)
private wealth or power in such a way that people conceived it to be a public
gift or contribution to the city, the citizenry or groups of citizens. Such civic
euergetism is the type of munificence we encounter most frequently in our
sources, and, I would like to stress, it is to *this* type of munificence that
the argument concerning euergetism's role and function in civic society
developed in this study applies. Of course, there existed other forms of
gift-giving behaviour that are also often grouped under the heading of
euergetism. I refer, for instance, to the small bequests of money to *collegia*
or other private clubs we hear about, often with the attached obligation to
use it for financing the performance of commemorative acts at the donor's
gravesite,[14] or to gifts by city grandees to their native village or to country
shrines.[15] I also leave out of account benefactions by the emperor,[16] and the

---

[13] *I.Smyrna* (*IK* 23–4) 637.
[14] For good discussion of this category of small foundations for private commemoration, mostly
involving the performance of funerary rites at the donor's gravesite, see Andreau (1977) 180ff.
[15] On rural euergetism, mainly with respect to the donation of domanial market facilities, see briefly
de Ligt (1993) 176–8. Note also the discussion in Schuler (1998) 278ff.
[16] On which see e.g. Veyne (1976) part IV.

euergetism of members of the imperial elite (senators and knights), except if the latter acted in their capacity as members of the local elite of their native town. I am aware of the fact that the boundaries between what I define as civic euergetism and the types of munificence just mentioned cannot always be drawn very clearly, but as a sort of working definition of the type of munificence most frequently attested in our sources, and the type on which I wish to focus in this study, civic euergetism as I have just described it will probably do. Euergetism had a long history, originating in the early Hellenistic period, and during the course of this history it assumed many shapes and forms, but only in its most common civic variety did it begin to play a very specific political and ideological role in Roman provincial civic society during the late first and second centuries AD. It is on this political function of civic euergetism during the period just referred to that I wish to concentrate in this study.

I should also add that my definition of civic euergetism is one that consciously and deliberately takes in forms of public expenditure by the rich that are usually termed liturgies (i.e costs associated with an office, which the holder was supposed to pay for out of his own pocket). I have a clear reason for defining the subject thus broadly, and that has much to do with what was, I think, the perspective of contemporaries on what precisely constituted an act of civic munificence. When one goes through the sources, it quickly becomes evident that, for the ancients, a wide and fairly flexible gamut of acts could, depending on circumstances, qualify as public benefactions. Of course there were some main trends in gift-giving, but on the whole the ancient conception of civic euergetism seems to have been fairly fluid. This fluidity had a clear function, which quickly becomes apparent when we interpret civic euergetism primarily as a form of politics and ideological ritual, aimed at easing social tensions, for it allowed parties to present a fairly wide range of actions and behaviours as acts of civic munificence, and hence to increase the amounts of social (prestige), political and ideological benefit that could be reaped from them. Thus, civic euergetism allowed pent-up political energies that otherwise might have been (and sometimes were) spent in fierce social conflicts between elite and non-elite groups to be transferred into a process of subtle and skilled political negotiation over gifts and counter-gifts between benefactors, their fellow elite-members and the demos. Such negotiation could take a variety of forms. Non-elite citizens could aim to please elite members by deliberately interpreting certain of their actions as benefactions and grant them honours for these, thus hoping to accumulate goodwill and extract more future benefactions from the elite individuals in question.

But it was only when the civic community (i.e. fellow elite-members and the demos) had accepted a certain contribution as constituting a public gift that it would qualify as an act of civic euergetism and generate the appropriate honours. Donors proposed gifts, but were in fact dependent on the outcome of the power games involving themselves, their peers and the demos, which were set in train by their proposals. Making a public donation did not automatically turn you into an *euergetes*; only public acceptance of your gift and the granting of the appropriate honours could do that.

To sum up, it was a political process (and a range of ideological conceptions that played a role in that process) that determined which act would qualify as civic euergetism.[17] Thus the fulfilment of a liturgy could qualify as a benefaction as easily as the apparently more spontaneous contributions modern historians usually designate with the term, especially in those cases where the liturgist spent more of his own money than law or custom required. At other times, even the *selling* of grain, albeit at a lower price than the current market price (but, in times of shortage, often at a higher one than the normal market price) could qualify as civic munificence. It is mostly modern historians who make the fine technical distinctions, not the authors of the honorific inscriptions. This is not to say that such modern distinctions have no merit. For the purpose of answering a certain range of, mostly technical, questions, they are even indispensable. However, since I am primarily interested in the ways in which civic euergetism functioned as a political and ideological process, it is the ancient, ideologically charged, perceptions of what counted as a civic benefaction and why which matter most to me, and it is on these that I shall concentrate.

Finally, we should briefly turn to the matter of the sheer variety of interpretations historians have advanced to explain euergetism. In this book, it may seem as if I present a rather monocausal explanation in explicitly relating euergetism to the legitimation of elite rule and the collective affirmation of civic ideals without paying much attention to alternative

---

[17] Hence I can also see little analytical value in retaining the distinction proposed by Veyne (1976) 103 between a more political form of euergetism (*ob honorem*) connected to office holding, such as paying the costs associated with your office out of your own pocket, or 'entrance fees' (*summae honorariae*) for offices and council membership, and 'disinterested' spontaneous gifts by non-office holding members of the elite (*mécénat*). If it was a process of political negotiation between the benefactors, their elite peers and the demos that determined which forms of elite behaviour could be classified as benefactions, then a 'politically disinterested' euergetism is a contradiction in terms. I therefore agree completely with Andreau, Schmitt and Schnapp (1978) 312 when they state that Veyne's distinction between the two kinds of euergetism makes no sense because 'tout l'évergétisme est politique'. For a further discussion of Veyne's views and how they relate to my own interpretation of euergetism see Chapter 6, pp. 113–14.

theories. However, I do acknowledge that scholars have brought forward a variety of interpretations of munificence, and that many of the factors they refer to will have had a role to play. Hence I do not wish to deny, to list only some of the more influential theories, that civic euergetism *was* a field of intense competition among members of local elites, that it was a source of prestige and symbolic capital for individual benefactors, that it was an important part of a specific elite lifestyle, that it did to some extent represent a safety net in times of harvest failure, did sporadically take the form of a contribution to public infrastructure, might sometimes benefit the poor, and so on.[18] My point is rather a different one. All of the theories just mentioned try first and foremost to account for the *existence* of euergetism, and, sure enough, they contribute to our understanding of why euergetism should have been a feature of Greco-Roman life in the first place, just as do my arguments about political legitimation and affirming civic ideals. In this book, however, I am not in the first place concerned with the reasons for euergetism's existence per se, but rather with explaining why we find such a *totally unprecedented proliferation* of elite benefactions in the eastern provincial cities during the early and high Empire. And in explaining not just the existence, but also this peculiar *proliferation*, of munificence, I argue that the factors of political legitimation and collective affirmation of civic ideals must necessarily take precedence over alternative explanations, which, although often insightful, do not provide us with a clear reason why there should have been such an explosion of elite public generosity during precisely this period. Here we have, in fact, the core argument of this book. It will be defended in much detail in Chapters 4, 5 and 6.

WHY ASIA MINOR?

In this study I focus on the Roman east, especially Asia Minor. I have several reasons for doing so. First, even though western areas such as Italy and North Africa have produced large quantities of inscriptions concerning munificence, the bulk of the evidence for civic euergetism during the early Empire is from the east. Asia Minor in particular witnessed a proliferation of public benefactions during the first two centuries AD unmatched in earlier or later periods of Roman history. Since it is precisely this remarkable proliferation of munificence (echoed, no doubt, in other provinces east and west) that this book sets out to explain, Asia Minor almost naturally presents itself as its subject area.

---

[18] See e.g., Gordon (1990); van Nijf (1997) 111ff. (euergetism and symbolic capital); Garnsey (1988) (euergetism as a safety net); Jones (1940) 237; Veyne (1976) 9 (benefactors and civic infrastructure); Hands (1968) (euergetism as charity).

A second reason for my concentration on the east has to do with the social and cultural origins of euergetism. Although later 'exported' to the west, where it easily blended in with the Roman traditions of patronage and (Republican) electoral benefactions, euergetism originated in the Greek world of the Hellenistic east. It represented perhaps the most successful offshoot of the old Greek tradition of generosity of elites amongst themselves or towards their communities, other manifestations of which were Dark Age and Archaic aristocratic largesse and the system of liturgies as it developed in Classical Athens. As I argue in Chapter 6, Greek notions of a 'just' division of power and wealth in society were strongly bound up with ideas of moral excellence. Only individuals who displayed the right set of moral virtues, and were able to show that they possessed them in sufficient quantity, were truly entitled to the possession of wealth and political power. Since this was an activist ethic, meaning that virtue had to show from one's deeds, I argue that elite public generosity (in whatever form) was a crucial instrument in the hands of Greek political leaders to display their innate virtuousness and hence justify their position of power. It is precisely this enduring aspect of Greek political culture as it, since the region's hellenisation, also existed in Asia Minor that provides us with part of the explanation for the unprecedented flourishing of euergetism in the east during the early Empire. As processes of oligarchisation and growing elite wealth put increasing pressure on polis society, an ever more oligarchic and powerful elite increasingly needed to show that their strongly elevated position was indeed the result of their possession of extraordinary amounts of virtue. And what better way to do so than to indulge in ever more sumptuous forms of public munificence? To some extent, very similar developments occurred in the west. There too the political structure of the cities, the cogs in the wheel of the Roman imperial machine, was strongly oligarchic. And yet there too the cities needed the political–ideological fiction that they were organic, closely-knit and cohesive citizen communities (instead of the polarised societies strongly divided by enormous disparities of wealth and political power that they were in reality) to be able to function at all.[19] Yet whereas most western cities were construed as functioning oligarchies from their very beginning, closely modelled as they were on late Republican Rome, the cities of the Greek east, as the socio-political and cultural heirs of Classical Greek civilisation, were still equipped with the full institutional apparatus of the Classical Greek democratic polis (council, assembly, courts). Indeed, the popular assemblies, however much depleted

---

[19] For a recent collection of papers on euergetism in Roman Italy, see Lomas and Cornell (2003).

of political power they might seem when compared to their Classical Athenian forebear, only disappear from view in the eastern provinces some time towards the end of the third century AD.[20] Informal oligarchisation of social and political life in the Greek cities had already begun during the later Hellenistic period, while many cities had never been radical democracies on the Athenian model at all. The informal domination of civic life by a small coterie of wealthy citizens then received legal and constitutional reinforcement with the advent of Roman rule, with Roman provincial legislation backing the transformation of city councils into mini-senates whose members sat for life, and with their families came to form a curial class on the Roman model. And yet, as I said, the eastern cities held on to the institutional structure, and, in their public inscriptions, kept using the political–institutional language, of the Classical democratic polis. Hence nowhere was the tension between the polis ideal of the city as a community of political equals and the stark political and socio-economic inequalities characterising everyday life experienced as strongly as in the Roman east. The proliferation of euergetism was partly an answer to this growing tension, as we shall see, and, crucially, it was also instrumental to the slow but significant change the polis ideal underwent during the high imperial period, as the Classical egalitarian notion of *isonomia* slowly transformed into a vision of the citizen community as a hierarchy of status groups.[21] Inclusion of developments in the west might indeed have cast an even more distinctive light on the specific role of euergetism in the social and political evolution of civic society in the east, yet such inclusion is beyond the scope of this study.[22]

ELITES AND NON-ELITES

Before we turn to a consideration of the data on civic munificence in Roman Asia Minor, one final problem of definition needs perhaps to be addressed, to avoid confusion. When, in this study, I speak of the demos or the non-elite citizenry, I refer to those citizens not belonging to the official political elite of the city. In socio-economic terms, this non-elite citizenry or demos was probably a rather differentiated group,

---

[20] Jones (1940) 177–8.   [21] See Chapter 5.
[22] Note that Veyne (1976) includes discussion of both the Republican electoral benefactions and the munificence of the Roman emperors in his classic, massive study of euergetism, in addition to a long section on benefactions in the Hellenistic and Roman east. Yet he never manages fully to integrate these separate parts of his book. More seriously even, he pays no attention to munificence in the west outside the city of Rome, either in Italy, or in the provinces.

ranging from individuals living at a level just above bare subsistence to individuals whose level of wealth may well have matched that of a lower ranking councillor.[23] The majority of individuals in this group will probably have belonged to what might be called the professional middle ranks of civic society, neither very rich nor very poor, i.e. shop-owners, small-scale traders, money dealers, craftsmen, some owning also some land or real estate, in short, the sort of people we would expect to find in the urban *collegia*,[24] and who would probably also make up the majority of those present during a public assembly.[25] I am well aware of the fact that most cities also counted an unknown number of inhabitants without full citizen status, including slaves, freedmen, resident aliens (metics), dependent non-citizen peasant groups such as could often be found in the surrounding countryside (*chora*) of poleis in Asia Minor, and perhaps some other, less clearly defined, categories. When, in the following chapters, I wish to include such non-citizen groups in the discussion, I explicitly mention them. When, on the other hand, I speak solely of the demos or non-elite citizenry, I mean exactly that: the non-elite *citizens*. The groups without full citizen status are then explicitly left out of consideration.

Conversely, when I speak of 'the elite', 'the civic elite' or 'the *ordo*' or 'bouleutic order', I mean the official political elite of the city, i.e. the citizens who were members of the council and who, together with their families, constituted the *ordo decurionum* or bouleutic order of the city. To be sure, every city would have counted a small number of citizens rich enough to be part of this political elite, who nonetheless, and for various reasons, shied away from magistracies and liturgies, or were legally exempt from taking them up, and hence did not become part of the bouleutic order. Such individuals, however, hardly figure in the sources for civic euergetism. Almost without exception, attested civic benefactors were politically active individuals, mostly belonging to the *ordo*. This is not surprising since it was the latter who really needed the political legitimation that euergetism could supply.[26] The few wealthy individuals who consciously remained outside the political elite had for this very reason not much use for such legitimation, and I shall leave them out of consideration in this study.

---

[23] See pp. 135–7 and Zuiderhoek (forthcoming).
[24] Van Nijf's (1997) study of the professional *collegia* in the Roman east indeed represents an attempt to reconstruct the socio-political position, cultural outlook and world view of precisely this part of the civic population.
[25] See Quass (1993) 355–65; van Nijf (1997) 20.   [26] See Chapter 6.

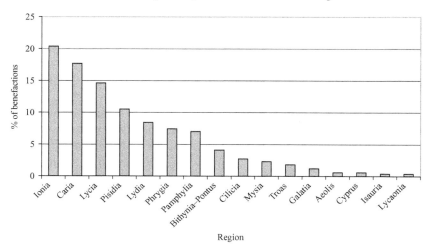

Figure 1.1 Regional distribution of benefactions in Roman Asia Minor (N = 514)

THE DATA

After these preliminary remarks, it is now time to take a closer look at
the raw data for public benefactions in Roman Asia Minor. I shall here
primarily be concerned with the chronological patterns exhibited by the
data. A detailed consideration of what benefactors actually gave follows in
Chapter 5 (for a quick overview see Fig. 5.1).

The empirical core of this study consists of a sample of a little over 500
epigraphically recorded benefactions from Roman Asia Minor.[27] I have
tried to gather them as randomly as possible from the published collections
of inscriptions. The sample has a wide geographical scope, covering most
of the peninsula (see Fig. 1.1). Chronologically, it ranges from just before
the beginning of our era until well into the fourth century AD. Yet, despite
such benefits, we ought to operate carefully. To an unknown extent, the
patterns in our data will reflect modern-day archaeological activity rather
than ancient developments. Archaeologists have tended to be interested
in sites that promised to be rich in finds. Hence, regions that appeared
to harbour few such promising sites (either because they were indeed less

---

[27] For source references see Appendix 1. The sample is – let me repeat – a collection of benefactions,
not a collection of inscriptions recording benefactions. Multiple benefactions recorded on a single
inscription have been listed separately, unless they clearly formed part of one single act of munificence. In assembling the data, I have benefited greatly from earlier collections of material such as
Laum (1914) and Broughton (1938), and from the catalogues of epigraphically attested bath buildings
and festivals provided by Farrington (1995) and Fagan (1999).

prosperous in antiquity, or because you could not so easily spot from the surface that the place once contained some fairly large cities) have suffered comparative neglect. On the other hand, promising sites, i.e. larger and more splendid cities, tend to be situated in relatively urbanised areas. So the fact that, nowadays, we still have more inscriptions from such sites and areas than from others probably more or less reflects ancient conditions, since epigraphy was mostly an urban phenomenon. Still, this last observation does not completely absolve us from taking into account the potentially distorting effects of modern research-preferences on our ancient data set. To mention yet another pitfall, my database has been compiled from *published* inscriptions. Now, as is well known, numerous inscriptions, though excavated and – sometimes – initially reported, remain unpublished, sometimes for long periods. Like archaeologists, epigraphic specialists have their own predilections.[28] Hence, the amount of known material that has been properly published (i.e. in accessible collections with sufficient commentary) varies considerably from region to region. I have had to rely on this published material and on the restorations and comments of the specialists who published it. Again, this reliance on published material may have created distorting effects of unknown magnitude or kind in my data set. The reader should therefore bear in mind that all arguments that follow below and that are based on patterns in the data are to a certain extent provisional and liable to change as more data become available in the future.

CHRONOLOGY

It is well known that the dating of inscriptions is often problematic. Only a relative minority of texts contain information of a sufficiently precise nature to allow us to assign a more or less exact date to them. A larger minority of texts can be dated to the reigns of individual emperors or to imperial dynasties. Many inscriptions, however, have to be dated on the basis of stylistic characteristics of text or monument or on the basis of the archaeological context in which they are found.[29] Needless to say, many such dates are imprecise ('second century AD', or, if one is lucky, 'second half of second century AD') and provisional. Finally, there is a category of texts of which nothing more can be said than that they belong to the imperial

---

[28] Or, equally often, simply lack funds, or a sufficient number of specialist colleagues to carry out all the work. The result is the same: hard choices have to be made.

[29] On the methods of dating Greek inscriptions from the Hellenistic and Roman imperial periods, and the problems involved, see the lucid discussion of McLean (2002) 149–78.

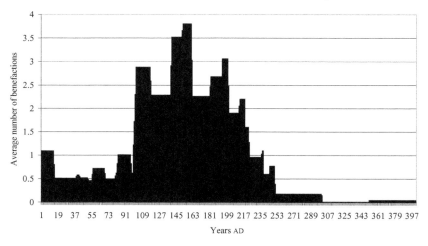

Figure 1.2 Average number of benefactions per year (N = 442)

period. These I have labelled 'not datable' for the purpose of the present enquiry, which is after all limited to the Roman imperial period alone. I have mostly taken over the dates provided by the most recent editions of the inscriptions. Figure 1.2 contains all datable benefactions in the sample, and gives a broad chronology.[30] The graph shows a clear overall rise in the average number of recorded benefactions per year during the second century AD, which lasts until the early decades of the third. An absolute peak occurs around the middle decades of the second century, with two minor peaks during its opening and closing decades. In between are two slight dents. Figure 1.2 however still suffers from some chronological imprecision, since it includes large numbers of benefactions recorded on inscriptions that could only be dated to a century or a half-century. I therefore present a second graph (Fig. 1.3), which only includes benefactions precisely datable to the reign of an individual emperor. The reader should be aware, however, that Fig. 1.3 covers only about 40 per cent of all data in the sample, whereas Fig. 1.2 covers more than 80 per cent. Increased chronological precision thus comes at a price.

---

[30] In order to arrive at the average number of benefactions for each year I somewhat artificially had to 'spread out' the data over centuries, half centuries and reigns respectively. This means that I have calculated averages per year for all benefactions *only* datable to a century (i.e. excluding those also datable to a half-century and/or a reign), those *only* datable to a half-century (excluding those also datable to a reign), and those datable to a reign. Next I added up the results for each year, and this gave me the average total number of benefactions for each year in the period.

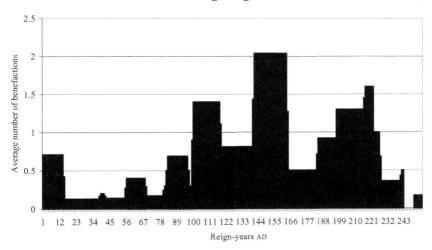

Figure 1.3 Average number of benefactions per reign-year (N = 202)

Figure 1.3 shows us roughly the same pattern for the second/early third-century proliferation of munificence as Fig. 1.2, but with some interesting (minor) differences. The build-up in the early second century, under Trajan, is still visible, as is the dent under Hadrian. We again see the absolute peak during the middle decades of the century, under Antoninus Pius. The dent in the later second century, during the reign of Marcus Aurelius, however appears far more pronounced here than in Fig. 1.2, as does, to some extent, the late second/early third-century (partial) recovery under Commodus and the early Severi. As in Fig. 1.2, decline sets in from the second quarter of the third century onwards.

It is not easy to account for all the irregularities exhibited by the data during the second/early third-century period of euergetism's greatest proliferation. The various peaks and dents may be as much a reflection of patterns in modern-day archaeological and epigraphic scholarship as of ancient reality. Nonetheless, the peak under Antoninus Pius seems in line with the general flowering of provincial civic culture in the east during his reign. More controversially, we may perhaps relate the steep dent under Marcus Aurelius as shown in Fig. 1.3 to the social disruption and high mortality resulting from the series of great smallpox epidemics that affected the Empire during his reign.[31] The early third-century partial recovery

---

[31] See Duncan-Jones (1996). Jongman (2006) in fact argues tentatively that the Antonine plague was a decisive turning point in the social, economic and political history of the Empire.

may then reflect Severan consolidation policies as they affected the eastern provinces, which were however not successful in the longer term, given the decline from the 220s onwards. All this is highly speculative, though we should not therefore dismiss it out of hand.[32] I should note however that at present I am unable to provide a sufficient explanation for the dent in the average number of recorded benefactions per year under Hadrian.[33] What matters most for the argument developed in this study, however, are not so much these irregularities, but the overall pattern exhibited by the data (best visible in Fig. 1.2): an unprecedented proliferation of euergetism during the late first, second and early third centuries AD, and steady decline afterwards. This, moreover, is a chronological pattern also visible in other archaeological data series from the Roman imperial period (see below). Overall, I think it broadly conforms to historical reality.

Before we enter into a discussion of the historical implications of this pattern, however (for which see Chapters 4, 5 and 6), we first have to face one fundamental methodological objection. Benefactions were recorded on inscriptions. And inscriptions, as we have all come to know, were the products of cultural choice. In other words, they were objects of fashion. The question therefore arises: does the chronological pattern we see in Figs. 1.2 and 1.3 represent the rise and fall of civic euergetism, or have we merely constructed a chronology of epigraphic fashion? Have we done no more than just document the rise and fall of the epigraphic habit in Roman Asia Minor?[34] If so, then munificence may well have operated more or less independently from it, sometimes becoming extremely visible to us during the high tide of epigraphic fashion, at other times disappearing from view, but nevertheless continuing. However, I do not think that my graphs merely document changes in the so-called epigraphic habit. I have two reasons for thinking they do not. The first is that the overall pattern we can discern in Fig. 1.2 broadly matches chronological patterns exhibited by other archaeological data series from the imperial period. We can observe a very similar pattern in, for instance, the chronology of dated shipwrecks from the Mediterranean, the construction of public buildings, and the incidence of meat consumption as reconstructed recently by Willem Jongman

---

[32] See the discussion of the third-century decline of euergetism in the Epilogue.

[33] Did the emperor's frequent travelling in the eastern provinces perhaps discourage local benefactors, making them realise that they were simply no match for serious imperial outlay? This is only a suggestion.

[34] For the classic analysis of the 'epigraphic habit' in the Roman Empire see MacMullen (1982); Meyer (1990) for further analysis with reference to epitaphs.

from the distribution of animal bones on datable sites.[35] The pattern is also repeated in the chronology of lead and copper pollution in the Greenland ice cap, which constitutes evidence for the intensity of Roman mining activity.[36] The chronologies of these data series all show roughly the same: a rise during the (later) first century AD, an absolute peak during the second and decline from the late second century or the (middle) third century onwards. The chronology of the epigraphic evidence for munificence from Roman Asia Minor thus more or less conforms to a broad pattern of rise and decline of aggregate production and consumption during the imperial period. Given such correspondence, the claim that the chronological pattern we observe in our data primarily reflects epigraphic fashion becomes much harder to sustain. As one commentator recently observed, it is precisely the convergence between the chronologies of these various data series which inspires confidence in the reality of the overall pattern they reveal, despite the doubts one may harbour with regard to each of them individually.[37]

There is, however, yet another reason why we should discard the epigraphic habit hypothesis. On my interpretation, euergetism consisted of a whole process of politico-ritualistic acts that primarily served to underwrite the ideal of the essential unity and centrality of the – hierarchically structured – citizen community, and the legitimation of the oligarchic division of power within that community. Honorific ritual was a crucial element in this process, and the honorific inscription, in turn, was an absolutely seminal component of honorific ritual. As the final result of the long sequence of giving, receiving and honouring, it was the lasting record of the benefactor's great virtue, his resulting generosity, and the honour and prestige awarded to him (of which the inscription, again, was the physical embodiment). In other words, inscriptions recording benefactions were an element integral to the very phenomenon of euergetism itself. Consequently, when such inscriptions decline in numbers from the early decades of the third century onwards, this means that euergetism in its 'classic' social and political form, as we know it from the Hellenistic period and the early Empire, either gradually disappeared, or underwent a profound transformation. Whichever way, the tentative conclusion would seem to

---

[35] For shipwrecks see Hopkins (1980) 106, and the same data rearranged with a clear peak in the period AD 1–150 in MacMullen (1988) 9, based on Cornell and Matthews (1982) 93. Public buildings: Jouffroy (1986), with Duncan-Jones (1996) 127 (Figs. 10–11). Meat consumption as attested by animal bones deposited per century: Jongman (2006) 245–6; (2007) 613–14, working with data collected by King (1999).

[36] Wilson (2002) 26–7. See now also de Callataÿ (2005).   [37] See Jongman (2006) 246.

be that the decline in recorded benefactions from the 220s onwards might signify the onset of a profound change in political culture, away from the ideological focus on the citizen community towards something new and different.[38] I shall return briefly to this process of cultural transformation in the epilogue to this study.

During the discussion of definitions and data in this chapter I have already sketched some of the main lines of interpretation that I will follow in this study. In the chapters to come, I shall first deal in detail with existing interpretations of euergetism, especially those that aim to explain its imperial proliferation primarily in economic terms, for it is such an economic perspective that still dominates most of the literature on munificence. It is to a consideration of this model, and the ways in which it proves inadequate as an explanation of euergetism's imperial boom, that the next two chapters are devoted. After that I shall turn to my own interpretation of euergetism and a consideration of the factors responsible for its unprecedented proliferation during the early and high Empire.

---

[38] See in particular Brown (2002) for a suggestive analysis.

CHAPTER 2

The size and nature of gifts

Many scholars adopt an economic explanation to account for the proliferation of euergetism in the cities of the early and high Roman Empire. In outline, the argument runs like this: the imperial government, greedy for taxes, left the provincial cities few revenues of their own. Hence, provincial civic governments suffered an endemic shortage of cash and were by and large unable to finance the necessary urban infrastructure and public amenities for their communities. Members of the local elite stepped in, however, to pay for the required amenities out of their own pocket. Thus elite public benefactions were crucial to the long-term economic survival of the cities of the Roman world.[1] This explanation of public benefactions in fact forms part of most textbook descriptions of euergetism. It gives, however, a distorted picture of the nature and functioning of elite public generosity in the Roman world. In this chapter and the following one I shall argue that none of the elements that make up the economic explanation stands up to close scrutiny.

I start with the observation that even if we base our estimate of the elite's average annual expenditure on munificence on a collection including some of the largest individual gifts on record it still amounts to no more than a small percentage of aggregate annual elite income. This might still be a sizeable sum, but it does not square with the traditional picture of euergetism as a dominant force in the urban economy.

Secondly, in most cities only a small number of elite families would have been able to finance substantial benefactions (i.e. entire public buildings or large public festivals) at all, let alone with some frequency. Most gifts were small-scale: in public building, the largest and most expensive sector of munificence, the majority of gifts consisted of donations of architectural elements for the purpose of embellishment or restoration. Also, with their

---

[1] See for instance Liebenam (1900) 21; Abbott and Johnson (1926) 143; Broughton (1938) 802; Jones (1940) 237; Veyne (1976) 9; Bogaert (1968) 407 with note 24; Sartre (1991) 133 with note 1; Mitchell (1993) 210. For more extended discussion see Chapter 3, pp. 40–9.

gifts, elite benefactors did not address the basic daily needs of the mass of ordinary citizens. Elite munificence did not improve poorer citizens' living standards, either directly or through unforeseen spin-off effects of the expenditure on benefactions.

Yet even a more modest estimate of elite expenditure on benefactions and a reinterpretation of euergetism's function in civic life, such as I attempt in this chapter, do not preclude entirely the possibility that munificence constituted a crucial addition to public funds if the cities were to have a decent public infrastructure. Hence in the following chapter we shall turn to civic finances and ask whether the cities could have coped without the benefactors. Now, however, we first turn to munificence itself.

ELITE MUNIFICENCE: A QUANTITATIVE ASSESSMENT

Ancient historians have frequently described elite benefactors as the economic pillars of post-Classical Greek and Roman cities. Tarn and Griffith once referred to a group of Hellenistic benefactors as men who carried entire cities on their shoulders. T. R. S. Broughton thought that 'the liturgies performed by rich citizens and the gifts these gave' formed the most important item on the civic budget of cities in Roman Asia Minor. In similar vein, both A. H. M. Jones and Paul Veyne argued that elite benefactors financed by far the greatest number of all public buildings in the cities of the Hellenistic and Roman east.[2] Yet how large a part of their income did the elite actually spend on munificence? Let us take a closer look at gifts towards public building. Inscriptions frequently record sums donated by benefactors for public building. Since buildings were among the most expensive forms of munificence, the sums expended on them should already give us some idea of the magnitude of public benefactions at their grandest.

I have collected a small sample of forty-four such sums, and they are listed in Table 2.1.[3]

The collection is rather heavily biased towards the Lycian inscriptions of the mid second century AD, but with good reason. First, from Lycia in this period we have on record some of the most spectacular expenditure by benefactors on public building known from Roman Asia Minor, including in particular the gifts of local grandees like Opramoas of Rhodiapolis,

---

[2] Tarn and Griffith (1952) 108–9; Broughton (1938) 802 (he also adds *summae honorariae*); Jones (1940) 237; Veyne (1976) 9.
[3] All sums are in denarii.

Table 2.1 *Sums donated for public building from Roman*
Asia Minor, c. *second–third century* AD

2,000,000	*IGR* III 804
300,000	Lanck. II no. 250
125,000	Balland (1981) no. 67
75,000	*FE* II 37
70,000	*IGR* IV 501
60,000	*IGR* III 739
56,000	Balland (1981) no. 67
50,000	*IGR* IV 1637
50,000	Balland (1981) no. 67
45,000	Balland (1981) no. 67
40,000	Balland (1981) no. 67
35,000	*PAS* III 426
35,000	*IGR* III 739
30,000	Balland (1981) no. 67
30,000	*IGR* III 739
30,000	Balland (1981) no. 67
30,000	Balland (1981) no. 67
27,100	*TAM* II 550–1
20,000	*Jahresh.* XXVIII (1933) Beibl. 100
20,000	*IGR* III 739
18,000	*IGR* III 739
18,000	*IGR* III 739
15,000	*IGR* III 833
15,000	*SEG* XXXVIII (1988) 1462
13,000	*IGR* III 351
12,100	Lanck. II no. 83
10,000	*IGR* III 342
10,000	*IGR* III 739
10,000	*IGR* III 739
10,000	*IGR* III 704
10,000	*R.Ph.* XI (1937) 334ff.
10,000	*IGR* III 704
9,000	*BCH* XXVIII (1904) 30
7,000	*IGR* III 739
5,000	*IGR* III 739
5,000	Balland (1981) no. 69
3,000	*IGR* III 639
2,500	*FE* III 66
1,750	*IGR* III 407
1,500	*IK* 48 no. 38
1,025	*IGR* III 833
1,000	Robert, *Ét. An.* 549f.
250	KP III 87
50	*AM* XX (1895) 344ff.

Iason of Cyaneae, and the Anonymous Benefactor from the Letoon near Xanthos. If such impressive outlays can nonetheless be shown to square with a minimalist model of average elite expenditure on civic munificence, this will strengthen my argument in favour of such a minimalist model. Second, focusing primarily (though not exclusively) on the material from Lycia, which mainly dates from *c.* AD 100–160 allows me to concentrate on a relatively short time span, the heyday, in fact, of civic public building in the east. Again, it would strengthen my argument if, even during the glory days of public building, benefactors' recorded contributions to this very expensive form of euergetism would fit a minimalist model of elite expenditure on munificence.

The total of the forty-four gifts is 3,316,275 denarii. The smallest gift in the sample, 50 denarii, equals the cost of about one and a half year's subsistence for an average Roman.[4] The largest gift, a sum of 2 million denarii, is about seven times greater than the minimum senatorial census requirement.[5] Both sums are outliers, however, as can be seen when they are compared to 75,369.9 denarii, the sample's mean (the average value, obtained by dividing the total sum by the number of donations), 16,500 denarii, its median (the value of the donation at the mid point of the series, but here the mean of the *two* donations at the mid point, since there is an even number of donations), and 10,000 denarii, its mode (the value that occurs most frequently in the series). The huge difference between the mean, on the one hand, and the median and mode on the other results from the incorporation in the mean of the three largest sums in the sample. Taken together, these three sums account for some 73 per cent of the sample's total. Since the distribution is so skewed, the median and mode offer a much better description of its central tendencies than the mean. I shall therefore use the median and the mode rather than the mean in the discussion that follows.

Let us assume that the sums in our sample offer a fairly representative picture of elite expenditure on munificence in the provinces. How large a proportion of elite income did they then constitute? A few speculative calculations may throw some light on the matter. I start with the assumption that, leaving aside Italy, the Empire contained some 2,000 cities. I assume further that the population of the Empire minus Italy consisted of 50 million inhabitants. This implies an average of 25,000 people per community, of whom perhaps some 2,500 to 5,000 were urban residents. Naturally, many cities would have been smaller than this, and a few much larger, but,

[4] See Chapter 1, note 3 above.   [5] Duncan-Jones (1982) 4 for a senatorial census of HS 1.2 million.

for an average provincial town, our estimate will do. How large a surplus would our community of 25,000 people have produced annually? If a year's subsistence for one individual cost HS 115, and if, as Keith Hopkins has suggested,[6] Gross Product in the Roman world was the equivalent of twice subsistence, then 25,000 people would have produced an annual surplus of about HS 3 million. What proportion of this surplus would have been taken up by elite income? A little less than 10 per cent at the minimum, if we reckon with an elite consisting of some fifty councillors, who each owned no more than their census minimum of HS 100,000.[7] Maximum elite income would of course have been the equivalent of our surplus of HS 3 million. In reality, aggregate elite income in a community of 25,000 people producing an annual surplus of HS 3 million may have to be located in a range of HS 1 to 2 million per annum.[8]

How large a proportion of this elite income would have been spent on munificence? Basing himself on the median averages of a large series of epigraphically attested building costs from a variety of provinces east and west, Ramsay MacMullen estimates that a sum of about HS 9 million would have been sufficient to equip a city the size of Pompeii with all its public buildings and amenities.[9] Pompeii was a large regional urban centre. For our medium-sized provincial town, perhaps HS 5 million would have sufficed. If we write off this sum over a period of hundred years, we arrive at an average annual expenditure on public buildings and amenities of HS 50,000, or 12,500 denarii. This is a sum that fits reasonably well with the epigraphically attested donations for public building listed in Table 2.1. It is only a little larger than the sample's mode of 10,000 denarii, though still a bit smaller than its median, 16,500 denarii. The sum constitutes about 3 per cent of an aggregate annual elite income of HS 2 million, and 5 per cent of an income of HS 1 million. This does not mean of course that in each and every provincial town of the Empire about 3 to 5 per cent of annual elite income was spent on munificence. These are estimates of *average* expenditure. The calculation, furthermore, is based on an assessment of the costs of public construction, but donating public buildings was only

---

[6] Hopkins (1980) 119–20.
[7] Assuming 5 per cent annual revenue on land, the total annual income of fifty councillors owning estates worth HS 100,000 would have been HS 250,000, or about 8.3 per cent of HS 3 million.
[8] As suggested by Wim Jongman, whose advice prevented me from letting my speculative calculations of elite expenditure on munificence take on too much Never-Never Land quality. At 5 per cent annual revenue on land, and provided that each councillor owned no more than the census minimum of HS 100,000, this range implies an *ordo* of 200–400 members. In reality, there was much socio-economic differentiation among councillors. The presence of much senatorial landownership in our town's territory would have put annual elite income rather nearer to the upper limit of the suggested range.
[9] MacMullen (1974) 142–5.

one area of euergetism, albeit by far the most expensive one. Members of the elite would also finance games, festivals, distributions and so forth. Money would also have to be spent on the activities associated with some of the buildings once the buildings themselves were in place. Public baths are the most obvious example – they required continuous expenditure on fuel for heating, and on oil for the gymnasium – but we may also think of sacrificial animals for temples. Then again, many public buildings may have been (partially) financed by civic governments instead of benefactors (compare Pliny's comments on the theatre at Nicaea in *Ep.* 10.39.3 which I discuss below). Regardless of such variation, however, it will be clear that even a maximum estimate of 5 per cent of annual elite income spent on munificence still does little to support the traditional picture of euergetism as a dominant force in the urban economy.[10]

THE SIZE AND NATURE OF BENEFACTORS' GIFTS

So far, we have established that expenditure on munificence took up only a modest part of total annual elite income. We can however further reinforce our case against the economic interpretation of euergetism by taking a closer look at the gifts themselves. Did the majority of benefactors frequently make substantial contributions towards the overall well-being of their non-elite fellow citizens? Or was most elite munificence rather more modest in scope (excepting the contributions of a small group of very wealthy benefactors), and did benefactions mostly serve a rather different purpose?

To begin with, let us look at the size of gifts. If we consider again the gifts towards buildings discussed above (see Table 2.1), we can see that, in theory, it required the effort of only a small number of local elite families to equip an average provincial town with its entire set of public buildings. This shows in particular when we compare estimates for building costs with epigraphically attested donations for public buildings. To mention only the most extreme case: the largest sum in our sample, the 2 million denarii which Ti. Claudius Erymneus donated to Aspendus in Pamphylia to pay for the construction of an aqueduct (see Table 2.1), would almost have sufficed to equip Pompeii with its complete set of public buildings, if MacMullen's estimate of HS 9 million, or 2,250,000 denarii, is roughly

---

[10] It is in the order of magnitude of Hopkins's estimate of tax paid to the Roman government, 5–7 per cent of actual GDP. Judged by this comparison, 5 per cent of aggregate annual elite income spent on munificence (our *maximum* estimate) cannot be called a negligible sum, but it does not allow us to conclude that benefactors' contributions were of major importance to the urban economy. Hopkins himself calls a Roman tax rate of 5–7 per cent 'objectively speaking, low'. See Hopkins (2002) 201.

correct. We should keep in mind, however, that only very few elite families would have been able to engage frequently in the most expensive form of munificence, which is what donating an entire public building was. In a study of North African municipal benefactions, Richard Duncan-Jones reveals the staggering social stratification of public generosity. More than half of the total sum of his sample of 206 recorded gifts was donated by only eleven individuals, that is, just over 5 per cent of the benefactors concerned.[11] A similar stratification can be reconstructed for Roman Asia Minor. Working with a sample of eighty-five recorded donations, we can see that 5–6 per cent of the donors (four out of sixty-eight) were responsible for over 50 per cent of the total sum of all gifts.[12] If we now assume that city councils normally contained some 200 to 400 individuals,[13] such a 5 per cent estimate leaves us with an average of some ten to twenty families per city who were financially capable of frequent large-scale expenditure on munificence.

The implication of such an estimate is that, in practice, most gifts must have been small-scale. This is in fact precisely what the evidence for munificence reveals, as a search of my database of benefactions from Roman Asia Minor confirms. As 'small gifts' I defined all those gifts that involved a sum lower than 1,000 denarii, that is, almost the annual income of a councillor owning no more than the census minimum of HS 100,000 or 25,000 denarii, assuming a 5 per cent return on landed property per annum. I also excluded gifts of entire public buildings. A survey of the database with these criteria in mind showed that some 60 per cent of all 530 gifts qualified as small. Naturally, this percentage is to be taken with a pinch of salt, since, due to the absence of sums or other specific information, the size of a gift cannot always be determined clearly from the inscription alone, especially in the case of games and festivals. We can nonetheless conclude that truly large gifts involving thousands of denarii, or big public buildings, were relatively scarce.[14]

[11] Duncan-Jones (1963) 165.
[12] The calculation is based on a sample of foundation capital sums donated by benefactors from all over Roman Asia Minor, including some material from Greece proper and the Aegean islands. See Appendix 2 for the data.
[13] For the size of councils see Liebenam (1900) 229, note 5; Broughton (1938) 814; Magie (1950) II 1505 and Mitchell (1993) 204. Although many small towns might have had councils numbering fewer than a hundred members (sixty at Cnidos, for instance), those of most larger towns and cities would have numbered several hundred (100 at Halicarnassos, 450 at Ephesos, 500–650 at Thyatira). Even a small city could have a large council, however, as the 500 members at Oenoanda in Lycia testify. See Broughton (1938) 814 for source references. About 200 to 400 members thus seems a reasonable guess for an average Greek city in Roman times.
[14] See Chapter 1, pp. 16–17 for a discussion of the characteristics of the database.

What form did such 'small gifts' usually take? Once again, it is instructive to look at contributions towards public building. Pliny the Younger's comments on the theatre at Nicaea in Bithynia provide an important clue. Complaining to Trajan about the waste of HS 10 million of public money on a project that was still unfinished, Pliny states that there had been 'many additions to the theatre promised by private individuals, such as a colonnade on either side and a gallery above the auditorium, but all these are now held up by the stoppage of work on the main building which must be finished first'.[15] This remark is interesting because it provides us with an example of the civic government functioning as the chief financier behind important and large-scale public works, but acting in concert with local benefactors. Examples of such dual financing schemes can also be found elsewhere in Asia Minor.[16] Given the fairly limited number of elite members in any given town rich enough to finance an entire public service completely out of their own pockets, financial co-operation of this kind between civic governments and private benefactors is likely to have been a popular and widespread mode of paying for public amenities.

Equally revealing, however, is the remark for the light it throws on the nature of the most common type of smaller-scale munificence. Pliny mentions that local benefactors had promised to embellish the theatre with colonnades and a gallery. Such gifts of architectural elements were in fact an extremely common form of munificence. The Nicaean elite's contributions towards their theatre find their almost exact parallel in a series of inscriptions from Aphrodisias, ranging from the first to the third century AD and recording gifts towards the theatre of the city. I quote the relevant lines of two of the texts in question:

To Aphrodite and the deified *Augusti*, the buttresses and the stairways, the ?paving? (?panelling), the blocks of seats, the vaults and all the seats (were given and dedicated) by Aristokles Molossos Kaikos(?), son of Artemidoros and Kaikos Papias, son of Artemidoros...

To the goddess Aphrodite, to Imperator Caesar Titus Aelius Hadrianus Antoninus Augustus Pius and Marcus Aurelius Verus Caesar and the whole household of the *Augusti*, and to his very dear country; Tib. Claudius Zelos, high priest, priest for life of the goddess Aphrodite, prepared and dedicated the columns and the entablature above them and the veneering of the wall and of the floor at his own expense.[17]

---

[15] *Ep.* 10.39.3: *Huic theatro ex privatorum pollicitationibus multa debentur, ut basilicae circa, ut porticus supra caveam. Quae nunc omnia differentur cessante eo, quod ante peragendum est.* Loeb tr.
[16] See Schwarz (2001) 221–7 and 237–9 for numerous attestations; also Zuiderhoek (2005) 172.
[17] See Reynolds (1991) for the texts, the translations and discussion.

We can add some other examples, almost entirely at random. At Thessaloniki in Macedon a benefactor contributed 10,000 wooden beams to the city's basilica.[18] Again at Aphrodisias, a series of inscriptions record the names of donors who contributed columns to the temple of Aphrodite,[19] while at Priene a benefactor contributed three steps to the temple of Athena Polias and Augustus.[20] At Assos, a foundation was set up for the restoration of buildings in the city. At Acmoneia, a benefactor paid for the restoration of an agora entrance. At Sagalassos, the priest Gbaimos financed repairs to the temple of Apollo, while at Stratonikeia benefactors restored both a public bath and a storehouse.[21] As these sources indicate, partial gifts towards public buildings need not preclude occasional substantial expenditure on the part of the benefactor, though such gifts were not nearly as costly as donating an entire gymnasium or theatre.

In the other main areas of euergetism, donations of games and festivals and distributions, it is more difficult to determine the size or nature of gifts, especially when there is no mention of costs. Gifts of games and festivals or, for instance, large distributions of money among all citizens, or of oil for the gymnasia, could be prohibitively expensive. This was especially so when the gift was made in the form of a foundation, i.e. a capital fund of which the revenues were to be used for the organisation of the game/festival/distribution at regular (annual or multi-annual) intervals.[22] Again, however, like donations of whole buildings, such large festive foundations were beyond the means of anyone outside the top echelons of the urban elite. Although the evidence is more ambiguous than it is in the case of public building, the proliferation in the epigraphic records of relatively small-scale money distributions among select groups of citizens, often the council and/or the *gerousia*, suggests that in these areas of munificence too relatively modest gifts predominated.[23]

Even if most gifts were relatively small-scale, however, there is still the possibility that what was given made a significant contribution to the standard of living and overall well-being of the non-elite citizenry. Here

---

[18] *SEG* II (1924) 410.   [19] See *CIG* 2748; LW 589, 591, 1578; *REG* XIX (1906) p. 220.

[20] *I.Priene* 159. For donations of parts of buildings in the east see Jones (1940) 237 with note 50 and Broughton (1938) 746–97 *passim*. For the west, see Duncan-Jones (1982) 92–3 and 160–2.

[21] See *I.Assos* (*IK* 4) 22–3; *IGR* IV 636 (Acmoneia); Lanck II, no. 201 (Sagalassos); Robert, *Ét. An.*, p. 549f., no. 8 (bath Stratonikeia); *BCH* XXVIII (1904) p. 30 (storehouse Stratonikeia). More evidence concerning the restoration activities of civic benefactors can be found in the lists of Broughton (1938) 746–97 *passim*. For the western provinces, see the material collected by Thomas and Witschel (1992).

[22] For the costs of foundations see Appendix 2.

[23] For some examples see for instance *Mus. Iznik (Nikaia)* (*IK* 9) 61; *I.Stratonikeia* (*IK* 21–2) 172, 237; *I.Side* (*IK* 44) 103.

we hit upon an important subsidiary element of the so-called economic interpretation of munificence, namely that the civic amenities financed by elite benefactors represented a decided improvement to the lot of the poor in their cities. Following this line of argument, euergetism might even be interpreted as the Greco-Roman forerunner of Christian charity and modern state-sponsored social aid. In his influential *Wohltätigkeit und Armenpflege im vorchristlichen Altertum*, H. Bolkestein had already concluded that the pagan philanthropy of Greco-Roman antiquity in fact contained the seeds of the late antique Christian 'love of the poor'. Detecting a shift in Roman morality from the classic notion of the public benefaction to something approaching *Armenpflege* from as early on as the first century AD, Bolkestein concluded that the early Christian notion of charity (*caritas*) was simply the equivalent of the pagan Greco-Roman *philanthropia* in its more restricted sense of *philoptochia*, love of the poor.[24] However, we find the charity-argument in its most fully developed form in A. R. Hands' *Charities and social aid in Greece and Rome*. Basing himself on a series of carefully selected documents from Classical Greece, the Hellenistic world and the Roman Empire, Hands sets out to show that, despite the absence of explicitly formulated charitable motives in the evidence for public giving, elite 'beneficence did nevertheless ameliorate the conditions of the poor'.[25] He selects three areas in particular: 'the provision of basic commodities', 'education and culture', and 'health and hygiene'.

The charity-argument founders, however, on the empirical evidence for the patterns in elite gift-giving, at least when *systematically* explored. In order to substantiate his theory that elite munificence did in fact ameliorate the lot of the poor, Hands works with a fairly small and very particular selection of documents with a very wide geographical distribution drawn from a very long period of time (Classical Greece until *c.* AD 250). What he does, in fact, is select the exceptions. For, indeed, benefactors did *sometimes* sell some grain below the market price, or contribute to a public grain fund, and they did *sometimes* distribute some food.[26] And indeed,

---

[24] Bolkestein (1967) 467–84, in particular 484: 'Die altchristliche *caritas*, die Liebestätigkeit, ist die antike φιλανθρωπία, die Menschenliebe, in der eingeschränkten Bedeutung von φιλοπτωχία, der Liebe zu den Armen.'

[25] Hands (1968) 13.

[26] See Balland (1981) 185–224, esp. 211–21 on distributions to (privileged sections of) the citizenry financed by benefactors in the cities of the Roman east. Contributions towards the municipal grain funds or incidental gifts of grain by private benefactors are on record, and might occasionally have contributed to the relief of a food shortage (see in general Garnsey (1988), who I think somewhat overemphasises the role of euergetism in warding off food crises). Such gifts, however,

benefactors *sometimes* contributed to the schooling of citizens' children,[27] or donated a library (which might however simultaneously serve as a magnificent burial chamber, as did the library of Celsus at Ephesos). Also, they may *from time to time* have made some contributions to citizens' health and hygiene, though we have every reason to question whether supplying non-chlorinated water to hot public baths did do much good for the visitors' health.[28] When, however, we systematically collect a fairly large amount of evidence (500+ items) on civic benefactions from a particular region of the Roman Empire, in our case Asia Minor, it quickly becomes clear that the type of benefactions Hands writes about constituted just a tiny minority. By far the largest number of all elite benefactions (*c.* 90 per cent of all those recorded in my database) in fact consisted of architecture of display, monumental public buildings associated with politics, entertainment and religion, games, festivals, and hierarchically structured distributions of oil, grain, wine or money (see Fig. 5.1 in Chapter 5, and the discussion there). And they were – and the importance of this fact cannot be overstressed – gifts to the city or the citizens (whatever their level of wealth), *not* to the poor. Even those forms of euergetism that carried a semblance of philanthropy, such as distributions of grain or money, were often targeted at those who least needed them. As inscriptions show, those at the top of the social hierarchy commonly received most.[29] A case in point is the distributions of money by the benefactress Menodora at Sillyon in Pamphylia. In her scheme, council members would receive eighty-six drachmae, members of the *gerousia* eighty, members of the assembly seventy-seven. Ordinary citizens received only nine drachmae, and freed slaves only three.[30] As Richard Gordon wrote, 'it is evident that the major purpose of this philanthropy is not to relieve poverty'. Instead, 'the hierarchy of the city is given

---

were comparatively rare. In my database of benefactions from Roman Asia Minor, contributions to the urban food supply make up only 3 per cent (fifteen instances) of all 530 benefactions. On municipal grain funds (*sitonia*) in Roman Asia Minor see Strubbe (1987) and (1989). See Zuiderhoek (2008) for a more extended discussion of the role of euergetism and municipal grain funds in the urban food supply.

[27] See Balland (1981) no. 67 for an example.

[28] Of course, supplying fresh *drinking* water would, but that is again something elite benefactors did only very rarely.

[29] See *IGR* III 800–2 (Sillyon); *I.Ephesos* (*IK* 11–17) 27 with Rogers (1991a); Balland (1981) no. 67 (Xanthos); *SEG* 38 (1988) 1462 (Oenoanda) with Wörrle (1988); *I.Histria* 57; *I.Stratonikeia* (*IK* 21–2) 662; Robert, *Ét. An.* p. 343–51, no. 4 (Sebastopolis); *IGR* III 409 (Pogla); *I.Selge* (*IK* 37) 17. The evidence for distributions of money where the size of individual handouts is known is set out in Chapter 5, table 5.2 and discussed on pp. 104–6.

[30] See *IGR* III 800–2. These are only the distributions recorded in *IGR* III 801. In fact, Menodora made three consecutive distributions. For a reconstruction of Menodora's family background see van Bremen (1994).

monetary expression'.[31] Whatever the symbolic and ideological function of such schemes, they clearly made but little difference to the situation of the poor. 'The poor', moreover, as Peter Brown has recently and convincingly argued, did in fact not exist as a social category in the pagan, Greco-Roman, civic world view. It required a complete shift in the social imagination, the development of a totally new, revolutionary model of society, constructed precisely in opposition to the pagan idea of *euergesia*, for charity and love of the poor to become dominant themes in civic discourse. Its inspiration was Judeo-Christian, and its agents were the bishops and their flocks. Christian charity and love of the poor had in fact little if anything to do with the pagan, Greco-Roman, ideals of elite public generosity and civic munificence.[32]

Yet, even if benefactions were not targeted directly at the needs of poorer citizens, could the expenditure on munificence not have generated indirect economic benefits? As economic theory teaches, the net effect on overall income and employment of a sum expended can be much larger than the original sum. This is due to the consumer re-spending effect: increase of income by new spending injections leads to more spending on consumer goods, which in turn increases the income of the people producing those consumer goods, and so on. It is however fairly unlikely that elite expenditure on munificence would often have generated such multiplier effects. Multiplier effects are generally strongest in (sectors of) economies operating below full capacity. Unused capacity may be caused by the so-called 'downward inflexibility of wages'. When labour supply outstrips demand, to retain full employment wages must fall until they reach a level employers are willing to pay. If, for some reason, this does not happen, unemployment, i.e. unused capacity, results. In Roman cities, the labour needed for building work and the more menial tasks associated with the organisation of large public events would most often have been provided by the poorest, unskilled, section of the urban population.[33] Since these people were usually casual wage earners who lived on a level of near subsistence, their bargaining power in negotiations with contractors and employers must have been limited. Thus, their wages are likely to have been fairly flexible and would have varied in accordance with fluctuations in the supply of labour or the demand for building.

---

[31] Gordon (1990) 229. See also van Nijf (1997) 152–6. See Duncan-Jones (1982) and Mrozek (1987) for evidence from the west.

[32] Brown (2002). For further (brief) discussion of the relation between pagan munificence and Christianity see the Epilogue below.

[33] For the use of free wage labour in building work, see Anderson (1997) 122–7.

We may also ask whether benefactions really constituted *extra* expenditure. Would the money not have been spent if the benefaction had not taken place? That benefactions constituted such extra expenditure seems unlikely for two reasons. First, if benefactors did not pay for public buildings, the civic government would probably pay for them from tax resources.[34] Second, the money the elite did not spend on public buildings now they might spend on their own houses and villas later. From an economic point of view it does of course not matter who spends the money, as long as the expenditure takes place at all.

CONCLUSION

Historians often argue that elite private benefactors financed the bulk of the public amenities in Roman cities, since, due to an endemic lack of disposable resources, the civic treasuries were by and large unable to do so. In this chapter I have argued against one of the two main elements that make up this traditional explanation of the proliferation of munificence in the Roman Empire, i.e. the assumption that euergetism was crucial to the economic functioning and survival of the Empire's cities. I have argued (a) that elite expenditure on benefactions commonly comprised just a small percentage of aggregate annual elite income; (b) that in most cities only a tiny number of elite families would have been able to finance major benefactions, such as the donation of a large public building or a big annual festival, with some regularity or at all; (c) that, consequently, such big gifts, even if often considered emblematic of Greco-Roman munificence by modern historians, must in reality have been comparatively rare, an observation that is borne out by the evidence for munificence itself, in which smaller-scale gifts generally predominate; (d) that the majority of gifts were targeted at the city, i.e. the citizens as a collective, not the poor, and concerned prestige projects or public events with strong political and ideological–symbolic overtones that did little or nothing to alleviate the situation of poorer citizens; and finally (e) that expenditure on benefactions is unlikely to have generated spin-offs that might have made a more indirect (and unintended) contribution to the welfare of the non-elite citizenry.

With this, the argument is not yet complete, however. We still have to counter the second main assumption of the traditional model, namely that civic governments were structurally unable to pay for urban infrastructure

[34] See Duncan-Jones (1990) 178–84 for the comparison of a town built by benefactors (Thugga in northern Tunisia) and a town built from public funds (Thamugadi in Numidia). For a discussion of civic governments' capability to finance public amenities from public resources see Chapter 3.

and amenities from public revenues. For even if the overall contribution by benefactors was far more modest than traditionally envisaged, and if their munificence did by and large not address the basic daily needs of the mass of ordinary citizens, this by itself does not prove that the cities could easily have paid for most amenities themselves. Thus in the next chapter we shall take a closer look at civic income and expenditure and, crucially, ask whether the cities could have managed without the benefactors.

CHAPTER 3

The icing on the cake?

According to the traditional view among ancient historians, the provincial cities of the Roman Empire suffered from an endemic shortage of public resources, brought about by a tax-greedy central government that left the cities few revenues of their own. Consequently, city governments were unable to finance much in the way of public amenities, and it was only the private money of elite citizens acting as public benefactors that prevented the permanent decline of the Empire's civic infrastructure. Euergetism, in short, was the motor of the civic economy. As we saw in the previous chapter, this latter part of the theory is evidently false. Overall elite expenditure on munificence was fairly modest and did not have much effect on the urban economy, most gifts were small-scale and the wide majority were non-utilitarian in nature, i.e. prestige projects and highly ideologically charged public events rather than direct contributions to the material or social welfare of the non-elite citizenry. Yet all of this again raises the question of the financial capabilities of civic governments. For if benefactors did not habitually finance the bulk of the civic infrastructure, even if they occasionally made substantial contributions, then it must have been the civic treasury that did so. From Pliny's letter to Trajan about the theatre at Nicaea in Bithynia, cited in the previous chapter, and from additional evidence it is clear that cities and private benefactors often acted together. However, to fully clinch our argument against the economic model, we have to ask the counterfactual question whether cities could actually have managed without the aid of private wealth. This is the issue with which we shall be concerned in the present chapter.

WHAT IF THERE WERE NO BENEFACTIONS?

Could the cities have coped without the benefactors? Or were they, as the economic model of munificence has it, fatally dependent on the private contributions of the elite? If we could plausibly argue that civic governments were able to provide their citizens with the usual public amenities *even if there had never existed any benefactions and liturgies*, then that constitutes the ultimate argument against an important economic role for civic euergetism. Naturally, such a claim can never be established with a great amount of certainty. For that, the data at our disposal are simply too fragmented and anecdotal. It is however possible to bypass the deficiencies of the data to some extent by constructing a hypothetical model of civic income and expenditure in the absence of munificence of any kind. This is what I intend to do in the pages that follow. I shall attempt to ground the model as far as possible in the information we have available in the sources.

Let us start with expenditure. What would a list of annual public expenditures in an average, medium-sized Greek city in Roman Asia Minor have looked like? We shall concentrate on public expenditure during a normal year, i.e. one without disasters (food crises, earthquakes) or unusual events (a visit by the emperor, the stationing of an army unit, the large-scale requisitioning of means of transport by imperial officials). Such a list would then have included figures for the cost of:

(1) The construction and upkeep of public buildings and amenities (including streets, water supply systems,[1] public latrines, sewers, but also statues, inscriptions and other decorative architectural elements). We can use again the figure of 12,500 denarii annually for the construction and maintenance of public buildings from our earlier discussion of annual elite expenditure on munificence in Chapter 2.

(2) The organisation of public events (games, festivals, distributions, public banquets, religious rituals, incidental or recurring). As we know from many inscriptions, games and festivals could be quite expensive. A large annual festival easily required a foundation capital of tens of thousands of denarii. Set at interest rates of, say, 6–12 per cent, such capitals would annually yield large sums for the organisation of the festivities.[2]

---

[1] At least, within the city. The aqueducts conducting water towards the cities were so prohibitively expensive that the imperial government usually paid for them. One exception is of course the aqueduct at Aspendos in Pamphylia, for which Ti. Claudius Erymneus donated 2 million denarii: see above p. 28.

[2] To list only a few examples, the capital sums donated to Aphrodisias by Fl. Lysimachus had to accrue to a mimimum (!) of 120,000 denarii before his planned musical games could be held for the first time: see *OGIS* 509 = *CIG* 2759 = Laum II 103; a certain Septicia donated a capital sum of 30,000 denarii to an unknown city to finance the prize money in a four-yearly contest: see *Dig.* 50.12.10 (Modestinus); the capital donated to Ephesos for a festival by C. Vibius Salutaris amounted to a total of 21,500 denarii: see *I.Ephesos* (*IK* 11–17) 27; the son of Metrodoros gave 70,000 drachmae to support the games in honour of Trajan founded by Antius Iulius Quadratus at Pergamum: *IGR* IV 337; finally, C. Iulius Demosthenes gave 4,450 denarii to Oenoanda for a penteteric musical contest: see Wörrle (1988) = *SEG* XXXVIII (1988) 1462. At interest rates of 6–12 per cent per annum, these capital sums would generate revenues of several hundreds to several thousands of denarii annually.

Thus we shall regard the expenditure on public events as equivalent to the most expensive item on the list of expenditures, public building and amenities, and set it at 12,500 denarii. By deliberately setting the annual public expenditures of our civic government at a high level, I am working against my argument that annual civic revenues would in normal years have sufficed to cover civic public expenditure, making the contributions of benefactors de facto superfluous.

(3) The provision of oil for the gymnasium and fuel for heating the baths, both rather expensive,[3] plus some annual expenditure on maintaining a municipal grain fund.[4]

(4) Salaries for certain professionals (doctors, teachers, professors of rhetoric, policemen) and allowances for public slaves and low status public personnel.[5]

(5) Incidental expenditure on embassies to governors or emperors.[6]

(6) Costs of upkeep and exploitation of public property (*ager publicus*, urban real estate, public workshops, natural resources in the city's territory and so forth).

Since so much is uncertain regarding the actual size of the expenditure on items (3), (4), (5) and (6), it is probably best only to give a maximum figure for total civic expenditure. I therefore propose to set the expenditure on items (3), (4), (5) and (6) taken together at 25,000 denarii annually, which is the equivalent of the expenditure on buildings and public events combined. The estimate for total annual public expenditure – in the *absence* of munificence and liturgies – in our model Greek city would then be 50,000 denarii. Assuming that a year's subsistence for an individual cost about 30 denarii, and that actual GDP was the equivalent of twice subsistence, the GDP of our community of 25,000 individuals would amount to some

Again, for comparison, one year's subsistence for an average Roman cost about 30 denarii: see above, p. 4, note 3. For interest rates in Roman Asia Minor see Broughton (1938) 900–2.

[3] At Gytheion in Laconia, Phaenia Aromation donated a sum of 8,000 denarii to provide free oil for the gymnasium in perpetuity: *SEG* XIII (1956) 258; at Iasos, a certain Caninius donated a capital of 5,000 denarii of which the revenues, 450 denarii at 9 per cent, served to finance the supply of oil to the gymnasium of the *neoi* during the sixth month: *REG* VI (1893) 156ff. On the cost of fuel for heating the baths see *Dig.* 50.4.18.5; *IG* XII.5 946.

[4] See p. 32, note 26 and Zuiderhoek (2008).

[5] For salaries and wages paid by the civic government see Jones (1940) 242–3 with note 58.

[6] We may wonder, however, how 'incidental' such embassies actually were. Pliny, *Ep.* 10.43 writes that the Byzantines had a habit of sending one embassy to greet the emperor (*à raison* of HS 12,000 or 3,000 denarii in travelling expenses) and another to greet the governor of Moesia (which cost them HS 3,000 or 750 denarii) *every year*. Though Pliny clearly considers this extravagant, given the intense competition between cities for honours and privileges, and the chances that a hearing before governor or emperor afforded for securing these, many cities may actually have behaved in a manner similar to that of Byzantium. Hence, 'incidental' embassies figure on our model city's list of annual expenditures.

1,500,000 denarii.[7] Our estimate of total annual public expenditure would thus constitute some 3.3 per cent of our city's GDP. The crucial question is now whether our model city would have been able to raise revenues to the extent of 3.3 per cent of its GDP.

So let us turn to civic income. Cities' main sources of revenue are generally taken to be:

(1) Public land and/or urban real estate owned by the civic government. Such possessions would secure the city a steady income from rents. We may add income from public workshops.[8]

(2) Payments for office by civic magistrates, priests and aspiring council members, the so-called *summae honorariae*.

(3) Fees for the use of public amenities (for example the baths), tolls, all sorts of fines.

(4) Indirect taxation, i.e. import and export taxes and levies on all kinds of economic activity (market dues, money changing).

To this list may be added the income generated by the exploitation of natural resources, if any, occasional direct taxes, usually levied among dependent non-citizen groups in the territory of a city, or on dependent villages, and income from public monopolies on some economic activities.[9] The question is now: would our model city have been able to raise revenues to the extent of 3.3 per cent of its GDP from these sources? Or, stated more generally, would customary public revenues have sufficed to pay for the normal public expenditures of Greek cities in the Roman east, given the – hypothetical – absence of benefactions, liturgies and so forth? To provide a proper answer, we first need to turn in some detail to the traditional interpretation of the state of public finances in the cities of the Roman Empire.

THE STATE OF CIVIC FINANCES

As we saw earlier, ancient historians have generally been pessimistic about the financial situation of the cities of the Roman Empire. Wilhelm

---

[7] For HS 115 or 30 denarii as the cost of a year's subsistence for an average Roman see Chapter 1, note 3. For actual GDP as twice aggregate subsistence see Hopkins (1980) 119–20. Our model city's GDP can be calculated as follows: 25,000 × 115 = 2,875,000 × 2 = 5,750,000, which I have rounded off at HS 6 million or 1,500,000 denarii.

[8] An inscription from Aphrodisias published by Reynolds (1996) 123–4 clearly speaks of public workshops (δημοσίοις ἐργαστηρίοις) as a source of revenue for the city, see lines 5–10. At Pompeii, the auctioneer L. Caecilius Iucundus rented a *fullonica* (fullers' workshop) from the city for HS 1,652 (413 denarii) a year: see Andreau (1974) 69ff; Jongman (1991) 216.

[9] On the revenues of cities in the Roman Empire in general see Liebenam (1900) 2–68. For the Roman east and Asia Minor see Broughton (1938) 797–803; Jones (1940) 244–50; Sartre (1991) 134ff.; Schwarz (2001) 205–337 (revenues and expenditures examined together).

Liebenam, in his fundamental if largely antiquarian study of civic finances published in 1900, argued – without much evidence – that the greedy imperial fiscus left the cities little tax revenue of their own. He did not specify exactly which sources of revenue should compensate for the lack of income from taxation.[10] Later historians of the subject, such as F. F. Abbott, A. C. Johnson and T. R. S. Broughton, were, however, quite clear about the sources of revenue that made up for the missing taxes: *summae honorariae*, but above all liturgies and benefactions.[11] Subsequent scholarship largely followed their lead,[12] and thus euergetism came to assume its prominent role in the literature as the primary means of economic survival for the Empire's cities.

As I hope the discussion in the previous chapter has made clear, there are good reasons to reject this traditional overestimation of euergetism's contribution to the economic well-being of the cities. The major flaw in the traditional interpretation of the state of civic finances in the Roman Empire lies however in the implicit assumption that the practice of private contributions to public amenities *by its very existence* already proves that the cities were incapable of covering all their expenditures with their customary public revenues. Of course, there is absolutely no reason why the mere existence of euergetism, or even its proliferation during the late first and second centuries AD, should imply that civic public finances were in a bad state (in the sense that civic governments suffered from a chronic shortage of revenues).

An additional, more prosaic, reason for the underestimation of civic public revenues and the related overestimation of private contributions and benefactions may be found in the character of our source material. As both Mireille Corbier and Werner Eck have noted, the epigraphic sources are heavily biased towards the expenditures and gifts made by private

---

[10] Liebenam (1900) 21. In his paragraph on municipal taxes he writes: 'Durchschnittlich haben die Städte in der Kaiserzeit unzweifelhaft nur in bescheidenem Masse auf derartige Einnahmen [i.e. income from municipal taxes, dues, tolls and so forth] rechnen können. Mehr und mehr hat der Staat [i.e. the imperial government] die ertragsfähigsten Steuerobjekte zu eignem Nutzen in Beschlag genommen.' For a good overview of the discussion on municipal finance in the Roman Empire since the publication of Liebenam's study see Schwarz (2001) 1–23. My own remarks owe much to her thoughtful treatment of the subject there.

[11] Abbott and Johnson (1926) 142–3; Broughton (1938) 802.

[12] See among others Jones (1940) 241: 'Finance was the weakest point of the cities. Few drew up anything like a budget'; 248: 'When the principal taxes had been appropriated by the kings, and later by Rome, the cities had not many important sources of revenue left to exploit', and 'the bulk of the expenditure on every department, and especially on public works, was contributed by the aristocracy'. Similarly Sartre (1991) 133 with note 1: 'la cité... n'a pas du budget et doit trouver pour la plupart des dépenses un financement particulier'. Note also in particular Stahl (1978) 111–25.

individuals, but hardly mention expenditure by the civic government.[13] This seems natural, given that epigraphic commemoration of their bene-factions constituted perhaps the most important motive for private citizens to be publicly generous. The expenditure of the civic government itself, by contrast, hardly merited such commemoration in honorific inscriptions. Consequently, public expenditure on civic amenities is heavily underrepre-sented in our sources, while the documentation for gifts and benefactions by private individuals is particularly abundant. This easily creates the false impression that private individuals financed the majority of buildings and amenities in the cities of the Empire.

It is however possible to avoid the positivist fallacy here, and to come to more realistic conclusions. In her recent, thorough study of civic public finances in Roman Asia Minor, Hertha Schwarz presents a convincingly revisionist picture of the financial situation of the cities in the eastern provinces. She shows that the claim of an Empire-wide crisis in the pub-lic finances of the cities due to Rome's tightening control over civic tax revenues – first propagated by Liebenam and taken over by virtually all subsequent scholars – has no solid basis in evidence, as there is no such evidence.[14] The correspondence between the Younger Pliny and Trajan concerning the Bithynian cities, often the only source called upon to back up the crisis argument, can actually be used as proof of the exact opposite. From Pliny's letters, we learn that the Bithynian cities had plenty of public money to burn. As we saw earlier, the city of Nicaea spent more than HS 10 million of public money on the construction of a theatre. We can be sure that these millions were public money, because a few sentences later Pliny talks about additional contributions to the theatre by private individuals (*ex privatorum pollicitationibus . . .*).[15] Similarly, the Nicomedi-ans spent HS 3,318,000 on an aqueduct, and an additional HS 200,000 on yet another water system.[16] No private benefactor is mentioned, nor does Pliny refer to additional private contributions. So once again we may conclude that we have a case of massive spending on public amenities *from public resources*.[17] Since, despite the massive government investments, all three projects were still unfinished when Pliny saw them, we may con-clude that the Bithynian cities did not lack public funds, but suffered from apparently deep-rooted and widespread corruption. This, incidentally, is precisely Pliny's own conclusion when he inspects the public accounts at Prusa: the funds are available in principle, but large sums are being held

---

[13] See Corbier (1991) 215; Eck (1997) 315–24, esp. 318–19; also Schwarz (2001) 25.
[14] Schwarz (2001) 7–20, esp. 13–20.   [15] *Ep.* 10.39.1–3.   [16] *Ep.* 10.37.1.   [17] Schwarz (2001) 51–2.

back, or are used for illegal purposes, and building contractors charge far higher prices than originally agreed upon.[18]

In fact, Schwarz finds no evidence indicating that, during the early centuries of the Empire, the cities of Asia Minor would have experienced anything like a chronic crisis in their public finances. During the second century AD, the period often taken to mark the beginning of the Empire-wide financial crisis of the cities, she notes many signs of widespread economic prosperity in her three regional case studies, Bithynia, Lycia and the city of Ephesos. All three regions showed a great upsurge in public building and the organisation of public events, financed by both the city and private individuals, while at the same time local economies seemed to have recovered quickly from several serious earthquakes. In none of the regions did the local elite show any sign of a decreasing willingness to hold office (the 'problem of the *decuriones*', generally regarded as an important part of the crisis of the cities). On the contrary, almost all individuals honoured in public inscriptions held one or more offices. Most importantly, though, there are many indications in the evidence that cities were generally quite capable of financing the bulk of their public amenities from public resources. Pliny's letters to Trajan on the public investments of the Bithynian cities certainly do not constitute an isolated example in this respect.

This becomes particularly clear in Schwarz's detailed discussion of civic revenues and expenditures in the second part of her book. With regard to revenues, which concern us most here, she is pessimistic about the actual contribution of *summae honorariae*, liturgies and benefactions, that is to say, all forms of contributions by private individuals to public revenues. *Summae honorariae* certainly existed in some form in the east (I do not agree with Schwarz that 'we may justifiably doubt the existence of this institution in Bithynia, Lycia and Ephesos'),[19] but that is almost all that can be said about them, given the sparse and often cryptic references in our sources.[20] Given such poor attestation I think, however, that Schwarz is

---

[18] See *Ep.* 10.17a.3 and 10.17b.2, with Schwarz (2001) 43–5.

[19] Schwarz (2001) 318–19: 'Zweifel an der Existenz dieser Einrichtung in Bithynien, Lykien und Ephesos [ist] berechtigt.'

[20] Pliny *Ep.* 10.112.1–3 specifies that, in Bithynia, only councillors who were admitted in addition to the legally fixed number of boule members had to pay an entrance fee of 1,000 or 2,000 denarii. A letter from Hadrian to the Ephesians could be interpreted as speaking of an entrance fee to the boule, see *I.Ephesos* (*IK* 11–17) 1487 = 1488. Quass (1993) 328–34 gives further (mostly epigraphic and often rather enigmatic) references to all kinds of payments for offices, which he interprets as *summae honorariae*.

right to conclude that entrance fees for the boule and payments for offices must have constituted only a minor item on the budget of many cities.[21]

Similarly for liturgies an overview of the sources from her three case studies – Bithynia, Lycia and Ephesos – leads Schwarz to conclude that they too cannot have counted for much. They are mentioned quite rarely, and it is often not entirely clear who exactly paid how much for what.[22] Yet could it not be argued that liturgies and *summae honorariae* were so common and expected that they were mostly passed over in silence in honorific inscriptions? The point, however, is that they were not, for we have them on record in inscriptions, where they are often mentioned along with the other benefactions made by the honorand.[23] Liturgic payments and *summae honorariae* seem therefore not to have been an *automatic* requirement for office holding or boule membership (at least not in Roman Asia Minor). Rather, I would argue, they were just particular types of munificence. When liturgic payments were made, or *summae honorariae* paid, the inscriptions tend to mention them, just as they mention other types of benefactions. As for 'normal' benefactions, Schwarz argues that, if it were true that benefactions by private individuals constituted the major source of revenue for most cities in the Empire, then the majority of benefactions should actually be targeted towards providing the citizen body at large with necessary public amenities.[24] The material from Schwarz's regional case studies by contrast shows that many benefactions were not aimed at the citizen body as such, but were made to all kinds of groups within the citizenry – clubs, *collegia*, but also political bodies such as the boule or the *gerousia*.[25] Some confusion seems to have crept into her argument here, however. For, even if benefactions did not constitute a major source of revenue for the cities, this need not preclude the possibility that most munificence was primarily targeted at the citizenry. In fact, virtually all benefactions were to citizens, whether to the citizen body as a whole or to subgroups within it. The fact that both the citizenry as a whole and various (privileged) civic subgroups were often recipients of benefactions points to the development of a more hierarchical conception of civic society, but the emphasis on citizens remains, clearly and unequivocally.[26] A better argument against assigning much economic importance to benefactions is

---

[21] Schwarz (2001) 313–19.   [22] Schwarz (2001) 319–25.
[23] See for instance Strubbe (1989) 108, 111 (referring to texts assembled in Strubbe (1987)) on inscriptions for *sitonai* (officials of the grain supply) that state that the *sitones* contributed to the costs associated with the office out of his own pocket.
[24] Schwarz (2001) 261–2.   [25] Schwarz (2001) 261–77.   [26] See Chapter 5 below.

that most of them consisted of prestige projects with primarily a symbolic and ideological function instead of a utilitarian one.[27]

Finally, as Schwarz remarks, 'all private expenditures had in common that they were random and sporadic in nature'.[28] The needs of the public, naturally, were of a continuous nature, and hence required continuous public expenditure. All things considered, euergetism can hardly be expected to have balanced the books in most cities at all times. Foundations providing for essential and expensive public needs, such as oil for the public baths or a municipal grain fund, of course constituted the major exception to this rule. Again, however, while all cities had baths that needed oil all the time, whether such foundations would be set up at all in a city depended on chance factors, primarily the whims of individual members of the urban elite.

How then did cities take care of themselves? Schwarz's answer is simple: by taxation. She argues that the (eastern) cities had recourse to a wide range of (mostly indirect) forms of taxation, and that the revenues the cities drew from these, together with revenues from other sources (public property, fees, fines and so forth) usually sufficed to cover customary public expenditures. First, she attacks Liebenam's old but unfounded theory that the Roman imperial fiscus over time laid claim to the bulk of the civic public revenues from indirect taxation. Most cities in the east had for centuries been part of larger politico-administrative systems (the Persian Empire, Leagues of cities, Hellenistic monarchies) before they were conquered by Rome. They had, therefore, long since learned to get by with a dual system of taxation: taxes were raised both by a higher authority and by the cities themselves. Upon their incorporation into the Roman Empire, the cities were therefore not faced with a fiscal situation completely different from their earlier experiences. For centuries, in fact, both forms of taxation had co-existed, and there is absolutely no indication, either in the Roman period, or earlier, that civic taxation was ever seriously hampered by royal or imperial fiscal claims.[29]

The evidence for civic taxes is admittedly sparse, scattered and often difficult to interpret. However, if we had only *epigraphic* sources for the public finances of Classical Athens (i.e., no *Athenaion Politeia* and no Attic Orators, texts which supply the bulk of our information on Athenian finance), we would know roughly as much about them as we do about

---

[27] For a more detailed exposition of this argument see Chapter 5.

[28] Schwarz (2001) 277: 'Alle privaten Spenden haben ein gemeinsames Merkmal, nämlich daß sie willkürlicher und sporadischer Natur waren.'

[29] Schwarz (2001) 348–62, esp. 348–9.

civic taxes in the imperial period. 'This means', writes Schwarz, 'that the absence of unequivocal and detailed information [on civic taxation] in imperial times does not allow us to conclude that civic taxation was non-existent.'[30] Absence of evidence is not evidence of absence, as the old archaeological maxim goes.

In fact, evidence, though not abundant, is far from absent. Direct civic taxes are attested above all in the speeches of Dio Chrysostom. Usually they were levied on non-citizen groups within the polis, or on dependent villages and communes in the city's territory.[31] The cities also levied a host of indirect taxes,[32] however, from which they probably drew the bulk of their income. There are many scattered references in the sources to all kinds of civic dues and fees on various economic activities.[33] However, the true variety of indirect taxes and their importance to the civic budget only becomes clear after study of several important documents, to the chance survival of which we owe most of our knowledge of civic taxation in the east during imperial times.[34] The first is the inscription recording the establishment of a festival at Oenoanda in Lycia by the benefactor C. Iulius Demosthenes.[35] At two places in the document, the organisers of the festival specify that, for the duration of the festivities, all goods bought and sold, imported or exported, should be exempt from taxation.[36] Such

---

[30] Schwarz (2001) 363: 'Das heißt daß aus dem Fehlen einschlägiger und detaillierter Nachrichten in der Kaiserzeit unter keinen Umständen zwinged auf das Fehlen von Steuern geschloßen werden darf.'

[31] See Dio Chrys. *Or.* 31.101 (dependent cities taxed by Rhodes); 35.14 (dependent cities and villages in the territory of Apamea Celaena on which it levies taxes). See Schwarz (2001) 363–9, who also discusses some additional but less straightforward passages in the speeches. Similarly, in the west the city of Nîmes is said to have had twenty-four dependent villages in its territory, on which it presumably levied direct taxes (Strabo 4.1.12).

[32] As did the Roman government: in addition to its direct taxes, the personal tax (*tributum capitis*) and the land tax (*tributum soli*), it also collected various indirect taxes, such as tolls (*portoria*) and taxes on manumission and inheritance (for Roman citizens only); see Corbier (1991) 226. It is important, but sometimes difficult, not to confuse imperial tolls and dues with those levied by cities. In fact, a failure to distinguish clearly between these two types of indirect taxation may be what lies behind Liebenam's misinterpretation of the fiscal situation of the imperial cities. See Schwarz (2001) 376.

[33] See Schwarz (2001) 371–2, who cites evidence for fees on the use of ferries (e.g. the ferry from Myra to Limyra in Lycia, *OGIS* 572), other transport facilities and market dues (on which see Wörrle (1988) 212–15 and the evidence listed by Broughton (1938) 800).

[34] All are discussed in detail by Schwarz (2001) 369–401.

[35] See Wörrle (1988) 4–17 = *SEG* xxxviii (1988) 1462.

[36] See lines 87ff. and 108ff. From the reply of the Roman governor, whom the city had asked to confirm the remission of taxes during festival days, it is clear that we are dealing with civic taxes here. See line 115: εἶναι δὲ ἀτέλειαν τὰς τοῦ ἀγῶ]νος ἡμέρας ἂν προνοήσητε ὅπως μηδὲν αἱ τῆς πόλεως πρόσοδ[ι μειωθῶσι, 'There shall be tax-free status during the days of the competition, if you take care that the city's revenues are in no way diminished.' Translation by Mitchell (1990).

temporary tax exemptions during festivals are also attested elsewhere.[37] The purpose of the exemption, as Wörrle suggests, was to encourage traders from other cities to come and do their business at Oenoanda, which would secure the city a large enough supply of goods to satisfy the demand of the festival crowd, and boost local sales.[38] This at least implies that tolls and market dues at Oenoanda were high enough for their temporary removal to generate a local trading boom. We may therefore expect that outside the festival period the city drew in handsome revenues from these taxes.[39]

The three other documents are all so-called tariff inscriptions, from Palmyra, Kaunos and Myra, which record all kinds of indirect taxes and the goods on which they fell.[40] There are indications that all three documents owe their existence solely to disputes over the extent and precise nature of the taxes in question.[41] As the Palmyrene document indicates, civic tolls and dues were generally levied according to old usage and custom, i.e. by unwritten law.[42] If so, the general dearth of detailed documentation on civic taxes should hardly surprise us, as Schwarz shrewdly points out.[43] Again, an exclusive focus on the quantity (instead of the quality) of surviving data may easily lead to a misjudgement of the actual importance of past phenomena.

Of the three texts, the Palmyrene tariff, with its rich tableau of tolls and dues and the goods on which they were levied, is by far the most informative. It shows how deeply the civic government was involved in the operation of the local economy by means of an intricate, and no doubt very remunerative, system of indirect taxation.[44] The text from Kaunos, though fragmentary and hence difficult to interpret, seems to reveal a similar picture. As in the case of the *Demostheneia* at Oenoanda, the document appears to concern a temporary remission, related to the

---

[37] See Wörrle (1988) 210 with note 158 for references; also de Ligt (1993) Appendices I.C and II.C for a fairly exhaustive listing of the evidence for festive *ateleia*, and 229–34 for discussion.

[38] Wörrle (1988) 214.

[39] Schwarz (2001) 369–70 discusses the passages in question, but she does not quite reach this conclusion.

[40] For the Palmyrene tariff see *OGIS* 629 = *IGR* III 1056, with an English translation in Matthews (1984). For the tariff from Kaunos see *SEG* XIV (1957) 639. For the Myra tariff see Wörrle (1975) 287.

[41] Schwarz (2001) 373 with note 141.

[42] Matthews (1984) 174. The council, in its opening decree, states that '[s]ince in former times most of the dues were not set down in the tax law but were exacted by convention, it being written into the contract that the tax collector should make his exactions in accordance with the law and with custom . . .'; Schwarz (2001) 372–3 argues that in the east most civic taxes were raised 'nach altem Brauch'.

[43] Schwarz (2001) 373.

[44] A long list of all taxes and goods mentioned in the tariff would take up too much space here, but a convenient summary can be found in Schwarz (2001) 375–6.

organisation of a festival, of a wide range of import and export taxes.[45]
The text further mentions that a local benefactor had agreed to make
good the resulting losses to the civic treasury by means of a foundation.
Like the Palmyrene tariff, the Kaunos document suggests a complex fiscal
involvement of the civic government in local economic activity.[46] Finally,
the document from Myra in Lycia speaks of an import and export tax of
2.5 per cent on goods brought into, sold and/or taken out of the city. From
the revenues it drew from this tax, the polis annually paid 7,000 denarii
(HS 28,000, or more than 200 times the annual subsistence budget of an
average Roman[47]) to the Lycian *koinon*. Since, however, it is fairly certain
that we are dealing with a civic tax here, and not with a federal or imperial
one, it seems reasonable to assume that the 7,000 denarii constituted only
a small part of the total revenue the city drew from this tax. This seems all
the more probable since the Lycian cities were not subjects of the *koinon*;
it could not forcibly exploit them by demanding high taxes. The 7,000
denarii should probably be interpreted as an annual contribution (probably
also paid by other cities, but we have no evidence to prove this) meant to
cover the organisational costs of the federal political institutions. To all
this may still be added an, admittedly late, passage from Herodian, where
we can deduce that cities normally had considerable public revenues at
their disposal to finance the sort of public amenities we also encounter
in the inscriptions for private benefactors. The passage describes how the
emperor Maximinus, in a frantic search for money to pay the troops, and
after ransacking the imperial elite, turned on the cities:

[H]e attacked public property (τὰ δημόσια). All the money belonging to the cities
that was collected for the feeding of the populace or for distribution among them,
or was devoted to theatres or to religious festivals, he diverted to his own use.[48]

Some of these civic funds no doubt had their origin in bequests from
private benefactors. Nonetheless the passage fits the scenario of largely self-
sufficient civic governments, able and willing to finance much in the way
of civic services and amenities from the sources of revenue at their disposal,
above all taxes.

We may conclude with Schwarz, then, that it is possible to construct
a picture of the state of civic public finances in the Roman Empire that
deviates considerably from the traditional pessimistic view. Unlike the traditional view, this new picture has a clear basis in the sources, no matter how

45 Schwarz (2001) 388–9.   46 Schwarz (2001) 385–95.
47 Assuming an annual subsistence budget of HS 115 or about 30 denarii; see Chapter 1, note 3.
48 Herodian 7.3.3–6. Translation by Rostovtzeff (1926) 399–400, slightly adapted.

scattered and enigmatic they sometimes are. Cities normally had recourse to a wide range of sources of revenue, among which (indirect) taxation was by far the most important. Though from time to time benefactions by private individuals certainly made a (sometimes not inconsiderable) contribution, they were by their nature of an irregular character and usually not targeted towards the more imminent needs of the population at large. Given the wide range of sources of revenue available to them, and given the absence of any indication that the fiscal demands of the central government in any way compromised the ability of the majority of cities to raise sufficient revenues, we must therefore conclude that civic public finances were generally in a healthy state during the early centuries of the Empire.

SUPERFLUOUS BENEFACTORS

If we accept this revisionist view of the state of civic public finances, the answer to our counterfactual question 'Would the cities have been able to cover their customary public expenses if there had never existed any benefactions, liturgies and so forth?' is most likely to be 'yes'. However, to be a little more precise, and carry the argument to its logical conclusion, we must return to our model of an average, medium-sized city in the eastern provinces.

Above I asked whether our model city could have raised revenues to the extent of 3.3 per cent of its GDP. The 3.3 per cent constituted my estimate of the cost of customary public expenditure, 50,000 denarii, set against a GDP for a community of 25,000 individuals of 1,500,000 denarii. Let us assume, in accordance with the revisionist picture of civic public finances just sketched, that the main source of public revenue for our city was indirect taxation, primarily of goods imported, exported and/or sold in the market. Now, in any urban community in the ancient world, a considerable number of inhabitants lived at a level just above bare subsistence. They would have spent a large proportion of their income (say, about 60 to 80 per cent)[49] on (low-quality) foodstuffs, mainly grain. Outside bad harvest years, most of the food consumed by these people grew within the city's territory, and was therefore not subjected to tolls. If bought or sold on the market, it would nonetheless be subject to market dues. In any ancient city, however, there would also have lived enough people whose

[49] An estimate for medieval and early modern Europe: see Cipolla (1994) 23. Things are unlikely to have been much different among the poor of antiquity.

living standards were at a level well above mere subsistence (artisans, shop-keepers, traders, money dealers and so forth). The standard of living of the urban elite, finally, was quite beyond the poor man's imagination. As we saw earlier, the census minimum of HS 100,000 or 25,000 denarii for a member of the urban council would feed over 800 average Romans at subsistence level for one year (or over forty average Romans 'for ever').[50] It should be noted, however, that the elite constituted only a tiny proportion of the population. Now, in addition to buying higher-quality foodstuffs, the section of the population with middling incomes and the elite would spend a far larger proportion of their incomes on non-food consumer goods than would be possible for the poor. It would not seem unreasonable to assume that many such goods were imported from outside polis territory, since most cities were part of regional and interregional trading networks. Imported goods were subject to tolls and, like all goods sold in the market, to market dues. Goods sold and then exported might again be subject to an export tax (see the Myra tariff discussed above). Now let us assume that aggregate above-subsistence consumption in our community of 25,000 individuals was more or less equivalent to its aggregate above-subsistence surplus. Let us also assume that most above-subsistence consumption consisted of goods subject to municipal taxation, either import taxes (tolls) or market dues. Here I should emphasise once more that market dues would of course also be levied on non-imported goods bought or sold in the city market.[51] Let us further assume an overall tax rate of 2–4 per cent. On this basis, the city would have been able to cover some 30–60 per cent of its total annual expenditure of 50,000 denarii from taxation alone.[52] Remember that I aimed at the highest possible estimate of total annual public expenditure. Even on the sole basis of revenues from ordinary tolls and market dues, set at relatively low rates, our model city is able to cover quite a large chunk of this high estimate of total public expenditure. The remaining part would naturally have to be paid from additional revenues – rents from public lands, public workshops and publicly owned real estate, fees, fines, the occasional *summae honorariae* and so forth. In aggregate, the

[50] See Chapter 1, note 3.
[51] Home-produced consumption goods consumed at home would of course not be taxed, but I think it is not unreasonable to assume that these represented only a small part of aggregate above-subsistence consumption.
[52] The above-subsistence surplus of our model community consisted of HS 3 million or 750,000 denarii (see Chapter 2, pp. 26–7); 2 per cent of 750,000 equals 15,000 denarii, or 30 per cent of our estimate of aggregate annual public expenditure of 50,000 denarii; 4 per cent of 750,000 equals 30,000 denarii, or 60 per cent of 50,000 denarii.

income derived from these sources may well have been quite substantial, though naturally this would differ from one city to another.

Given this outcome of our attempt at modelling civic income and expenditure, and given the high public expenditures we have on record for cities in the Roman east,[53] I think we may well assume that most cities were able to cover the bulk of their expenditures from customary public revenues. They did not need benefactors. Given the large-scale public expenditure on single buildings in the Bithynian cities or the wide range of indirect taxes attested for Palmyra, we could probably argue that some cities were even able to build up reserves, to be spent on occasional special projects such as a new theatre. Finally, if there is any justification in comparing the rate of indirect taxation in ancient pre-industrial cities with the rate of direct taxation in pre-industrial states, we may add the following. Hopkins estimates that the Roman central government's direct taxes amounted to some 5–7 per cent of GDP.[54] He calls these taxes low.[55] Early modern European states probably drew in tax revenues to the extent of 5 to 8 per cent of national income.[56] It is difficult to see, in the light of this comparison and the arguments presented above, how our model provincial city could have failed to draw in a meagre 3.3 per cent of GDP in indirect taxes and other revenues to cover its expenses.

CONCLUSION

I am well aware of the fact that the model of civic income and expenditure outlined above is highly hypothetical, and that it is based on many unprovable, though not unreasonable, assumptions. However, the model, together with the empirical arguments that can be made in support of a revisionist and indeed far more sensible picture of civic public finances, at least strongly suggest that the cities could indeed have managed without the benefactors. Far from being essential to the economic survival of the cities, euergetism was largely surplus to requirements in most cities most of the time, no matter how large individual outlays may sometimes have been. As this chapter and the previous one have shown, benefactors were no Atlases carrying the cities on their shoulders. What they provided, rather, was the icing on the richly decorated cake of civic life.

In this chapter and the previous one, we have mainly been concerned with what euergetism was not. In the chapters to come we shall, in turn,

---

[53] See for instance the passages from Pliny the Younger's letters discussed at pp. 42–3.
[54] Hopkins (2002) 201.   [55] *Ibid.*   [56] Cipolla (1994) 40.

look at what it actually *was*. In the next chapter we turn first to the main long-term developments in imperial society that, I argue, were responsible for the proliferation of elite munificence in the east during the high Empire. Subsequently, in Chapters 5 and 6, we shall take a closer look at the gifts benefactors gave, and what it was precisely that they got in return for their generosity. Here I shall argue that the main driving forces of euergetism were of a political and ideological rather than an economic nature. More specifically, they concerned the symbolic affirmation of civic social and political ideals, and the elite's need for affirmation and legitimation of their power and prestige.

CHAPTER 4

The concentration of wealth and power

In a Greek horoscope dating from the second century AD we read the following, apt, summary of an ancient success-story career:

> . . . then later, getting an inheritance and improving his means by shrewd enter-prises, he became ambitious, dominant and munificent . . . and he provided tem-ples and public works, and gained perpetual remembrance.[1]

There was, as I shall try to show, nothing accidental about the link the horoscope text makes between the accumulation of wealth, political domi-nance and munificence. In this chapter, we shall consider several long-term developments in imperial Greek civic society during the first two centuries AD that, I argue, provided the most important stimulus for the unprece-dented proliferation of euergetism in the eastern cities at the time. These developments can be summarised as a growing accumulation and con-centration of wealth and social and political power in the hands of elite citizens, and the social antagonism that resulted from this. We shall start with the first factor, the rise of elite incomes.

GROWING ELITE WEALTH

A simple neo-Ricardian model can easily account for slow but inex-orably increasing inequalities of wealth between urban elites consisting of large estate-owners on the one hand and small landowners and the non-landowning population on the other during the first two centuries AD. In such a model, population is the crucial variable. If population grows, then land becomes scarce relative to labour. Owners of large estates, as were most members of urban elites in the Roman Empire, become better off because rents start to rise. Small peasant farmers, tenants and wage labourers on the contrary become worse off because the first have now less

---

[1] Neugebauer and van Hoesen (1959) 97. Cited by Johnston (1985) 105.

land to feed their families, the second have to pay higher rents, and the third receive lower wages. Hence, social inequality increases. There is now increasing consensus among ancient historians that the population of the Empire rose slowly during the first two centuries AD, grinding to a halt only with the onset of the Antonine plague from the 170s onwards.[2] The annual rate of growth may have been modest, but its cumulative effect over the course of nearly two centuries will have been impressive.[3] Hence, it is likely that, during the first and second centuries AD, the Empire as a whole experienced precisely the development just sketched: an increasing accumulation of wealth in the hands of the landowning urban elite that went together with growing rural misery.[4]

The crucial issue for us now is to determine what effect this development had on urban society. Generally, the model just sketched would predict that the income of the urban-based, landowning elites rose significantly during the period in question, since, as estate-owners, they were the only clear beneficiaries of the declining land–labour ratio. The effects on the elite will have been twofold. First, urban elites will have broadened. This was due to the fact that the census criterion for entry into the boule (HS 100,000 or 25,000 denarii) remained fixed, while, due to the general growth of prosperity among the landowning elite, the number of middling landowners just able to meet it continuously increased.[5] Here is one explanation for the frequently attested large (i.e. 100+) councils in the east.[6] Second, and undoubtedly partly because of this broadening of their base, urban elites became more stratified internally. In most cities a core group of families owning (truly) large estates (and buying up ever more land as rents continued to increase) came to stand over and against a relatively large group of moderately wealthy elite families owning not much more than

---

[2] See Frier (2000) 813–16 and (2001); Scheidel (2001b) 78, alluding to climatic causes. See Alcock (2007) 676–7 for the eastern Mediterranean.

[3] For example, an annual rate of growth of 0.15 per cent will double the population every 4.6 centuries, while a still very modest rate of 0.5 per cent per annum will achieve the same effect every 1.4 centuries.

[4] See for instance Jongman's analysis of Pompeian agriculture (as a *pars pro toto* for the Roman economy) in terms of a 'peasant model' of rising population, *morcellement* of landholdings, declining labour productivity, rising rents, increasing peasant misery and rising social inequality: Jongman (1991) 85–95, 199–203. See also Jongman (2002a) for a similar 'more of the same' analysis of the Roman imperial economy: impressive expansion of aggregate production went together with low per capita productivity.

[5] For growing city councils in the east during the early second century see Pliny *Ep.* 10.112; Dio Chrys. *Or.* 40.14.

[6] Though I admit this begs the question with regard to the west, where councils were generally only a hundred or less strong, while population and hence elite income rose throughout the Empire and while the same census criterion held in both east and west. Perhaps we should imagine that, in the west, larger sections of the elite remained politically passive (at least formally, by not becoming council members) than in the east. For evidence of large eastern councils see Broughton (1938) 814.

the prescribed property qualification.[7] It seems safe to conclude, however, that, as a collective, the elite became ever richer.

But what happened to the incomes of the non-elite, non-landowning urban population? The model predicts that those of them depending on wage labour for their livelihood (primarily building workers, probably a sizeable section of the urban population in many cities, but also others) will have become poorer due to the increased competition on the labour market. Others (small-scale traders, manufacturers, shopkeepers, providers of all kinds of services) may have experienced a slight rise in their incomes as elite demand increased. Such spin-off effects are not likely to have been sustained, however, since marginal propensities to consume (here, among the urban elite) tend (eventually) to decline as income rises. We should also not ignore the smallish group(s) of more well-to-do people (successful traders, richer manufacturers and so forth) who might eventually enter the lower ranks of the bouleutic order.[8] Their incomes of course fluctuated with the success or failure of their businesses, but they are unlikely to have experienced a sustained increase of income unless they invested in land or employed relatively large numbers of people (with population growth causing a reduction of their wage bill). It should be noted, nonetheless, that there is some indication that the incomes of the non-elite urban population may have risen somewhat throughout the first and second centuries AD.[9] If this is what really happened, then we should note that even a very modest increase in living standards for the mass of the (urban) population is actually quite a remarkable achievement for a pre-industrial society, even more so because it occurred at a time when population grew. As such it is suggestive of the potential of the Roman economy during the first two centuries AD. That, however, is not what mainly concerns us here. What matters primarily for my argument is that the declining land–labour ratio and other evidence that I shall present in a moment suggest a rise of

---

[7] See Chapter 6, pp. 134–7 for a reconstruction of the dimensions of this internal elite stratification.

[8] See Chapter 6, pp. 134–7.

[9] See Jongman (2006), esp. 245–6, who argues, on the basis of a huge database of animal bones from sites all over the Empire collected by King (1999), that meat consumption in the Roman Empire rose dramatically from the late Republic onwards, to peak in the first and second centuries AD. This may point to a modest increase in per capita incomes among sections of the non-elite population, since '[meat] reflects prosperity at a level just a bit above subsistence. If you really live at bare subsistence, meat will be too expensive. If you live at a level many times above subsistence you are unlikely to consume a great deal more than if you are only living at a few times subsistence. In short, it may be a sensitive indicator of intermediate prosperity' (Jongman (2006) 245). To judge from this, the urban professional middle groups of Roman society, who made up a sizeable part of the demos or non-elite citizenry, seem indeed a likely candidate if we are looking for a group of consumers who started to eat (more) meat.

elite incomes on an incomparably larger scale. Ordinary citizens did not
necessarily become poorer; on the contrary, there is some evidence that
they, or at least some of them, may even have gained a bit. Landowning
elite citizens, however, became truly vastly richer, and it was precisely the
ever-widening gap created by this unprecedented concentration of new
wealth at the top, which, crucially, *combined* with previously unheard of
levels of social and political oligarchisation, that began to cause political
and ideological problems in imperial polis society. We should nonetheless
add that if a contemporary modest increase of living standards among
the non-elite citizens has some relevance to the argument developed here,
this relevance lies perhaps in the possibility that the expectations of the
non-elite citizens rose together with their incomes. As fellow-citizens of
their elite counterparts, they may have felt politically entitled to a share
of the vast new wealth they saw accumulating in the hands of the families
at the very top of the social hierarchy. If it was precisely the strong political oligarchisation characteristic of the period that prevented them from
receiving their due share of this wealth directly, it was also precisely the
potential for socio-political conflict which the non-elite citizens embodied *because* they were denied such access to this newly accumulating elite
wealth that, as I shall argue in the next two chapters, partly led to the
unprecedented second-century proliferation of munificence. Even if this
munificence did not achieve much in the way of an actual redistribution
of wealth among the non-elite citizenry, it at least offered some symbolic
and ideological confirmation of the continuing political relevance of their
citizen status, besides affording them some amount of political leverage.[10]
As the boule–demos conflicts attested with some frequency in the sources
for our period testify, this particular 'solution' did not always work entirely
as expected.[11] Yet I shall argue that euergetism contributed significantly
to the smooth running of socio-political life in most cities most of the
time.

Models aside, do we have any concrete evidence for an increase of
wealth among eastern urban elites during the early Empire? Risking a slight
circularity of argument, I would suggest that a first instance is provided
by euergetism itself. I am thinking not so much of the rise and fall of the
phenomenon as a whole over time, but of the rise and fall of a *specific type* of
euergetism, i.e. that of the truly big gift. But how big is big? For the purpose
of analysis, I have defined a gift as 'big' when it conformed to one or both
of the following criteria:

[10] See Chapter 6, pp. 126–9.   [11] See pp. 66–70 below.

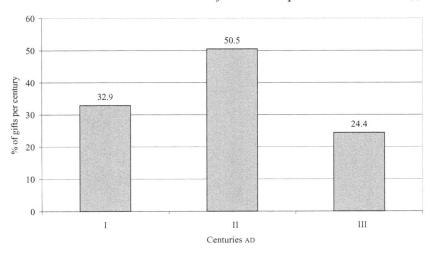

Figure 4.1 Gifts of 1,000 denarii or more or of entire public buildings as a percentage of gifts per century

- It concerned a donation of at least 1,000 denarii (HS 4,000) or more. The sum of 1,000 denarii represents a little over thirty times the costs of one year's subsistence for an average Roman.[12] More significantly perhaps, it also represents about 80 per cent of the annual income (1,250 denarii) of an urban councillor (*bouleutes*) owning no more than the census minimum of 25,000 denarii (HS 100,000).[13] Clearly, gifts in this category would have been financially crippling for many lower-ranking councillors.
- It concerned the donation of an entire public building of the major variety, i.e. bath buildings, gymnasia, theatres, temples and suchlike. Building was frightfully expensive in the Roman world, and the wholesale donation of major public buildings probably constituted the most costly form of euergetism.

A search of my database of benefactions with these criteria in mind produced the following results. Expressed as a percentage of the number of gifts per century, 32.9 per cent of all recorded first-century gifts in my database may be ranked as 'big', as against 50.5 per cent of all second-century, and 24.4 per cent of all third-century gifts (see Fig. 4.1) (all in all, some

[12] For a subsistence budget for an average Roman of HS 115 or about 30 denarii see Chapter 1, note 3 above.
[13] If we assume an annual income from landed possessions in the order of 5 per cent, for which see Duncan-Jones (1982) 33.

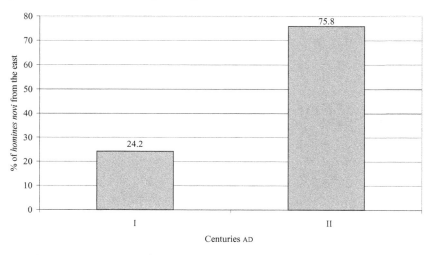

Figure 4.2 *Homines novi* from the east entering the Senate per century (N = 99)

40 per cent of all 530 benefactions in the database can be classified as 'big'). The number of 'big' gifts expressed as a percentage of recorded gifts per century thus clearly peaks in the second century AD and declines again in the third. Hence, 'big' gifts exhibit roughly the same chronological pattern as all benefactions aggregated (see Fig. 1.2 in Chapter 1). We have already established that the chronology of recorded benefactions cannot merely be a reflection of epigraphic habits. Comparison of Figs. 1.2 and 4.1 therefore indicates that, as euergetism became more widespread in the second century, it also became more expensive, with 'big' gifts constituting about half of all recorded gifts, as against about a third in the first century, and about a quarter in the third.[14] But does this rise in the number of big gifts also imply an increase of elite wealth during the second century AD? A sceptic might argue that the wealth that was channelled into euergetism in the second century was simply used for different purposes in the first and the third. However, the chronology of big gifts as pictured in Fig. 4.1 clearly conforms to the chronological development of other indicators of wealth among eastern provincial elites. Consider the distribution over time of eastern provincial elite members' entries into the Roman Senate. As Fig. 4.2 shows, roughly 75 per cent of all such entries took place during the second

[14] Assuming, naturally, that my sample of over 500 benefactions is roughly representative, and not too much distorted by modern archaeological activity.

century, as against only 24 per cent in the first.[15] Given the level of wealth
and political influence provincials required to enter the Senate – formally,
the census minimum of HS 1 million (250,000 denarii) would suffice, but
in practice, quite a bit more was often required[16] – the dramatic increase in
the number of eastern *homines novi* in the Senate during the second century
clearly points to a significant rise in prosperity among eastern urban elites
in that period. The contemporary occurrence, in the second century AD,
of a peak in the frequency of big gifts – 1,000 denarii or more, or large
public buildings – in Asia Minor can therefore hardly be a coincidence,
and serves only to reinforce the impression of ever-increasing upper-class
wealth. Indeed, Halfmann's data on eastern senators closely matches T. R. S.
Broughton's observations from a few decades earlier, which were based
on a wide-ranging survey of the then available material for Roman Asia
Minor:

The concentration of families wealthy enough to head the provincial assemblies,
or meet the census requirements for the equestrian order or the senate, agrees with
the concentration in space and the distribution in time of the benefactors, and
supports the impression they give that the period of the expansion of city life, of
economic activity, of general prosperity, and increase in wealth, at least in that
portion of society that held a high position and was called upon to make a public
display, reached its peak under Marcus Aurelius, and maintained a good but slowly
declining position under the Severi.[17]

Hence, empirical observation does seem to bear out the increase in wealth
among the eastern urban ruling classes during the early Empire predicted
by our population–resources model. Indeed, the data on big gifts, entry
of eastern elite members into the Senate, the equestrian order and high
provincial offices (Asiarchy and so forth) – the latter two as observed by
Broughton – do suggest a veritable surge in local elite wealth during the
second century AD.

---

[15] The data are collected by Halfmann (1979) 78–81. Unfortunately, he provides no data for the third
century.
[16] Contemporary sources sometimes indicate that a fortune in the order of HS 8 million was considered
appropriate for a senator. See Duncan-Jones (1982) 18.
[17] Broughton (1938) 795. It is interesting to note how Broughton's chronology of attested benefactions
deviates slightly from the one I was able to construct from my database. He sees a high point under
Marcus Aurelius, while my database suggests a peak during the reigns of Hadrian and Antoninus
Pius (see Fig. 1.3 in Chapter 1), and a rather steep drop under Marcus Aurelius and Commodus.
It may be that the dating of some of the material Broughton used has been improved or narrowed
down since his time (I have used where possible the most recent edition of each text). This, together
with the inclusion in my database of new material not yet available in Broughton's day, most likely
accounts for the slight difference in chronology between the two samples.

INCREASING OLIGARCHISATION

We shall now turn to the second factor mentioned at the beginning of this chapter, the growing accumulation of social and political power in the hands of the few, or oligarchisation. Inscriptions of the later Hellenistic and Roman imperial periods almost invariably announce that boule and demos of city so-and-so have decided or done this or that.[18] When we look at the broader social and political developments in these periods, however, the remarkable consistency and continuity of the institutional language of Greek democracy proves for the most part a façade. Political life had become increasingly oligarchic, a development exemplified above all by the ever more prominent role of the boule, or city council. I will treat only the Roman phase of this development, and be brief about its undeniable Hellenistic origins. My argument is that the oligarchisation of civic society progressed ever further during the early Empire, and reached its apogee during the later second century AD. Three separate, though interconnected, strands can be detected in it. First, there was *political* oligarchisation, in the sense that government increasingly became the prerogative of a small and wealthy citizen elite. Its members monopolised the important magistracies and turned the boule of which they were all members into the most important organ of government, at the expense of the popular assembly. Second, these bouleutic elites were themselves subject to a process of 'internal oligarchisation' (the term is H. W. Pleket's). In most cities, a tiny number of very wealthy and influential families came to dominate the elite and became the de facto leaders of society. This process of internal oligarchisation of the provincial urban elites seems primarily a development of the Roman Principate, and is in fact our clearest indicator of the progressively increasing oligarchisation of political life during that period. Third, urban society as a whole underwent a process of increasing hierarchisation, which meant that hierarchical divisions within the citizen body proper became increasingly visible, accepted and institutionalised. In effect, the increasing differentiation within the urban elites just referred to can also be viewed as part of this broader process of social hierarchisation. Finally, the processes of (internal) oligarchisation and hierarchisation were to some extent aided, but also significantly constrained, by the characteristics of the prevailing demographic regime.

---

[18] We also come across decrees in which the boule seems to have acted alone. Other decrees on the contrary have the demos as the sole decision-making body. For an exhaustive listing of the evidence and good discussion see Rhodes and Lewis (1997).

From the (later) Hellenistic period onwards, the boule ceased to be a mere advisory board of the popular assembly. Instead, monopolised, like the major magistracies, by the richer citizens, it became the effective governing institution of the city. Historians give various explanations for this development, but the necessity of negotiation between cities and kings and emperors coupled with the latter's preference for civic ambassadors from an elevated social background, and the financial burden of civic office holding characterised as it was by expensive liturgies, certainly played their part.[19] During the imperial period, the council more and more acquired the characteristics of a Roman *ordo*. Aspiring councillors had to be of a minimum age, had to come from respectable elite families, and mostly had to have held some important magistracy. New members either followed in their fathers' footsteps or were co-opted by sitting members. If there were still popular elections (i.e. for magistracies implying council membership), as in some cities, then councillors drew up the list of candidates. As in the west, there was a property qualification for membership, and we hear of urban censors (τιμηταί).[20] Occasionally, aspiring members also had to pay an entrance fee (*summa honoraria*).[21] Once admitted, council members sat for life. Clearly, then, by Roman imperial times, the principle of wealth as a *conditio sine qua non* of political power had become firmly entrenched both legally and institutionally in the cities of the east. When and how had this development taken place?

From Pliny's letters we know that the cities in Bithynia and Pontus acquired a Roman constitutional structure with the *lex Pompeia* of 65 BC.[22] This implied senate-like urban councils with the characteristics just sketched. The cities of Lycia too seem to have had urban councils on the Roman model, likewise as the consequence of a *lex provinciae*, perhaps by Vespasian.[23] Elsewhere in Asia Minor, we have many indications that local councils functioned more or less according to Roman constitutional principles, and that councillors and their families increasingly began to exhibit

---

[19] Quass (1993) is fundamental, see esp. 382–94; see Dmitriev (2005) for a detailed survey of Greek civic institutions during the Hellenistic and Roman periods. See also Pleket (1998) for a masterly short overview of the whole process; Jones (1940) 167–91; Mitchell (1993) 210. De Ste. Croix (1981) Appendix iv abundantly documents the oligarchisation of the eastern cities, or, as he describes it, 'the destruction of Greek democracy in the Roman period'.

[20] Minimum age, respectable background and office holding as entry requirements: see Pliny *Ep.* 10.79, on Bithynia, but councils probably had the same characteristic in most other eastern cities, see Quass (1993) 384ff. On co-optation of candidates or nomination of successors by councillors see Pleket (1998) 206 with references. On the existence of a census qualification of HS 100,000 (25,000 denarii) for councillors in the east see Sherwin-White (1966) on Pliny *Ep.* 10.110.2; Jones (1978) 96; Quass (1993) 343 and 383; Pleket (1998) 206. Finally, on urban censors see Quass (1993) 385.

[21] Quass (1993) 328ff., 387.   [22] See Pliny *Ep.* 10.79.   [23] Wörrle (1988) 96–100, 123.

the characteristics of a true *ordo decurionum*. Urban censors are fairly widely attested, and many inscriptions refer to individuals as being both citizens *and* councillors; like citizenship, council membership had become an aspect of one's social persona, rather than just an office. Annual lists refer to the same individuals as councillors year after year, a clear indication that the position had become one for life.[24] Local elites began to refer to themselves as the βουλευτικὸν τάγμα (bouleutic order), thus revealing a sense of corporate identity as a curial class.[25] Such a sense of corporate identity also manifested itself in the form of a distinct elite lifestyle which became ever more prominently visible during the high Empire. Gymnasial athletics, literature and distinct forms of literary expression, especially rhetoric, and, naturally, munificence, were some of the ingredients essential to this lifestyle, and they served to create cultural barriers between mass and elite in addition to the existing social, economic and political ones.[26] No matter from what angle we look at the Greek cities of the early and high Roman Empire, what we see, almost uniformly, is distinctly oligarchic societies, where the social distance separating ordinary citizens from a small ruling citizen elite was considerable, and continued to increase.

With that, however, our picture is not yet complete, for neither the non-elite citizenry nor the bouleutic order was a uniform social entity. Among the non-elite citizens, there existed wealthier groups, some of whose members might eventually even make it into the lower echelons of the bouleutic order, to fill up the vacancies when high mortality generated shortages of *honesti viri*.[27] The elite likewise were a highly differentiated group.[28] The attempt to turn local elites into hereditary status groups was a vital element of their transformation into a true Roman *ordo*. Inscriptions and literary sources, mostly dating from the second century AD, continuously stress this aspect, by enumerating, or often just vaguely referring to, long lines of ancestors who had also held high magistracies and consequently

---

[24] See Quass (1993) 385–9 for references.

[25] Quass (1993) 388; Jones (1940) 179–80 with note 46; Pleket (1998) 205–6.

[26] On athletics as a form of elite self-representation in the Roman east see van Nijf (2001) and (2003).

[27] Studies of the demographic characteristics of the Roman Senate, the wider imperial elite and provincial urban elites have revealed that, behind a strong ideological façade of unchanging hierarchy and rigid social stratification, there existed a high rate of social turnover in elite circles (see Hopkins (1983) Chapters 2 and 3 on the Senate; Saller (1994) and Scheidel (1999) on the wider imperial elite; Tacoma (2006) on the urban elites of Roman Egypt). On the effects of the mortality regime on elite family strategies in the Roman east (with special emphasis on the role of women) see van Bremen (1996) Chapter 8, esp. 252–61. See also Tacoma (2006) on Roman Egypt and Jongman (1991) 317–29 on Canusium in Italy. For further discussion of the implications of all this for our interpretation of euergetism see Chapter 6, pp. 134–7 and Zuiderhoek (forthcoming).

[28] See Chapter 6, pp. 134–7 and Zuiderhoek (forthcoming).

had been council members. Given the high rate of social turnover among elites resulting from the severe Roman mortality regime, many such claims must have been fictitious. Yet it was precisely the high rate of turnover in the context of an increasingly oligarchic political regime that made it vital for elite members continuously to uphold the legitimating fiction of social continuity in power.[29] In reality, there were always many new-comers, replacing those elite members whose families had become extinct or impoverished, and most of them would enter the lower ranks of the bouleutic elite. However, due to the high variation of chances of survival around the mean, the same demographic volatility that produced all this social mobility also generated continuity in the elite's most elevated ranks. There would always be a small, randomly 'selected' number of families who were, demographically speaking, 'lucky winners'. Their members would, for a few successive generations, live long lives and have a small number of surviving offspring, just enough to replace them in their position. Conse-quently, such families would have a far longer time span available to them for the accumulation of wealth, power and prestige than competing but demographically 'unluckier' families. Within a strongly oligarchic society, the demographic lottery thus almost automatically led to the formation of an elite within the elite, or internal oligarchisation.[30] Naturally, the 'win-ning' families would also be in a good position to arrange continuation of their powerful position by means of clever strategies of adoption and suc-cession once their luck ran out. Evidence for internal oligarchisation and the existence of social cleavages within the bouleutic elite is fairly plentiful. In the epigraphic records for individual cities, the names of a small number of local families constantly reappear. Other indications may be found in Pliny's letters to Trajan, and in various passages of the *Digest*.[31]

Interestingly, the internal stratification of the urban elite is reflected in the patterns of civic munificence. For instance, the frequent occurrence of partial contributions to public buildings, discussed in Chapter 1, is in itself indicative of the elite's internal stratification. Building was prohibitively expensive, so donating entire public buildings would generally have been something only the richest elite families could afford. The majority of less

---

[29] See Chapter 6, pp. 140–6 for a more detailed discussion of these issues.

[30] Or, as Jongman (2003) 194 phrases it, 'any system where chances of survival vary as much around the mean as they did [in the Roman world] is bound to have a small number of lucky winners. We are wrong to assume that in a game of dice those who keep throwing sixes are any different from those who don't. They do win, however.' I have borrowed the term 'demographic lottery' from Tacoma (2006).

[31] Pliny *Ep.* 10.79, and *Dig.* 50.2.12 (Callistratus), 50.4.6 (Ulpian), 50.4.11.1 (Ulpian), 50.7.5.5 (Mar-cianus). See Chapter 6, pp. 134–7 and Zuiderhoek (forthcoming).

wealthy elite families would mostly have had to make do with contributing parts. Foundations (i.e. gifts of a capital, either land or money, from the revenues of which a benefaction would be financed at recurring intervals) provide another telling example of how munificence reflects the internal stratification of the urban elite. Foundations were costly. Assuming a 12 per cent annual interest on loans or annual revenues from landholding in the order of 5 per cent, foundations would generally be some eight to twenty times more expensive than single gifts. Barring a category of very small foundations that were usually set up for personal commemoration, foundations would by and large have been affordable only to the richer members of the urban elite. This can be illustrated from a small collection of foundation capitals from the eastern provinces that I have assembled (see Appendix 2). The sums range from 500,000 to 120 denarii. If we look at this material, we see that most foundation capitals (89.4 per cent) amount to 1,000 denarii or more. This means that a large majority of benefactors in our sample donated foundations with a value of at least (almost) once to, in the most extreme case, 400 times the annual income of a councillor possessing the census minimum of HS 100,000 or 25,000 denarii.[32] This would broadly seem to support the hypothesis that foundation donors mostly belonged to the wealthier sections of the urban elite.

We can also point out the stratification among the foundation donors. Assuming a rough correlation between size and number of gifts and level of wealth, we may attempt a tentative reconstruction of the distribution of wealth within our group of sixty-eight individual donors. What immediately strikes the eye is the very steep internal stratification of the group, mirroring the stratification within the urban elite as a whole and, one might say, Roman society in general. Almost the entire total of all capital sums (96.8 per cent) was donated by a little under half of all benefactors in the sample (32, or 47 per cent). This implies that, taken together, the donations of the remaining thirty-six benefactors amounted to no more than a few percentages of the total sum. We can still sharpen our focus somewhat by concentrating on the first twelve sums in the sample, which are all in the range from 500,000–100,000 denarii. Together, these constitute 76.8 per cent of the total sum, while they were donated by only ten individuals (14.7 per cent of all benefactors). Finally, the first five sums in the sample, which together constitute a little over half (50.7 per cent) of the total sum, were donated by just four individuals, or 5.9 per cent of all benefactors.

---

[32] Again, assuming a 5 per cent annual return on landed property, for which see Duncan-Jones (1982) 33. The annual income of a *bouleutes* possessing the census minimum would then be 1,250 denarii.

These last two calculations in particular reveal that at the urban provincial level the concentration of large-scale surpluses in a few hands was just as extreme as among senators and *equites* at the very top of the imperial hierarchy.[33]

The increasing political oligarchisation and the internal oligarchisation of the bouleutic elite in fact fit a wider trend towards a growing hierarchisation of urban society in the Greek east during the early and high Empire. Inscriptions from the period reveal the existence within the citizenry of a wide array of more or less privileged subgroups of citizens, who, as far as we can determine, were mostly located socially (just) below the *ordo*.[34] This process of hierarchisation did by no means lead to the creation of a standardised structure that held in each city, at least not beyond the crude outline, with the boule at the top and those without citizenship more or less at the bottom, that we find almost universally. Flexibility and fluidity are indeed key characteristics of the process: flexibility with regard to the criteria constituting a group qua group – age (*neoi,* ephebes, gerousiasts), religious or professional activities (*collegia* and clubs)[35], political activities and privileges, social and legal status (the *bouleutai,* naturally, but also the notorious *ekklesiastai* and *sitometroumenoi andres*), to name but a few; flexibility also, however, with regard to the structure of the hierarchy itself – as I shall show in my discussion of civic processions and public distributions in Chapter 5, we find (slightly) different visions of the ideal social hierarchy in inscriptions from different cities and/or referring to the activities of different benefactors.[36]

What matters now is not the existence as such of many of the various groups I have just mentioned. Some already had a much longer history, and their origins date back to earlier periods of Greek history, even though they might have undergone a significant change in character during the intervening period. Rather, what concerns me here is their increasing *visibility* in our sources from the Roman period, and their apparently increasingly self-conscious attempts to negotiate a recognised place for themselves in 'the' civic hierarchy, which was itself of course at least partly only a product of such strivings and struggles. This process of struggle by groups within the citizenry for an accepted position within the social hierarchy, a position exemplified par excellence by their participation as recognised, legitimate corporate entities in civic public events and rituals, has been aptly termed *ordo*-making. In his study of professional *collegia,* Onno van Nijf has

---

[33] See Duncan-Jones (1963) 165 for a very similar stratification among benefactors in imperial North Africa.
[34] For references see Chapter 5, Table 5.2.   [35] See van Nijf (1997).   [36] See Chapter 5, pp. 94–106.

defined this process as an ongoing attempt of various civic subgroups to order their world according to 'a hierarchical conception of society in which identity was derived from membership of a status group constructed along the lines of a Roman *ordo*'.[37] He thereby explicitly recognises the influence of Roman models of social hierarchy and patronage on the Greek cities of the time, an influence that we already saw at work in the transformation of the boule.[38] What matters for the argument put forward in this study, however, is that this trend towards increasing hierarchisation of the citizen community easily blended in with, and was up to a point strongly stimulated by, elite benefactors' attempts to organise their munificence around a distinctly hierarchical ideal of civic society. The reasons for such a fundamental shift in civic ideology are not hard to find. Clearly, the Classical Greek model of political egalitarianism made little sense in the oligarchic political world of the cities in the Roman east. Nonetheless, in the face of increasing oligarchisation and growing disparities of wealth, the maintenance of social stability in the cities was predicated precisely on the need to retain a sense of social and political cohesion within the citizen body. A hierarchical model of civic society, in which nevertheless the special status of even the poorest member of the citizen community was still highlighted by allowing him/her unlimited access to the essentials of the citizen lifestyle, clearly fitted the bill exactly. As we shall see in the discussion of gifts in Chapter 5, euergetism was a vital instrument in the continuing attempts to turn this 'new' civic ideal into a living reality. *Continuing* attempts, because both elements that made up the ideal, the hierarchical and the participatory, were constantly being threatened by strong countervailing forces – the participatory element suffering from the by now well-known duo of increasing oligarchisation and growing income-disparities within the citizenry, and the hierarchical being constantly undermined by the great demographic volatility resulting from the harsh mortality regime.

GROWING SOCIAL TENSIONS

The growing accumulation of wealth and power in the hands of the few did not fail to elicit a response from the many. In his exhaustive survey of the then available source material for the economic history of Roman Asia Minor, a quick perusal of which does more than anything to bring out the extent of the material and immaterial riches accruing in the hands of the region's upper classes at the time, T. R. S. Broughton noted that, despite

---

[37] Van Nijf (1997) 245, also 134, 168, 187, 217.   [38] See pp. 60–2 above.

appearances, 'all was not well'. There is 'evidence of a considerable amount of civic discord in such widely separated regions as Bithynia and Cilicia'.[39] And indeed, the sources for the first and second centuries AD convey a distinct impression of tension constantly brewing beneath the skin of civic life, and not infrequently erupting. The refrain of *homonoia* (concord) is repeated endlessly on coins and inscriptions from the region's numerous towns and cities.[40] Yet the continuous proclamation of peace only points to its absence, as the sources make abundantly clear. The information is scattered and sometimes difficult to interpret, but the pattern is evident: in many cities boule and demos frequently clashed during our period.[41] In his advisory text for aspiring politicians, Plutarch uses the example of the Classical Athenian demos to comment on the behaviour of the people in the Greek cities of his own day: 'easily moved to anger'.[42] A letter of Apollonius of Tyana to the people of Sardis hints darkly at considerable civic discord in that city, while the great rift separating the wealthy few from the mass of poorer citizens in most cities of Roman Asia Minor at the time is brought sharply into focus by the artificially induced shortage at Aspendus in Pamphylia, where 'the rich men (*hoi dynatoi*) had shut up all the corn and were holding it up for export from the *chora*' instead of selling it at the local marketplace. Public anger and indignation ran to such heights that Apollonius was barely able to prevent the burning alive of a local magistrate and a mass raid of elite estates.[43] Elsewhere, Philostratus writes about endemic conflict between 'the men of the upper part of the *chora*' and 'those on the seashore' at Smyrna, which the sophist Antonius Polemo managed to bring to an end.[44] At Rhodes, Aelius Aristides found rich and poor citizens at each other's throats, and rebuked them in a famous speech.[45] Dio Chrysostom spoke at Tarsus in an attempt to resolve long-lasting conflicts between the council, the people and the *gerousia*, while at Nicaea the orator delivered an eulogy on *homonoia* in the aftermath of violent civic strife in that city.[46] Dio was no stranger to civic conflicts; as Giovanni Salmeri notes, *homonoia* (concord), 'which he [Dio] saw as a guarantee for the continued power of the notables, his peers', is actually one of the most pervasive and recurring themes in Dio's political speeches.[47] The orator's native Prusa was frequently torn by conflicts between the

---

[39] Broughton (1938) 810.   [40] For the coinage see Pera (1984).
[41] On social conflicts in Roman Asia Minor see e.g. Sartre (1991) 187–90; Mitchell (1993) 203; Salmeri (2000) 71ff.
[42] *Prae. ger. reip.* 799c.
[43] For the letter to Sardis see Philostratus, *Letters of Apollonius* 56; for the Aspendus episode: Philostratus *Vit. Apoll.* 1.15.
[44] *Vit. Soph.* 1.25, p. 531.   [45] *Oration to the Rhodians: concerning concord (Or.* 24), *passim.*
[46] *Or.* 34.16–20 (Tarsus); 39 (Nicaea).   [47] Salmeri (2000) 75–81. The quote is from p. 77.

citizens. In fact, Dio's speeches on Prusan affairs are probably our best source for civic politics in the east during the early Empire, and as such they are highly indicative of the volatile and turbulent nature of elite–non-elite relations in the imperial Greek cities. The pattern is the same as in the sources already referred to, only it can be seen more clearly: most conflicts arose out of attempts by the non-elite citizenry to retain or regain a measure of control over the running of their communities, and out of anger and suspicion about oligarchic excesses and what the demos perceived as abuses of power by the bouleutic elite. As in Aspendus, the people stormed the houses of the elite, including Dio's, during a food shortage, suspecting the notables of speculative hoarding.[48] On other occasions, the people's anger was provoked by the notables' illegally holding on to public funds, and the latter's failure to live up to promises to contribute to the rebuilding of the city.[49] Dio's speeches also allow us to view the demos through the eyes of the elite in a situation where the people were not present: in a speech before the council, Dio assures his elite peers that his occasional displays of sympathy with the plight of the common people should by no means be taken to imply 'that I am on more friendly terms with them than with you'.[50] His basic policy was to try to restrain the demos. His speeches to the assembly are littered with admonishments to the people to conduct themselves in an orderly fashion, to obey the notables and not to antagonise the Roman authorities through conflict.[51] All to little avail: probably following particularly vicious conflict between demos and notables, the Prusan assembly lost its right to meet.[52] Nor was the assembly the only medium through which the non-elite citizenry gave voice to their discontent. As the correspondence between the emperor Trajan and Pliny the Younger makes clear, lower-class associations and clubs were notorious vehicles for political disturbances as well.[53]

    The apparent contrast between the consistent pattern of civic distur-bances revealed by the sources and the unmistakable boom in civic splen-dour in Asia Minor during the first two centuries AD has given historians some headaches.[54] There is, however, another way to view the situation.

[48] *Or.* 46.   [49] *Or.* 47.19; 48.9. See Salmeri (2000) 73.   [50] *Or.* 50.3.
[51] Salmeri (2000) 72. Here lies the key to the reaction of urban elites to lower-class discontent. As Salmeri (2000) 74 writes: 'It was...in the interests of the upper classes for harmony and order to reign in the cities; indeed, it was an indispensable condition for them to be able to enjoy their economic well-being, and to prevent the intervention of the Roman governors.' For concern over Roman intervention because of civic disorder see Dio Chrys. *Or.* 46.14; Plut. *Prae. ger. reip.* 814f–815a.
[52] *Or.* 48. The proconsul Varenus Rufus restored it, probably around AD 102.
[53] Pliny *Ep.* 10.34: the emperor would not even allow permanent fire brigades in the cities.
[54] See for instance Broughton (1938) 810–12.

The changing status of the civic elite towards one of growing and increasingly institutionalised oligarchic exclusiveness (at least in political, if not in demographic, terms), brought about by the inclusion of the eastern cities into the Roman imperial structure, coupled with the unprecedented growth of elite incomes, put severe strains on the Classical *isonomic* model of polis society, which throughout the Hellenistic period and into the early Empire had still provided the ideological, if not always the practical, underpinning of civic society.[55] As a result, the polis model bent, and adapted, but the process was far from painless. It is therefore no coincidence, I would argue, that we have such an extensive record of civic conflict and tension precisely at a time when the accumulation of wealth at the top of the social hierarchy, and the concomitant civic splendour, were at their greatest. In fact, the surge in elite wealth and income, together with the growing oligarchisation of social and political life, significantly increased the potential for class antagonism and social disruption in the eastern cities. Those protesting were not always the very poor, they were the ordinary citizens, the *plebs media* who made up the larger part of the demos, people able to raise their voices in the popular assembly, citizens who were perhaps slightly more well-off than their grandfathers had been, and who saw their landowning fellow citizens at the top of the social hierarchy achieving vast new wealth, to a level totally unprecedented in provincial civic society. Perhaps more importantly still, they saw them assuming oligarchic power to an extreme not seen before in the poleis of the Greek east. Here I think lay the root of the social and political disturbances between elite and non-elite citizens of which the sources so frequently speak.

Yet violent conflict, though frequent, was not the rule. More often, actual violence and open struggle were avoided, and the antagonism between rich and poor was expressed in a different way. This is where euergetism comes in. What I have in mind here is an analysis somewhat akin to the idea of the 'moral economy' as developed by the British social historian E. P. Thompson.[56] Analysing food riots in eighteenth-century England, Thompson argued that rioters were not in the first place motivated by hunger and deprivation. Rather, the poor acted upon what they perceived as a violation of 'justice' in the workings of the food market (very high prices, a dearth of food on the market) or in the behaviour of authorities in the event of shortages. In former centuries, authorities had usually

---

[55] See Jones (1940) Chapters 10 and 11; Dmitriev (2005) 335 speaks of a 'discrepancy between "democratic constitutions" of Greek cities in the Roman east and the "aristocratic nature" of the societies of these cities'.

[56] Thompson (1971), reprinted in Thompson (1991) along with a reply to critics and adherents.

intervened when grain was in short supply, and had ensured that local landowners and merchants sold their stocks at an artificially low price. The eighteenth-century crowds now expected the same principles of justice to operate when shortages occurred. When, due to the new liberal, laissez-faire ideology, authorities and elites failed to co-operate, the crowds felt entitled to take matters into their own hands.

What matters to me in this analysis is that in sixteenth- and early seventeenth-century England there was apparently a pattern of traditional expectations that somehow created ties of reciprocal obligation between governing elites and urban masses. The masses acquiesced in the existing inequalities of wealth and power, thus ensuring social stability and the secure enjoyment of privilege by the elite, but only on the condition that the latter lived up to their 'duty' and provided the poor with access to sustenance in times of dearth. My argument is that similar notions of reciprocal obligation existed among elite and non-elite citizens in the cities of the Roman east.[57] On this interpretation, non-elite citizens would be prepared to accept as politically legitimate the disparities of wealth and power separating them from their elite fellow citizens, as long, and only as long, as the latter fulfilled the – unwritten – obligation to provide them with all the amenities necessary for life as proper Greek (Greco-Roman) citizens. In the next chapter, I shall try to show that this was in fact precisely what elite benefactors did, even if, to judge from the evidence we have for civic conflicts, their generosity did not unfailingly succeed in keeping the peace.

---

[57] See Erdkamp (2002) on food riots in the Roman world for a recent, more direct, application of Thompson's theories to ancient society.

CHAPTER 5

The politics of public generosity

Why did elite benefactors give what they gave? This will be the central question of the present chapter. In previous chapters we saw that euergetism was not driven primarily by economic or charitable impulses. But if this is true then what did drive it? I will argue that the strain put on the polis model of society by the growing accumulation of wealth and power in the hands of small coteries of rich families encouraged elite benefactors to emphasise the continuing importance of the citizen community. Public munificence thus constituted a celebration of citizenship and the civic ideal, but it also helped to modify that ideal by allowing benefactors, whether deliberately or unconsciously, to move the focus away from the Classical notion of political egalitarianism towards a glorification of hierarchy within the citizen community. This latter aspect can be seen particularly clearly when we study the festivals and public handouts organised by members of the elite. In this way, euergetism served to re-emphasise the age-old collectivist ideal of the polis as a community of citizens in the face of the threats posed by contemporary economic and socio-political developments (for which see the previous chapter), while at the same time providing legitimation for the increasingly hierarchical and oligarchic nature of Greek civic society under the Empire.

BENEFACTIONS: THE CIVIC IDEAL AND CIVIC HIERARCHY

The old polis ideal, which defined the city essentially as a community of people, of citizens, had remained central to Greek civic ideology during the Roman imperial period. This is evident, for instance, from the way cities always described themselves, or were referred to, as a community of people – the Athenians, the Pergamenes, the Prusans – instead of a place.[1] It also shows from the great value people attached to their civic affiliation,

---

[1] See Reynolds (1988) 15; Millar (1993) 246–7.

71

referring to it whenever possible, in inscriptions, papyri and so forth. It shows from the fact that Roman citizenship, which became increasingly widespread in the east during the second century AD, *never* managed to replace local citizenship. Instead, the two statuses simply co-existed. And it shows from the fact that cities regarded the grant of *their* citizenship to outsiders who had done them well as one of the highest honours they could bestow, at least on a foreigner.[2] Members of the urban elites, however powerful, wealthy or influential in the wider world of the Empire, first and foremost felt themselves to be citizens of their native communities, and, most importantly, *fellow* citizens of their poorer compatriots. Dio Chrysostom told the assembly of his native Prusa that no praise was dearer to him than that of his fellow citizens, 'even if the whole Greek world and the Roman people too, were to admire and praise me'. He went on to say that he would not have preferred even Athens, Argos or Sparta, 'the first and most famous of the Greek cities', to Prusa:

For although many people in many lands have invited me both to make my home with them and to take charge of their public affairs . . . yet I never accepted such a proposal even by so much as a single word, and I did not even acquire a house or a plot of ground anywhere abroad, so that I might have nothing to suggest a home-land anywhere but here.[3]

We should of course allow for the rhetoric, but even if we do, the sentiment still strikes sincere. Dio, we should remember, was something of a celebrity. He had travelled widely and seen many of the Empire's great cities, including Rome, with his own eyes. He had high friends everywhere, and was even an acquaintance of the emperors Nerva and Trajan. And yet, he devoted much of his life and energies to politics and munificence in small-town Bithynian Prusa, in spite of considerable and frequently nasty opposition from jealous local rivals. It is a pattern known also from the careers of other eastern grandees. In a recent study Giovanni Salmeri provides a whole list of eastern aristocrats who, despite great wealth and wide political influence, chose to devote much of their lives to Greek municipal politics in the east, sometimes even aborting senatorial or equestrian careers for the purpose. Among them are the sophist M. Antonius Polemo, the grand Lycian benefactor Opramoas of Rhodiapolis (who was not even a Roman citizen), the historians-cum-senators Flavius Arrianus and A. Claudius Charax, the

---

[2] Roman emperors could and did acknowledge the importance polis ideals and institutions held for their Greek-speaking subjects. For a startling recent example see the letter by the (admittedly philhellene) emperor Hadrian to the citizens of Naryka in eastern Locris published by Jones (2006).

[3] *Or.* 44.1, 6. Loeb translation, slightly adapted.

equestrian C. Iulius Demosthenes of Oenoanda, and, famously, Herodes Atticus.[4] Like Dio and (probably) the individuals just mentioned, Plutarch too extols the ideal of service to one's native community, criticising those wealthy eastern citizens who scorned local politics out of eagerness for a career in the Roman administration.[5] Local patriotism and love of one's fellow citizens is also the motive most frequently encountered in inscriptions recording gifts by generous members of the urban elite. Hence when elite donors motivate their gifts by saying that they have 'loved my dearest homeland from my earliest youth' or wish 'to requite the native town that bred and loves me' we have no reason to doubt their sincerity.[6] As always, the discourse of praise of honorific inscriptions is instructive: as Peter Brown notes, a rich benefactor was invariably praised 'for being a *philopatris*, a "lover of his home-city", never for being a *philoptôchos*, a "lover of the poor."'[7]

As these last two examples indicate, it is euergetism which perhaps allows us to appreciate best just how central the notion of citizen community was to the civic ideology of the imperial Greek cities. As I shall demonstrate in this section, benefactors by means of their gifts to the citizen community helped to define that community in a very real sense. Through the character and structure of their public generosity, elite benefactors managed to endow their communities with a specific sense of corporate, collective identity. Their selection of what to donate and what not betrays a clear and sharply defined sense of what was needed for 'the good life' of the Greco-Roman citizen, and this was what they provided their fellow citizens with. Given its central ideological focus on the citizen community and the citizen 'good life', it is no wonder that euergetism proliferated precisely during the second century AD. As we saw in the previous chapter, it was during this period that great disparities of wealth between elite and non-elite citizens became increasingly strongly felt in urban society, as civic elites reached new and unprecedented levels of riches, while a socially and politically restive demos, some of whom perhaps saw their income rise a little as well (though not nearly as fast or on so large a scale as those of the elite), staked out a claim to a share of the new elite wealth. Also, political power had largely become the prerogative of a privileged group of very rich elite

---

[4] Salmeri (2000) 58–60.
[5] *De tranq. anim.* 470c; *Prae. ger. reip.* 811b–c, 814d. See Salmeri (2000) 61–2.
[6] Wörrle (1988) (C. Iulius Demosthenes, Oenoanda) line 8: [ἀπὸ] πρώτης ἡλικίας τὴν γλυκυτάτην μου πατρίδα πεφιληκώς; Buckler (1937) (Varus Aurelius Marcus, Orcistus) A lines 5–6: Πατρίδα ἀμείβεσθαι τὴν θρέψα[σα]ν καὶ φιλοῦσαν.
[7] Brown (2002) 5.

families active in the urban council, whose members acquired ever more characteristics of a true *ordo*, separated culturally, socially, politically and economically from the mass of ordinary citizens. These developments had the potential to erode the unifying ideal of citizen community, the very ideological notion that provided much of the basis for social and political stability in the post-Classical Greek cities. Open large-scale social conflict was perhaps rare, but contemporary commentators were acutely aware of the tension that was constantly brewing under the skin of civic life, as was Plutarch when he implored elite politicians by all means not to neglect their role as benefactors.[8] Moreover, we frequently hear of what were sometimes violent clashes between elite and non-elite citizens in the late first and second centuries AD. These, as we saw in the previous chapter, usually took the shape of conflicts between the boule/the notables on the one hand, and the demos on the other.

Given the continuous threat of social antagonism as a consequence of contemporary economic and socio-political developments, the unifying ideal of citizen community increasingly needed to be re-emphasised, and euergetism turned out to be the ideal instrument to do just that. Not only did most benefactors emphasise with their gifts the importance of the citizen community and the civic way of life, but also the very process of exchange that constituted euergetism can be said to have exemplified the ideological centrality of the citizen body. By means of a sort of unspoken, perhaps even largely unconscious, 'pact' elite citizens through their munificence made it in fact possible for their poorer fellow citizens to enjoy those amenities essential to the life of the true Greco-Roman citizen. In exchange, the non-elite citizenry, despite occasional struggles, in the end accepted the rule of the rich bouleutic families and through their consent legitimated the latter's position of power. Euergetism thus prevented the unifying notions of citizenship and citizen-community from losing their meaning completely in an age of ever-growing disparities of wealth and political power within the citizen body. By allowing poorer citizens unhindered access to all the amenities necessary for the citizen-'good life' – gymnasia, baths, theatres, temples, games, festivals, distributions – euergetism did not just serve to define the very notion of the Greco-Roman 'good life'. By unceasingly honouring the entitlements implicit in citizenship, euergetism also powerfully and unequivocally underlined the fact that citizenship still constituted the primary organising principle of civic life.[9] Consequently,

---

[8] *Prae. ger. reip.* 822a.
[9] For the concept of entitlement see Sen (1982) 1–8. Broadly following Sen, I think we could define entitlements as those aspects of an individual's legal, social, political and economic position that

largely because of euergetism, it still meant something to be a citizen of a polis during the high Roman Empire. In plain terms, citizenship often allowed you a larger share of the cake than you would have received had you simply been a non-citizen resident. Euergetism thus functioned as the primary distribution mechanism that turned citizenship-entitlements from a theoretical possibility into an everyday reality. As such, euergetism's palliative social effects were increasingly needed during the second century AD, when the divisions of wealth and power within the citizen body slowly reached their apex and their corroding influence on civic unity needed to be battled against on all fronts. It is no coincidence that the theme of *homonoia* figures so prominently in the literature and epigraphy of the east during the high Empire. Euergetism did much to make *homonoia* possible and to ensure its continuous existence; non-elite citizens considered it only natural that the elite did their best to allow them their rightful share of the increasingly sumptuous forms of civic life the new wealth made possible.[10] The balance, however, was precarious. As Plutarch realised, the elite had better live up to the facts of nature . . .

We should however note that, over the course of many centuries since the Classical period, the civic ideal did not remain unchanged. The notion of the polis as a community of political equals, which had prevailed in Classical times, started to make less and less sense in the far more oligarchic Greek civic world which came into existence from the later Hellenistic period onwards. Consequently, during the Roman imperial period, when the oligarchisation and hierarchisation of urban society became increasingly visible and institutionally formalised, the civic ideal had taken on a decidedly new form. The citizen community was, as we just saw, still *the* central element around which civic ideology was constructed, but it was now refashioned into a far more hierarchical shape. We can see this clearly in various areas of euergetism. Public distributions almost invariably

---

determine the extent to which he has access to the resources he needs. In the words of Sen (1982) 8, economists often tend to argue 'in terms of what *exists* rather than in terms of who can *command* what' (Sen's emphasis). A citizen of a Greek polis or the Roman Republic/Empire could, in various ways, more easily command access to (vital) resources than a non-citizen, hence in the ancient world citizenship functioned as a form of entitlement. See also Jongman (2002b) and (2006) for the benefits Roman citizenship might confer.

10 This 'naturalness' was underwritten ideologically by the populace's use of 'family language' while addressing or honouring generous elite members, calling them 'fathers' or 'mothers' of the city or demos: see Pleket (1998) 213–14 for evidence and literature. What is more natural for fathers or mothers than to desire to feed their children, and to provide them, as far as possible, with the essentials they need to lead a proper and fulfilling life? The notion must however also have been congenial to an oligarchic elite, since it implied a patriarchal, deferential society in which the poor 'children' are submissive and obey the rich 'fathers'. See also van Rossum (1988) 152–5; Robert (1966) 85–6; Zuiderhoek (2008).

focused on citizens, and if they sometimes included non-citizen groups, these mostly received (far) less than citizens. However, within the citizenry, as we shall see, a variety of privileged groups received handouts that were sometimes considerably larger than those granted to ordinary citizens (*politai*).[11] Festivals usually expressly involved the entire citizen body, and even glorified its unity, as citizens together worshipped their gods, honoured their traditions, commemorated their collective past and collectively enjoyed and participated in games and athletics. On closer inspection, however, there are often many hints suggesting that this same citizen body was now perceived as structured in a distinctly hierarchical way.[12]

Such a hierarchical definition of civic society made far more ideological sense in a society where power structures were so explicitly founded on a highly unequal division of wealth, power and prestige. Indeed, I would argue that it was precisely this redefinition of the citizen community in terms of a hierarchy of status groups that allowed the oligarchic urban societies of the Roman east to retain their sense of civic unity. By integrating the concept of status hierarchy into their idealised picture of the citizen community, the urban societies of the Roman east managed to devise an ideological justification for the huge social cleavages dividing their citizen bodies. The compromise was frequently an uneasy one, as our evidence for social tensions reveals, but it tended to work reasonably well provided that its central message was continuously reinforced and the elite lived up to their side of the bargain. Once more we see how crucial euergetism was to the stable functioning of urban society in the Roman east.

That, at least, is my theory. But is it borne out by the evidence? Does elite munificence in Roman Asia Minor indeed conform to the picture just sketched? Let us first look at the overall characteristics of elite gifts, and subsequently have a closer look at various main categories of donations. The overall characteristics of civic munificence in Roman Asia Minor are fairly clear (see Fig. 5.1). By far the largest number of all benefactions in the sample (88 per cent) concern games and festivals, distributions or public buildings, with gifts towards building constituting an absolute majority. Under the heading 'miscellaneous' I have grouped those benefactions of which too few are attested to make it worthwhile to list them as separate categories (at least, this cannot be done without messing up the graph). They include mainly embassies to the emperor, unspecified gifts of money or land to the city, the council or the *gerousia*, gifts of grain, or of money to buy grain, foundations that perpetually covered the costs of certain offices,

---

[11] I discuss such distributions in far more detail at pp. 98–106.   [12] See pp. 86–98.

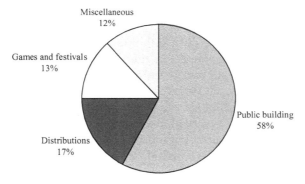

Figure 5.1 Frequency of benefaction-types (N = 529)

gifts which relieved people from taxes or debts and so forth. Reviewing the material in the aggregate, I want, without wishing to anticipate too much the subsequent discussion of individual benefaction-types, to make an important preliminary observation. Looking at the sample as a whole, it appears that so-called 'utilitarian' gifts (infrastructural contributions such as aqueducts, sewers, roads, or forms of relief of immediate needs of poorer citizens, i.e. food in times of dearth, tax or debt relief) were relatively few in number. They did exist, certainly, but there are so few of them on record that they do not even constitute a significant minority. Instead, gifts that evoke a distinctly Greco-Roman civic lifestyle predominate. These comprise gifts towards buildings and public events associated with civic religion, cultural life and entertainment that underwrote civic ideology and emphasised civic hierarchy. In addition, we find much architecture of display, and representational monuments. These observations in fact constitute the basis for my argument that with their gifts elite civic benefactors were primarily emphasising a specifically (eastern provincial) Greco-Roman ideal of civic life. By donating what they did, they allowed the recipient non-elite citizens to enjoy precisely the amenities that were deemed indispensable to the life of the true citizen. By thus preventing increased oligarchisation and ever-growing elite wealth from turning citizenship entitlements into a dead letter for the majority of non-elite citizens, the oligarchies of rich citizens managed more or less to preserve social stability and the ideal of civic unity. However, as I noted above, and as is clearly visible in the benefactions, that same civic ideal had also come to be redefined in a far more hierarchical sense. We shall now turn to the main categories of public gifts – buildings, festivals and distributions – in some more detail in order to substantiate further this specific interpretation of the role of public generosity.

CIVIC SURROUNDINGS: GIFTS TOWARDS PUBLIC BUILDING

A polis or *civitas* was essentially a community of people. We have already seen that, among the inhabitants of the Greek cities of Roman imperial times, this notion was still just as central as it had been among their cultural forebears in Classical Greece. A citizen, however, needed appropriate surroundings. Public buildings, festivals or games were all essential ingredients of the complicated cultural mix the Greeks and Romans thought of as urban civilisation. Civilisation, indeed, was virtually synonymous with the city. Without urbanism, civilisation could not exist. And urbanity presupposed public building: no true civic culture could exist in a town with 'no government buildings, no gymnasium, no theatre, no agora, no water conducted to a fountain, and where the people live in hovels like mountain cabins on the edge of a ravine'. As Pausanias indicated in this contemptuous description of the little town of Panopeus in Phokis, northern Greece, such a place had no right to call itself a polis.[13] '[E]very self respecting city', A. H. M. Jones noted, needed at least 'colonnaded streets [stoas] and market squares [agoras], aqueducts and fountains, temples, gymnasia, baths, a stadium, a hippodrome, a theatre, an odeum. To these may be added buildings to house the various administrative services – the offices of the several boards of magistrates, the record office, the treasury, and the council chamber [*bouleuterion*].'[14] As we shall see, many such buildings were provided or contributed to by benefactors, and cities vied with one another over who had the most beautiful and extravagant set. Dio Chrysostom explicitly included 'buildings and festivals' among a list of items which 'would make it natural for the pride of cities to be enhanced and the dignity of the community to be increased and for it to receive fuller honour both from the strangers within their gates and from the proconsuls as well'.[15] His own continuous efforts, much frustrated by peer political opposition, to turn his native Prusa into 'a good-looking city, more open to the air, with open spaces, shade in summer, shelter in winter, and instead of mean and sordid ruins, lofty buildings worthy of a great city'[16] testify again to the high value civic communities placed on splendid public buildings.

It comes therefore as no surprise that an aspect of civic culture deemed so essential to civic life and identity, which went to the heart, even, of

---

[13] Pausanias 10.3.4.

[14] Jones (1940) 236. For a recent collection of some excellent archaeological studies of urbanism in Roman Asia Minor see Parrish (2001).

[15] *Or.* 40.10. Loeb translation.   [16] *Or.* 47.15, with Jones (1978) 111–14; Mitchell (1993) 212.

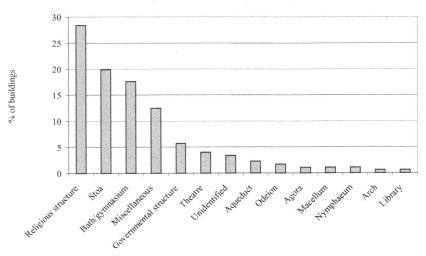

Figure 5.2 Whole buildings donated (N = 176)

the very notion of urbanity, was also the most important area of munif-icence. Urban life, citizen life, was not possible without public buildings. Hence nowhere does euergetism betray its focus on the provision of the essentials necessary for a true citizen lifestyle clearer than in the evident preponderance of gifts towards public building in our sample of recorded benefactions from Roman Asia Minor (see Fig. 5.1). We can appreciate this even better if we split up the recorded contributions according to the types of building donated. Figure 5.2 shows which types of building elite benefactors in Roman Asia Minor most frequently donated. It is a graph of whole buildings. Of course, many benefactors made only partial contributions to public buildings, for instance by donating some architectural element, or by financing repairs.[17] I did not include such partial contributions (restorations, embellishments) in the graph because these gifts are often fairly hard to classify. How, for instance, would one classify the gift of a statue group of gods, or a small shrine, which was to be placed in the theatre: as a religious structure or as a contribution to the theatre, as a 'whole building' or as a 'partial contribution'? In such cases I have mostly opted for the larger structure into which the gift was to be placed (in this case, the theatre), and hence for classification as a 'partial contribution'. However, to present

---

[17] See Chapter 2, pp. 28–31.

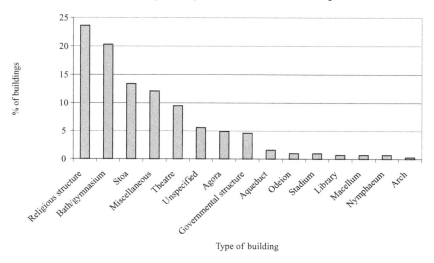

Figure 5.3 Types of public building donated or contributed to (N = 305)

as clear a pattern as possible of munificence-preferences in public build-ing, I have initially excluded this category of gifts from Fig. 5.2 (though see Fig. 5.3). It should be noted further that the terms 'whole building' and 'partial contribution' can sometimes be misleading, particularly with regard to the size of the gift concerned. In my classification, a tiny stoa, or a very small sanctuary (not much more than an altar, for instance) would count as a 'whole building', whereas a donation of, say, fifty columns to a very large temple complex would count as a partial contribution. Occa-sionally, therefore, 'partial contributions' may have been far more expensive gifts than 'whole buildings'. In general, however, most partial contributions were indeed fairly small, whereas most whole buildings were relatively large structures. Given the extremely high costs of construction in the ancient world, the donation of normal-sized public buildings (gymnasia, temples and so forth) will easily have constituted the most expensive form of civic munificence. Hence, give or take a few relatively cheap 'whole buildings', the pattern we observe in Fig. 5.2 is likely to be fairly representative of the preferences, at least in the area of public building, of the richest and most influential subset of public benefactors among the urban elite.

What pattern do these preferences reveal? First, I have to specify which types of building I listed under 'miscellaneous'. These include several statue groups, some towers, a public kitchen, a weighing house, storerooms, and a few booths. It is thus in this category that we find some types of building that we might term 'utilitarian'. The aqueducts are another such category, and perhaps we should also include the agoras and the *macelli*, though especially the agoras were often as much centres of symbolic display as functional marketplaces. On the whole, however, Fig. 5.2 reveals that in elite munificence towards buildings the emphasis was clearly on those types of public buildings that made a city 'civic' in the Greco-Roman sense. Temples, stoas, baths, gymnasia, *bouleuteria*, theatres, in short, the stock set of public buildings that according to Pausanias and modern archaeological findings ought to dominate the cityscape of every true polis, were the most favoured objects of munificence in public building. We shall treat the various categories one by one, turning to the religious structures first.

Although the ancient world knew rural shrines and temples, the city was in many ways a focal point of religious activity. Moreover, collective engagement in religious cults, festivals and ceremonies created strong symbolic bonds between citizens, thus reinforcing their sense of unity and corporate identity. Hence, a true polis was rich in temples, shrines, sanctuaries, altars, statues of the gods, and munificence abundantly reflects this. The preponderance of donations of religious structures which Fig. 5.2 reveals is indicative of a pronounced religious dimension of euergetism that, as will become evident below, we can also discern in many donated games and festivals. If euergetism was, as I argue, strongly bound up with ideas of civic identity and Greco-Roman ideals of urban civilisation and civic life, then the religious aspect of many forms of munificence indicates how deeply religiously embedded such ideas and ideals were. The inhabitants of the cities of the eastern Roman Empire in the second century AD still very much lived in a world full of gods. This was no pagan world in decline, as some older authors would have us believe, and euergetism decidedly shows this.[18] Many elite benefactors had been priests at some stage in their career, and not a few actually donated in that capacity. We should note that among benefactors' contributions, temples and sanctuaries for Roman emperors and the imperial cult figure almost as frequently as structures for other Greek, Greco-Roman or local deities. Here we touch on the almost seamless integration of the religious and the political in Greco-Roman civic life that was so strongly emphasised by Simon Price in his brilliant study of the Roman imperial cult in Asia Minor.[19] At the local level, this integration might manifest itself in the community's political mythology,

[18] See Lane Fox (1986) for an evocative sketch of the thriving pagan religious culture of the Empire's cities during the Flavian and Antonine periods. For festive religious life in action see Rogers (1991a).
[19] Price (1984).

which might relate the foundation and history of the city to important deities, or events and places important to the life of gods or demi-gods. Empire-wide, it showed in the cultivation of the religious connections between the deified Roman emperors and the faithful cities that were their subjects. The recurring ritual celebration of the community's relations with the divine, whether in the shape of a living or deceased emperor, Olympian gods, demi-gods or local deities, strongly stimulated a sense of civic unity by symbolically placing the community as a corporate entity over and against its gods. Small wonder, therefore, that elites, interested as they were in maintaining such a sense of unity among the citizenry in the face of growing disparities of wealth and power within it, made religion such a prominent area of their munificence. As with Price's study of the imperial cult, it is the *integration* of religion and politics that provides the key to the explanation.

The second most popular type of structure among elite benefactors, as Fig. 5.2 indicates, appears to have been the stoa. Here, financial calculation may have played a part. Stoas of course could be frightfully expensive, especially large and sumptuous ones. On the whole, however, it seems reasonable to think that a normal-sized stoa would have been a cheaper option, if one wished to donate an entire new building and not merely to make a contribution to an existing structure, than, say, an entire theatre or bath–gymnasium complex. Hence budgetary shrewdness might go a long way towards explaining the popularity of the stoa among civic benefactors, but financial considerations are not the whole story. The eastern stoa or colonnaded avenue, with its air of luxurious urbanity, was a highly appreciated architectural form in the cities of imperial Asia Minor, and we find it almost everywhere. As a combination of the traditional Greek stoa and the Roman *via portica*, it was a crucial element of what has been termed the typical 'Asiatic urbanism' of the cities of Asia Minor in imperial times, a creative synthesis of Hellenistic and Roman architectural ideas that revitalised the 'Romanized Greek polis in luxurious, nearly Baroque architectural forms'.[20] The so-called 'Syrian' colonnades – the first large one was built by Herod the Great in Syrian Antioch around 20 BC – provided an essential material backdrop to civic life (much like skyscrapers have become the emblematic structures of modern American cities), as the ruins of modern Turkey still testify.[21] They surrounded agoras and the courts of gymnasia, lined major streets and functioned as covered walks

[20] Hanfmann (1975) 48–9.
[21] In addition to the earliest attested one at Syrian Antioch, Boëthius and Ward-Perkins (1970) 395, 417 discuss examples from Corinth, Ephesos, Nicaea, Pergamon and Hierapolis.

wherever they could be squeezed into the urban layout. Dio Chrysostom went to great lengths to have one constructed at Prusa, as part of his grand scheme to turn his native town into a proper city worthy of the name.[22] Elite benefactors, eager to transform their cities into magnificent civic landscapes, found in the colonnaded avenue their perfect form. Stoas, colonnaded streets, were civic surroundings par excellence.

Next are baths and gymnasia. In Roman Asia Minor, these two were usually combined in one single complex, a synthesis of the Hellenistic gymnasium and the Roman bath building.[23] As such, like the colonnaded streets, these complexes can also be considered part of the great 'Asiatic' architectural renewal of the Greek cities in Asia Minor.[24] In Greek culture, physical exercise and athletics in the gymnasium had always constituted an essential part of what it meant to be a citizen, as had bathing and its facilities in Rome (though the Greeks had their baths too). However, the proliferation of the bath–gymnasium complexes in Roman imperial Asia Minor was strongly associated with a general 'renaissance' of gymnasial culture, as evidenced by the contemporaneous craze for agonistic games and festivals, to which members of the civic elite contributed significantly both as benefactors and participants.[25] The significance of the bath–gymnasium complexes for civic life and culture was, however, not confined to providing a context for agonistic contests. In many ways (and very much like the agoras of the Greek cities at this time)[26], through their multiplicity of functions, the bath–gymnasium complexes became focal points of civic life and citizen interaction in the public sphere, combining leisure, sport, religion (most bath–gymnasium complexes included a sanctuary for the imperial cult)[27], education and sociability, all in one building. In the words of the archaeologist George Hanfmann, '[w]ith its multiple functions as civic center, club house, leisure area, school, and place of worship of the emperors, the gymnasium now replaced the palace and the temples as the major concern of the Asiatic cities'.[28] Given this centrality of bath–gymnasium complexes to contemporary civic culture, we can only

[22] *Or.* 47.16–19 and 40.3–9. For Dio's building scheme, never entirely brought to completion, see also *Or.* 45.12–14 and the quotes at p. 78.
[23] See Yegül (2000) 144; also Yegül (1975) and (1986), on the bath–gymnasium complex at Sardis; Boëthius and Ward-Perkins (1970) 399–403; Hanfmann (1975) 48; Farrington (1987) and (1995) on the baths of Roman Lycia.
[24] Hanfmann (1975) 48.
[25] See van Nijf (2001), (2003) and the discussion of games and festivals at pp. 86–94 below.
[26] Here I draw attention to Chris Dickenson's research for his forthcoming PhD thesis at the Department of History, University of Groningen on the role and function of the agora in the Greek cities of the Hellenistic and Roman periods.
[27] See Yegül (1982).   [28] Hanfmann (1975) 48.

conclude that elite benefactors' fondness for donating them once again betrays their focus on providing their fellow citizens with the amenities essential to a proper citizen existence.

From here on the discussion becomes slightly more complicated. Figure 5.2, the graph of whole buildings, gives the category 'miscellaneous' next, followed by the category 'governmental structures'. However, if we look at Fig. 5.3, which is a graph that includes *all* contributions to public buildings in my database, i.e. also the partial ones, a somewhat different pattern emerges. We should of course bear in mind the classificatory problems associated with partial contributions discussed above, which make the classification in Fig. 5.3 somewhat more arbitrary than that in Fig. 5.2. Note that there are a few striking differences between the two graphs. First, when we include all recorded contributions to public building, the bath–gymnasium complex emerges as a more popular target for munificence than the stoa (in Fig. 5.2, it is the other way around). Second, whereas in Fig. 5.2 governmental structures (council houses, offices for the *agoranomoi* and so forth) surpass theatres, in Fig. 5.3 the theatre stands out as the more popular object of benefactions. The agora too appears as a more favoured object when we include all contributions (as in Fig. 5.3), instead of just donations of whole buildings (as in Fig. 5.2). The same is true, if only just, for libraries, while stadiums make their sole appearance in Fig. 5.3. In all these cases, I think the explanation for the difference between the two graphs is similar. Bath–gymnasium complexes, theatres, agoras, libraries and stadiums were often huge and complex structures, and hence frightfully expensive. Only the richest of the richest local elite families could afford to donate such buildings in their entirety. Given the prominence of bath–gymnasium complexes among the donations of whole buildings set out in Fig. 5.2, these seem to have been the least costly of the structures just mentioned. It is also quite conceivable that as gifts they were so popular among the citizenry, and hence brought donors such enormous prestige, that people were willing virtually to ruin themselves just to be able to provide one.[29] As for religious structures, many of these would have been rather smallish shrines, not big temples (although these are also present among recorded gifts), and hence not extremely expensive. Their prominence in the subset of whole buildings (Fig. 5.2) should therefore not surprise us. The relative cheapness of stoas (not universal: we know of very extensive and sumptuous examples too) we have already discussed.

[29] Another indication for the enormous popularity of baths/gymnasia and all the events and accessories associated with them is the proliferation among recorded benefactions of agonistic festivals and distributions of oil. I shall discuss these at pp. 88–92.

What all buildings with different locations in Figs. 5.2 and 5.3, perhaps with the exception of libraries (bath–gymnasium complexes, theatres, agoras, stadiums) have in common is that they were both expensive *and* essential to civic life and a proper citizen existence. I have just discussed bath–gymnasium complexes. Theatres were used for plays, shows, gladiatorial combats, wild beast hunts, all kinds of festivities, religious happenings, but also for mass meetings of the citizenry, in assembly, to honour a benefactor, or welcome a governor. Thus, theatres provided the citizenry with crucial venues for collective entertainment, festivity, and the expression of communal feeling and popular political will. The centrality of the agora to civic life hardly needs explaining. Most agoras combined the functions of local market, place of worship, venue for social interaction and sociability, centre of competitive elite display (in the form of monuments and statues) and stage for general architectural and sculptural splendour. Hence, in a very literal sense, the agora was a centre of civic life. The stadium, again, would be crucial to certain types of public entertainment, the absence of which would be unthinkable in a truly civilised Greek urban community. As a venue for horse racing, athletics and other forms of sport and competition, with citizens as both spectators and participants, the stadium was indispensable. In fact, the comparison between Figs. 5.2 and 5.3 underscores in a crucial way the sheer importance to civic life of the structures just discussed, and hence their popularity among elite benefactors. For what the comparison primarily reveals is the absolute determination of elite benefactors to contribute to just *this* set of structures, despite the highly costly nature of many of the buildings in question. These were the buildings a benefactor was supposed to provide his fellow citizens with, no matter how expensive they were. If that meant that many such benefactions could only be partial contributions (embellishments, restorations, and gifts of architectural elements), then this did not trouble most donors too much. What mattered was that one was seen to be contributing to precisely those public buildings that so crucially marked out the civic character of the community, and that were so essential to the day-to-day experience of civic life. By contributing to these types of buildings, elite members would thus be able both (as individuals) to maximise prestige and (as a collective) to show that they lived up to their part of the bargain by providing their non-elite fellow citizens with precisely those architectural amenities which were indispensable to civic life. I could go on to discuss the structures we have not yet touched upon – government buildings, important to civic administration but also, in their monumentality, to the community's perception of itself as a political entity, the *odeion*, the *nymphaeum*, structures for entertainment and display – but I think that by now my main point is fairly clear. Provision of the right civic surroundings, i.e. those structures without which a proper, civilised, citizen existence was well nigh impossible, was clearly a major concern for elite benefactors. These surroundings, in turn, provided the context for that other great area of civic munificence, the major public events and celebrations, the games, festivals and distributions which marked out the annual rhythm of civic life. It is to these that we shall now turn.

CITIZENS AND HIERARCHIES: GIFTS OF GAMES, FESTIVALS AND DISTRIBUTIONS

No occasion was better suited to the collective celebration of a sense of civic unity than the festival, and ancient cities were full of them. Particularly from Roman Asia Minor we have a considerable amount of mainly epigraphic documentation concerning festive life. The first thing to strike anyone is the enormous variety of festive forms. Festivals could include religious celebrations, processions and many sorts of contests (athletic, musical, dramatic, mimetic, rhetoric), but also communal meals, distributions, lotteries. Many festivals, moreover, combined several of these elements. At almost any time during the year, some part of the civic population was involved in some form of festive celebration, and many festivals even involved the entire civic community. So central indeed were festivals to ancient civic life that, following Walter Burkert, the ancient city may well be called a 'festive community' (*Festgemeinschaft*).[30] This centrality of the festival in the civic life of the Roman east should not surprise us, given that, as recent research has particularly emphasised, the festival was an important occasion for the celebration of civic unity and civic identity.[31] As we saw earlier, it was precisely this sense of unity and harmony within the citizen body that was badly needed, and had to be constantly re-emphasised in most cities, in an age of increasing oligarchisation and growing disparities of wealth within the citizenry.

Games and festivals, therefore, were a popular form of munificence. In many ways, they precisely fitted the bill of what an oligarchic elite of rich citizens in a Greek city of Roman times needed in order to maintain social harmony. Festivals often involved the entire citizen community in festive celebrations consisting of a potent mix of cultic activity (honouring the

---

[30] Burkert (1987); see also van Nijf (1997) 131–7 for a graphic description of festive life in the cities of the Roman east.
[31] See Wörrle (1988); Rogers (1991a); van Nijf (1997) Chapters 3–6.

city's patron deities and the emperor), agonistic contests, processions, distributions and a whole range of less clearly defined festive sociable activities. Festivals allowed great scope for rituals and symbolic statements emphasising the community's shared past, its foundation myths, its special relation with some gods, in short, its uniqueness as a corporate entity in a sacred, mythical and historical sense.[32] Festivals, moreover, offered elite benefactors an excellent opportunity to demonstrate their willingness to honour the entitlement aspect implicit in citizenship by granting their poorer fellow citizens free access to the essential amenities of civilised life. They often consisted of (combinations of) games and gymnastic contests to watch and participate in, theatrical shows, religious celebrations, public meals and distributions of such civic necessities as oil, wine, wheat or money. In most of these handouts, citizenship was the bottom-line criterion of distribution.[33] Viewed from this general perspective, festivals may partly be interpreted as short, intense, ritualised 'performances' of an ideal image of civic life, a strongly normative 'display' of what the community *ought* to look like, and how its citizens *ought* to live and relate to each other. This brings us to another attractive feature of festivals as a form of munificence, at least from the perspective of elite benefactors. Festivals, van Nijf has argued, were 'serious play', in the sense that '[p]ublic spectacles and civic celebrations were used to make serious political statements about the kind of community their organisers [i.e. members of the urban elite, acting as benefactors] thought they were living in'.[34] Festivals were indeed prime occasions not only for emphasising the centrality of the citizen community and the continuing importance of citizen status but also, and very importantly, for making symbolic statements about the community's internal socio-political structure. Moreover, as I have already argued earlier, and will show more fully in a moment, the conception of the citizen body's internal make-up, as represented in the structure of the festivals and distributions, was a distinctly hierarchical one. As we saw earlier, the move towards more hierarchical forms of social organisation (neatly falling in line with the trend towards ever-greater political oligarchisation) is clearly evident in the cities of the Greek east during the high Empire. Elite efforts to provide idealised hierarchical definitions of the social order should thus be viewed as part of this ongoing process, but also as an attempt both to naturalise and re-emphasise the ideal continuously. Such constant re-emphasising was important, since, for various important reasons to be

---

[32] This aspect of festive life is discussed with great insight in Rogers (1991a).
[33] See the discussion at pp. 104–5.   [34] Van Nijf (1997) 135.

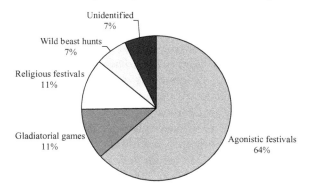

Figure 5.4 Types of festival donated (N = 71)

discussed below, social reality never quite came to match the hierarchical ideal.

Let us, with these considerations in mind, now have a closer look at what types of festival elite benefactors most commonly donated (see Fig. 5.4). I hasten to add that Fig. 5.4 should be understood as a very rough attempt at classification. As I noted earlier, an important characteristic of many civic festivals was precisely the integration of religious and agonistic elements. The separation of the two in Fig. 5.4 is therefore somewhat arbitrary. Yet, as I will show, it is not entirely useless either. I have classified festivals as 'agonistic' when, despite possible religious elements or undertones, athletic or other contests seemed the prime purpose of the event, and then applied the same principle, *mutatis mutandis*, to classifying festivals as 'religious'.

Whatever one's reservations about these classifications, the prominence of agonistic festivals is obvious. Festivals that involved contests of any kind, often athletic, but also musical, theatrical and so forth, seem to have been an extremely popular form of munificence among benefactors in Roman Asia Minor. Why? For an attempt to answer this question, we first have to return to Fig. 5.2, the graph of whole buildings donated. Remember that this graph showed that, despite the frightfully high costs involved in building them, bath–gymnasium complexes constituted the third most popular type of structure among elite donors in Asia Minor. With partial gifts included, they even made it to second place (see Fig. 5.3). A further step is to pre-empt our discussion of public distributions to some extent,

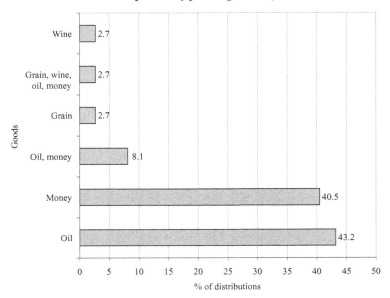

Figure 5.5 Goods distributed (N = 37)

and have a look at the frequency at which various (combinations of) goods were distributed, and to whom (see Fig. 5.5). As is clear from Fig. 5.5, oil was one of the most popular types of goods distributed by benefactors. And as Table 5.1 shows, the citizen population at large was among the chief beneficiaries of such oil distributions.[35] All but three of the twenty-seven distributions of oil where we know the recipient group(s) involve the citizen body as a collective (see Table 5.1).

What are we to make of this remarkable proliferation of bath–gymnasium complexes, agonistic festivals and oil distributions to the citizen body in the records of civic munificence from Asia Minor? I would argue that the patterns we see here in the gift-giving of local elite benefactors are in fact representative of a broad 'renaissance' of gymnasial culture in the

---

[35] NB: cit. = citizens; co. = councillors; ger. = gerousiasts; oth. = others. Note that the term 'others' in this table refers to a wide array of citizen and non-citizen subgroups (e.g. *sitometroumenoi andres, ekklesiastai*, ephebes, *neoi*, priests, women, children, resident Romans, *katoikoi, paroikoi, metoikoi*, slaves and so forth). Many of these will receive some attention in the discussion of money distributions below (see especially Table 5.2). In the present table, however, I have for the sake of clarity and simplicity decided to concentrate on the subgroups most commonly mentioned in epigraphic records of civic munificence, i.e. ordinary citizens (*politai*), councillors (*bouleutai*) and gerousiasts.

Table 5.1 *Goods distributed: who gets what?*

	cit.	cit., oth.	co.	co., cit.	co., cit., oth.	co., ger.	co., ger., cit., oth.	co., ger., oth.	co., oth.	ger.	ger., oth.
Grain	1	–	–	–	–	–	–	–	–	–	–
Grain, wine, oil, money	1	–	–	–	–	–	–	–	–	–	–
Money	9	2	14	1	–	5	2	1	4	4	–
Oil	20	–	–	–	–	–	–	–	–	–	2
Oil, money	1	–	2	–	–	–	–	–	–	–	–
Wine	–	–	–	–	–	–	–	–	–	1	–
Money, grain	–	–	–	–	–	–	–	–	1	–	–

eastern provinces during the high Empire. Van Nijf has linked the proliferation of agonistic festivals in the eastern cities during this period to a general
(re)invention of the traditions of cultural Hellenism, which was 'not politically innocent'. '[T]hese festivals', he writes, 'were not just the antiquarian
fads of schoolmasters. All over the eastern provinces, Hellenism was a major
ideological force in the hands of local elites, used to provide a common
identity to dominant groups in widely divergent cities and provinces.'[36]
And indeed he is able to show that, contrary to received opinion, participation in gymnasial athletics was an important element of a specific
elite lifestyle in the cities of the eastern provinces. The attestations of sons
of city councillors in the inscriptions commemorating athletic victories at
festivals are simply too numerous to ignore.[37] I think, however, that van
Nijf's identity-argument is socially too exclusive. It was not just the elite,
the 'dominant groups', for whom the engagement with gymnasial culture
constituted an important element in their self-fashioning. Rather, I think,
as I said above, that we should view the proliferation of bath–gymnasium
complexes, agonistic festivals and oil distributions to the citizenry as the
constituent parts of one large gymnasial renaissance. And if we do so, it
immediately becomes clear from the evidence for munificence that we are
here dealing with a cultural and ideological phenomenon involving not
just the elite, but the citizen body as a whole. The frequent attestation of
bath–gymnasium complexes, both in the evidence for munificence and in
the archaeology of cities (large cities such as Ephesos often had several of
them), and the frequent distributions of oil, indispensable to the activities
in the gymnasium, to all the citizens, are indicative of the popularity of
gymnasial culture among all social strata. It is this general popularity of
gymnasial culture that provides the context for the flourishing of agonistic
festivals, and it explains why rich citizens donated or contributed to them
with such frequency. Naturally, even though most citizens would probably
spend some time in the gymnasium on an almost daily basis, only the sons
of richer families would have the leisure time available for a really intensive
training programme. Hence it is only to be expected that it is mostly they
who appear as participants and victors in the evidence for athletic *agones*.
As the evidence for civic munificence makes clear, however, participation
in gymnasial culture in the more general sense just defined probably constituted an important component of civic identity for all citizens, elite
and non-elite. Hence, it served to reinforce their sense of belonging to a

---

[36] Van Nijf (2001) 317. See Swain (1996) for similar arguments with regard to the Greek literature of
the period.
[37] Van Nijf (2001) 321–9 and (2003) *passim*.

status group with a specific and unique corporate identity.[38] Participation in gymnasial culture thus formed an important part of what it meant to be a citizen of a Greek polis under the Roman Empire.[39] This explains why bath–gymnasium complexes, oil distributions and agonistic festivals are so commonly found among public gifts. Once more, we see that with their munificence elite benefactors aimed to stress the unity and corporate identity of the citizen body, by providing citizens of all social strata, rich and poor, with access to the amenities deemed indispensable to the life of a true citizen.

Returning to a somewhat earlier point, we may note that the lack of political innocence in the revival of cultural Hellenism in the east during the high Empire, of which the renaissance of gymnasial culture formed a constitutive part, can be overstated. Recent literature has made much of so-called cultural resistance against Rome among the elites of the eastern provinces, and has sometimes interpreted the revival of Hellenism as an act of covert opposition, aimed to emphasise the superiority of Greek culture over Roman.[40] Such a resistance model does not, however, seem the best way to approach the evidence for civic munificence in Roman Asia Minor. We have already seen briefly how, in the munificence towards religious structures, contributions to temples and sanctuaries for the Roman

[38] The fact that festivals experience a longer drawn-out period of prominence, lasting into the early decades of the third century, than public buildings and distributions does not really affect this argument. *Pace* Mitchell (1990) 189–90, the difference in timing is not as dramatic as is often supposed. In my database, festivals peak at the same time as public buildings and distributions. The only difference is that their decline was much slower. They continue to be donated with some frequency well into the early Severan period (for a rough chronology see the chart in Appendix 3). Explanations for this slower decline might be: (1) that, by the later second century AD, most cities had most of the public buildings they needed, and the period of great rebuilding began to wane, and (2) that the impact of the Antonine plague, and the social disruption that followed, severely reduced the spending power of local elites. In either case, it seems likely that festivals would have been popular among local benefactors during the Severan restoration, in the case of explanation (1) because they were an attractive alternative to buildings, and in the case of (2) because they were often actually somewhat cheaper to donate than large public buildings.

[39] With regard to *agones*, I do not of course mean to imply that only local citizens participated in the contests; there is much evidence to indicate that the participation of foreign athletes, musicians, artists and so forth was quite normal. Rather, I argue that being a spectator of – and, for a more select, i.e. well-trained, group of citizens, participating in – agonistic festivals was considered an essential part of the citizen lifestyle, of what it meant to live life as a proper member of a polis community in Roman times. It was primarily the element of public, collective enjoyment and celebration that turned agonistic festivals donated by rich citizens into events strengthening the internal cohesion of the citizen body as a whole. Participation of accomplished professional foreign athletes would only heighten the thrill. Benefactors could however make a specific allowance for the participation of local citizens, as did C. Iulius Demosthenes in the penteteric agonistic festival he donated to Oenoanda, see Wörrle (1988) 8, lines 46–7.

[40] See for instance Swain (1996); Goldhill (2001).

emperor went together with those to temples for Greek and local deities in an apparently unproblematic fashion. In festivals too, as both Guy Rogers and Michael Wörrle have clearly shown, the imperial cult and the ideology of empire were very much present alongside the more traditional Hellenistic elements.[41] And as Simon Price has emphasised in his study of the imperial cult in Asia Minor, and as is evident from the records of munificence, religious/ideological allegiance to Rome was mostly a product of *local* elite initiative.[42] Similarly, and that is the point I wish to make here, we frequently find Roman-type games, such as gladiatorial shows and wild beast hunts (*venationes*) scattered among the evidence for the more 'Greek' types of festival we have been discussing so far (see Fig. 5.4). As far as can be judged from the inscriptions, neither benefactors nor recipients in the cities of the east considered such Roman games in any way problematic, with the exception of the odd intellectual such as Plutarch (but he had problems with 'Greek' theatrical shows too).[43] What I mean to say is that there is no obvious evidence of cultural friction, and it is questionable whether we have the right to assume its presence a priori. This is a subject that does not belong to the main themes of this chapter, and consequently I shall not devote a great deal of space to it. Nonetheless I would suggest that, given the apparent seamless interweaving of 'Greek' and 'Roman' elements in the evidence for civic munificence from the Roman east, it should be stressed that the *integration* of Greek and Roman elements is in fact the defining aspect of eastern civic culture. Instead of 'cultural resistance', what we see in the east during the high Empire, in civic munificence, and hence in festive life, art and architecture, is the genesis and flowering of a new provincial culture representing a creative and dynamic synthesis of Hellenistic and Roman cultural elements.[44]

This, I would suggest, is the background against which we should interpret the conspicuous presence of gladiatorial games and *venationes* among the benefactions in Asia Minor. By the time of the high Empire, these types of games had simply become part and parcel of the normal repertoire of events and amenities defining civic life in the east. A citizen of an eastern city would go to watch a gladiatorial combat hosted by a local benefactor just as he would go and watch, or participate in, an athletics contest organised by another benefactor. He would simply regard both events as belonging to that specific category of elements emblematic of civilised

[41] Wörrle (1988); Rogers (1991a).   [42] Price (1984).   [43] Plutarch *Prae. ger. reip.* 821f.
[44] A point particularly stressed by archaeologists and art historians working on the eastern provinces: see Ward-Perkins (1947) 19; Hanfmann (1975) 56; Yegül (1991) 346, 355 and (2000) 139ff.

urban life, and would probably register no immediate cultural differences between the two. That, at least, is what the apparently frictionless inclusion of Roman-type games among elite benefactors' gifts of games and festivals in Roman Asia Minor seems to suggest.

I have already discussed, in my treatment of gifts towards religious structures above, how central the collective religious experience was to maintaining a sense of civic community. It seems therefore relatively pointless to go over much the same argument again in a discussion of religious festivals. Festivals for the gods had from times immemorial constituted a central aspect of polis religion, and they continued to do so right into the late Roman period. In a sense, the festival and the temple or sanctuary were inseparable; as houses of the gods, the temples and sanctuaries were fronted by the altars that constituted the central places of cultic activity, and they were thus inextricably bound up with festive religious life. Given these characteristics of religious festivals, we can easily understand why they became and remained important targets of civic munificence. Again, however, I want to draw attention to the element of arbitrariness in my categorisation in Fig. 5.4; most agonistic festivals contained religious elements, many religious festivals agonistic ones. Up to a point, the distinction we have made here is artificial, and will not have been nearly as clear-cut in the minds of most benefactors and recipients.

Until now I have mainly discussed the integrative, unifying character of festivals and distributions. However, as I have already stated earlier, while euergetism did lead to a strengthening of social cohesion within and a re-affirmation of the corporate identity of the citizen body, it also contributed to the formulation of a new ideal of the civic social order. This new civic social ideal was of a distinctly hierarchical character. Such a hierarchical conception of the civic community of course fitted far better, and also partly reinforced, the tendencies towards oligarchisation and hierarchisation that already existed in the urban societies of the Roman east. However, there are additional reasons for the adoption of such a model, which go somewhat deeper than this.

Euergetism, of course, *presupposes* social inequality, i.e. hierarchy. It could only exist and function when there were enough sufficiently wealthy people who were able to act as benefactors. Its aim was not to abolish inequality, but to ensure the stable functioning of an oligarchic political system. To that end, a bargain was struck between mass and elite, involving an exchange of gifts that confirmed the non-elite members of the community in their citizenship status through realisation of the entitlements implicit in it, for honours that, in the aggregate, amounted to a legitimation of the oligarchic political order.[45] Ideological acceptance of a hierarchically structured civic community – as advertised by euergetism – was therefore an essential precondition for the system to function at all. Euergetism's endorsement of civic hierarchy was a natural consequence of its role in the political structure of the post-Classical Greek city. To this we should add that, as a consequence of the prevailing mortality regime, the configuration of individuals inhabiting positions at the various levels within the civic hierarchy was in a constant state of flux.[46] Social disruption, due to increasing income-disparities between elite and non-elite citizens and oligarchisation, did not constitute the sole threat to the hierarchical, oligarchic urban social order. The constant upward and downward social mobility of individuals through the social hierarchy meant that, generation after generation, civic communities were harnessing their ideological energies towards a continued restatement of the same. The threat posed by the constantly changing social composition of the elite, sub-elites, and other privileged groups within the citizenry needed to be countered by a continuous process of symbolically 'fixing' the prevailing hierarchy in time, by taking every opportunity to make the hierarchical system seem eternal and unchangeable. This is precisely what the distributions of money and the processions during festivals donated by benefactors did in a most graphic form. Together, these two factors – social inequality as a precondition for munificence, and demographic volatility – explain why a social phenomenon aimed at maintaining *homonoia* between the citizen elite and their non-elite fellow citizens could nonetheless also contribute to the glorification of a distinctly hierarchical ideal of civic society.

As I have already argued, it is primarily in festive processions and money distributions that we can best discern elite benefactors' general endorsement of a hierarchical ideal of civic community. Let us therefore have a closer look at both these phenomena.

Festive processions were an integral part of ancient Greek and Roman religion.[47] In most cities, some kind of procession would be threading its way through the avenues and streets almost every day. Many festivals donated by benefactors involved processions of some sort, and in several cases, due to the haphazard survival of some lengthy inscriptions containing detailed specifications, we are particularly well informed about their

[45] See Chapter 6.
[46] See Chapter 6, pp. 134–8 for a more extensive analysis of the relation between elite demography and munificence. See also Zuiderhoek (forthcoming).
[47] See Burkert (1985) 99–101 on Greek religion; Price (1984) 107–14 and 188–91 on processions associated with the imperial cult.

structure and internal organisation. First, there is the procession that was part of the festive foundation donated by the wealthy Ephesian notable C. Vibius Salutaris early in the second century AD. According to the terms of Salutaris' foundation, throughout the year, roughly every two weeks, a procession carrying statues would progress through the city along a set route marked by Ephesos' architectural–historical hotspots. It started from the Roman road in the upper city and, after passing various historical landmarks (*Embolos*, Marble Street, theatre, Stadion Street), ended at the Koressian gate and the Artemision, places associated with the city's historical and mythological origins. According to Guy Rogers, the Ephesians thus symbolically re-enacted their history in reverse order, moving from the present-day Roman period slowly back into the city's distant and mythical past.[48]

What primarily interests me here, however, is another aspect of the procession: the representation and personification of various deities, individuals and groups in the statuary carried by the participants.[49] First there came the statues of the reigning emperor Trajan and his wife, Plotina. Then followed a whole range of groups of three statues, each containing one statue of Artemis, personifications of Roman political institutions (Senate, equestrian order, the Roman people), deities and legendary and historical figures associated with the city's past, and of Ephesian social and political institutions. It is the latter that are most important to me here, for if we look at their arrangement in the procession we can discern a distinctly hierarchical conception of the city's social and political order. First came the statue of the boule; then, in the second group of three statues, followed the statue of the *gerousia*, the council of elders. In the third group came the statue representing the *ephebeia*, and then, in the subsequent statue groups, followed the personifications of the demos and the city's tribes.[50] Thus the city's hierarchical and oligarchic social and political structure was clearly articulated in the Salutaris procession: the council, as the political organ of the ruling elite, was put squarely in the front. The *gerousia*, which contained many aged council members, but which might also, as recent research has uncovered, contain rich citizens from outside the bouleutic *ordo*,[51] followed next, an arrangement closely repeated in several known money distributions, as we shall see presently. Third came the ephebes, whose prominent position, *before* the demos, might be explained by the fact that they both contained many sons of councillors and constituted the

---

[48] Rogers (1991a) 80–135; van Nijf (1997) 191–3.   [49] See Rogers (1991a) 83–5, esp. his Table 9.
[50] Rogers (1991a) 84–5, Table 9.   [51] Van Rossum (1988).

majority among the statue bearers; the procession was partly *their* ritual.[52] Next, finally, there followed the personifications of the citizen body in a broader sense, the demos and the tribes. Clearly, we are far removed here from the Classical Athenian conception of the primacy of the demos in the social and political order, both in representation and in political practice. The procession neatly encapsulates the oligarchic and hierarchical structure of Ephesian society, setting it in the context of both the wider hierarchical world of the Empire and the glorious foundation history of the city. This was a world in which the citizen body was still of fundamental importance, both as an ideological construct and as a living reality (as we have seen above), but it was also, again fundamentally, a world in which some citizens were conspicuously more important than others.

Another very detailed description of the regulations for a festival can be found in the long inscription concerning the endowment of a penteteric festival by C. Iulius Demosthenes, a wealthy notable from the small city of Oenoanda in Lycia.[53] This festival, the endowment of which was almost contemporary with that of Salutaris at Ephesos, also contained an impressive civic procession, in which we may again discern how benefactors and their fellow citizens organised their civic world according to strict hierarchical principles. In the case of Demosthenes' festival and procession, however, the civic hierarchy was not represented in the form of statues. Rather, we find that various festival officials (the agonothete, *panegyriarchai, sebastophoroi, mastigophoroi, agelarchai*) were selected from the different subsections of the citizenry. Thus the agonothete and the *panegyriarchai* were chosen from among the councillors (*bouleutai*), the *sebastophoroi* and *mastigophoroi* from among the ordinary citizens (*politai*), and the *agelarchai* from among the 'well-born' (i.e. aristocratic) boys.[54] The civic procession itself consisted of the festive officials, the priest and priestess of the imperial cult, representatives of the city's various political institutions (the secretary of the council, *agoranomoi, gymnasiarchoi, tamiai, paraphylakes, ephebarchoi,* the *paidonomos,* and the overseer of public building), and from dependent villages in Oenoanda's territory. All had to bring one or more bulls for the sacrifice.[55] Again, as with Salutaris' foundation at Ephesos, we see an elite benefactor and his fellow citizens

---

[52] Rogers (1991a) 112 argues that the prominent role of the ephebes can be explained by interpreting the procession, with its representation of the socio-political hierarchy and symbolic re-enactment of the Ephesian past, as part of an attempt to socialise young elite males into the political and historical 'world' of their community. See also van Nijf (1997) 193.

[53] See Wörrle (1988); Rogers (1991b).   [54] See Wörrle (1988) 10, lines 59–66.

[55] Wörrle (1988) 12, lines 68–80.

putting their world in order by means of a festive representation of the civic social structure in strictly hierarchical terms.[56] Here, the civic hierarchy was represented by the officials drawn from the various socio-political groupings within the citizenry, and linked to both the wider world of the Empire and the surrounding countryside by the presence of imperial priests and village representatives respectively.[57] Hence, as these and other examples clearly show, 'processions expressed current ideas about the corporate structure of society and about the essence of its civic hierarchy'.[58] Thus, they constitute one of our best sources for arguing that elite benefactors and their citizen recipients did indeed conceptualise their social world in terms of a hierarchy of status groups.

Conceptions of civic hierarchy very similar to those visible in civic processions, however, appear also in yet another form of munificence similarly closely bound up with festive life, i.e. public distributions. Many festivals included public distributions. However, very often distributions also appear in our records as an independent form of benefaction. The majority of those in my database are such 'independent' benefactions. As far as I could judge from the inscriptions concerned, the distributions in question were not tied to specific festivals, though, like festivals, many were set up as foundations and hence constituted periodically recurring events. Of course, this categorisation is to some extent arbitrary; perhaps the distinction between 'distribution' and 'festival' is far too artificial, since both would constitute festive public occasions. However, for the purpose of analysis, some kind of distinction has to be made. In that spirit I have also included under the heading 'distributions' such major distributions that *were* part of specific festivals, but which seemed to constitute a separate element within them, a specific 'chapter' of the festival script, so to speak, and hence a distinctive entity. Two distributions in this latter category were part of the festival foundations of Salutaris and Demosthenes just discussed, and we shall come to speak of them in a moment.

---

[56] 'Putting their world in order' paraphrases the title of Darnton's (1984) study, an illuminating discussion of an eighteenth-century civic procession in the city of Montpellier as perceived by a contemporary bourgeois onlooker. Another interesting early modern parallel for the type of hierarchically structured civic procession that existed in the Roman east can be found in Muir (1981) Chapter 5 on the ducal processions in Renaissance Venice.

[57] See Rogers (1991b) 96–9 and van Nijf (1997) 193–4.

[58] Van Nijf (1997) 194. His discussion of the participation of private associations (*collegia*) in civic processions on 131–6 and 195–200 provides another good example of how contemporaries perceived such parades as convincing and powerful representations of the social hierarchy. If you wanted your group's place in the hierarchy to be recognised publicly, you had to negotiate your way into the processions and other civic rituals, and this was precisely what *collegia* did.

Epigraphic texts that record public distributions organised by elite benefactors in some detail come in roughly two kinds. There are those texts
that simply inform us about, say, 'a distribution of money to the council
and the *gerousia*' given by so-and-so, and there are those which provide
detailed information on the size of the individual handouts to the members
of the recipient group(s). The latter represent a rather small subcategory
of all distributions. I have listed the most detailed of these in Table 5.2
below, and we will turn to them shortly. First, however, we should have
a closer look at the evidence for recipient groups of distributions in Asia
Minor as a whole. My sample gives the following results (see Fig. 5.6).
Again, as in Table 5.1, I have focused on the most important civic categories, and subsumed a whole variety of smaller subgroups under the heading of 'others'. We shall come to speak in some more detail about these
'others' when discussing the evidence for individual handouts.

There could hardly be a clearer ideological statement by elite benefactors about the type of community they thought they were living in than
that provided by the data presented in Fig. 5.6. A little over 40 per cent
of all distributions (mainly of oil, as we saw in Table 5.1) from Roman
Asia Minor assembled in my database had the citizen community proper
as sole recipient. Here we see the centrality of the citizen body, the polis
community, to both civic ideology and political practice in the Greek
cities of Roman imperial times stand out as nowhere before. If we simply
consider all benefactions involving citizens, we can see that ordinary citizens were among the recipients, or were the sole recipients, of 44 out of
78 recorded distributions. Equally, however, the data show us the extent
to which the citizen communities of the Roman east were perceived (by
elite benefactors) to be oligarchic and hierarchically structured societies.
Councillors and gerousiasts are prominently represented among recipients
(see Fig. 5.6), and if we add up all the distributions in which councillors
were involved as sole recipients, or as recipients alongside other groups,
we arrive at 35 out of 78 recorded distributions. However, those distributions that involve, alongside each other, the councillors, ordinary citizens
and other groups provide perhaps the best evidence of oligarchisation and
hierarchisation and their ideological glorification. By openly including the
various status groups, the distribution itself became an explicit, positive
recognition of the hierarchical social order, and of the desirability of its
continued existence. Thus, as a festive public ritual, the distribution both
confirmed for all present the legitimacy of a hierarchical social order as
such, and, at the same time, presented to onlookers and participants its
own particular version of that hierarchy as a normative ideal which society

Table 5.2 *Money distributions with specification of individual handouts*

	i	ii	iii	iv	v	vi	vii	viii	ix	x	xi	xii	xiii	xiv	xv	xvi	xvii	xviii	xix	xx	xxi
Councillors (*bouleutai*)	20	85	88*	2	3	1.3	65	!	12	–	24	–	2#	250	–	1	–	–	1	3	–
Honorary members (*teteimenoi*) (of the council?)	–	–	–	–	–	–	–	–	–	–	–	–	–	–	–	1	–	–	–	–	–
Priests	–	–	–	–	–	–	–	–	–	–	–	–	–	–	–	–	–	–	1	–	–
Gerousiastai	18	80	81*	2	–	–	–	–	–	–	–	–	–	–	–	–	–	–	–	–	–
Ekklesiastai	18	77	78*	–	–	–	–	–	–	–	–	–	–	–	–	–	–	4	–	–	–
Wives of councillors	–	3	3	–	–	–	–	–	–	–	–	–	–	–	–	–	–	–	–	–	–
Wives of *gerousiastai*	–	3	3	–	–	–	–	–	–	–	–	–	–	–	–	–	–	–	–	–	–
Wives of *ekklesiastai*	–	3	3	–	–	–	–	–	–	–	–	–	–	–	–	–	–	–	–	–	–
Children of councillors	–	–	–	–	–	–	–	–	–	–	–	–	2#	–	–	–	–	–	–	–	–
Sitometroumenoi andres	–	–	–	–	3	–	–	!	–	1	–	–	–	–	–	–	–	–	–	–	–
Taureastai	–	–	–	2	–	–	–	–	–	–	–	–	–	–	1	–	–	–	–	–	–
Physicians	–	–	–	2	–	–	–	–	–	–	–	–	–	–	–	–	–	–	–	–	–
Teachers	–	–	–	2	–	–	–	–	–	–	–	–	–	–	–	–	10	–	–	–	–
Citizens (*politai*)	2	9	–	–	+	1	10	10	–	–	12	4	–	–	–	–	10	–	–	–	3
Freedmen	1	3	4	–	+	–	–	–	–	–	–	–	–	–	–	–	–	–	–	–	–
Vindictarii (freedmen)	–	3	4	–	–	–	–	–	–	–	–	–	–	–	–	–	–	–	–	–	–
Paroikoi	1	3	–	–	+	–	–	–	–	–	–	–	–	–	–	–	–	–	–	–	2

Metoikoi	–	–	–	–	–	–	–	–	–	–	–	–	–	–	10	–	–	–	–	–	–
Romans	–	–	–	–	–	–	–	–	–	–	–	5	–	–	–	–	–	–	–	–	2
'Others'	–	–	–	–	–	–	–	–	–	–	–	–	–	–	–	–	–	–	–	–	–

Legend

Bold print: individuals with citizen status

<u>Underlined</u>: individuals with semi-citizen status

Normal print: individuals without citizen status

– not included in distribution

* plus one *modius* of grain each

¶ plus a distribution of wine to 'those in tribes who were assigned to groups of fifty', the *hymnoidoi*, the builders, the *Hieroplateitai* and the *Herakleiastai*.

+ included in distribution, but size of individual handouts unknown

! each group receives 1,000 denarii, to be divided among its members

plus four *modii* of grain each

References

i = *IGR* III 800 (Sillyon); ii = *IGR* III 801 (Sillyon); iii = *IGR* III 802 (Sillyon); iv = *I.Histria* 57; v = *SEG* xxxvIII (1988) 1462/Wörrle (1988) (Oenoanda); vi = Robert, *Ét. An.* 343–52, no. 4 (Sebastopolis); vii = *I.Stratonikeia* (*IK* 21–2) 662; viii = Balland (1981) no. 67 (Xanthos); ix = *SEG* xxxIV (1984) 1175 (Miletos); x = *SEG* xxvII (1977) 938 (Tlos); xi = *IGR* IV 1127 (Rhodes); xii = *I.Ephesos* (*IK* 11–17) 2061 II; xiii = *IGR* III 492 (Oenoanda); xiv = *I.Tralleis* (*IK* 36.1) 145/Laum II 95; xv = *TAM* II 578–9 (Tlos); xvi = *IGR* IV 1222/de Hoz 22.9 (Thyatira); xvii = *IGR* III 493 (Oenoanda); xviii = *Mus. Iznik (Nikaia)* (*IK* 9) 61; xix = *I.Ephesos* (*IK* 11–17) 690; xx = *I.Stratonikeia* (*IK* 21–2) 237; xxi = *I.Stratonikeia* (*IK* 21–2) 527.

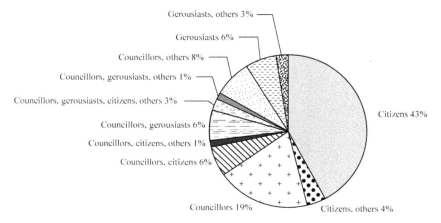

Figure 5.6 Recipients of distributions (N = 78)

should strive to attain. For, as we shall see below, though there are some almost universal constants, different benefactors provided in their respective distributions (slightly) different versions of the social hierarchy. These versions partly reflected the benefactors' own predilections and the nature of their patronage networks, but also the compromises they had had to strike in the complicated background negotiations with boule and demos that surrounded every major benefaction.[59]

We can see these different hierarchies best reflected in the subgroup of texts which, alongside other information, also record the size of individual handouts to members of the various status groups included in the distribution. Inscriptions recording such details are comparatively rare. In Table 5.2 I have listed the examples included in my database so as to make it possible to compare the various ideals of hierarchical order proposed.[60] One very intricate example I have left out of this table, however, both because it is simply too complex to include without severely reducing the clarity of the table, and because it has already been very ably analysed by another historian. This is the distribution that was part of the festival foundation of Vibius Salutaris at Ephesos discussed earlier, and we shall turn to it first (the festival of Demosthenes at Oenoanda also included a distribution, but that one is included in Table 5.2 under (v)).

---

[59] I will return to these processes of negotiation, which have assumed particular importance in recent literature, towards the end of this chapter.
[60] All sums are in denarii.

The scheme of lotteries and distributions set up by Salutaris at Ephesos was complex and served a variety of purposes. These included providing certain groups and officials within the city with the capital needed to take care of the statuary Salutaris donated and to perform specific ritual tasks during the days of the festival. The most important function of the scheme, however, as Rogers has made abundantly clear, was to provide an image of the civic hierarchy at Ephesos as it was perceived to stand in AD 104.[61] In this sense, the scheme served a purpose similar to Salutaris' civic procession, which we discussed above. Like the procession, the scheme was also tied to some of the overarching ideas behind the foundation as a whole, and this might account for some of the idiosyncrasies that can be perceived in the hierarchy it sets out to represent. Hence it was the festival's specific emphasis on the distinguished history and foundation legends of Ephesos that allowed the members of the Ephesian tribes (i.e. some 1,500 citizens, represented by the phylarchs) to receive the largest endowment. The tribes' prominence in the scheme was tied to their important role in the legendary foundation history of the city. For it was the Ephesian tribes which were said to have first come into being at the time when the first colonists from Athens settled on the spot that would later become the city of Ephesos. After the phylarchs, however, the hierarchy assumes familiar shape again, with the boule and the *gerousia* (roughly, the Ephesian elite) receiving the second and third largest endowments for distributions and lotteries. After these institutions representing the top ranks of Ephesian society there followed the various youth organisations and their representatives, somewhat surprisingly placed above the functionaries of the imperial cult and the Artemision. However, as in the case of Salutaris' procession, this prominence of the youth organisations can be explained by the fact that an important aim of the festival was to socialise and acculturate the Ephesian youth into the social and political world of their native city, its history and traditions.[62] Most interesting, though, are all those groups or individuals to whom Salutaris accorded only a low position, or whom he left out of the scheme altogether. Functionaries of the imperial cult were not nearly as important in the scheme as they were in the procession. The ritual of the lotteries and distributions, with its strong concentration on the Ephesian past, Rogers suggests, still belonged to Artemis and the Ephesian polis, not to the world of the Romans.[63] Women, as a group, are conspicuously absent (whereas they are present in some other known distributions, see

---

[61] Rogers (1991a) Chapter 2. For a quick overview of the scheme see his Table 1 at p. 42.
[62] Rogers (1991a) 42 and 66–9. [63] Rogers (1991a) 70.

Table 5.2), something which is not surprising, Rogers argues, in an 'endowment [that] was structured to help bring *young men* into a male-dominated
civic structure'.[64] Perhaps the most glaring omission, however, is that of
functionaries and groups representing the entire economic infrastructure
of Ephesos. The *oikonomos*, the *agoranomos* and, most importantly, the professional associations (*collegia*), all these are absent. Since their functions
and wealth were associated with trade, commerce and production, Rogers
comments, these functionaries, but especially the *collegia*, did not easily fit
into the idealised world view of the landowning elite inhabiting the boule.
Hence, 'they became invisible when Salutaris and the Ephesian aristocracy
explicated their civic ideal'.[65]

I have dwelt for some time on Salutaris' distribution at Ephesos because
it illustrates so well how individual distributions, though all expressing a
broadly hierarchical view of the civic community, might in their representations be tailored to the specific preferences of benefactors and their
communities at any point in time. If we now take a closer look at Table
5.2, in which I have set out a number of other money distributions where
we know the size of individual handouts, the subtle differences between
the various conceptions of the civic hierarchy immediately catch the eye.

We start with some broad similarities, however. If we survey the table
from left to right, we can see that the two groups that are most commonly
included in money distributions are the councillors (*bouleutai*) and the
ordinary citizens (*politai*). It is also apparent that, in those distributions
that include both councillors and ordinary citizens, the councillors receive
a significantly larger handout than the *politai*. Hence we find repeated a
pattern that we already knew, more or less, from Fig. 5.6, namely that
distributions tend to stress the continuing relevance of the citizen community to ideology and political practice, but at the same time also glorify
the oligarchic/hierarchical structure of society by singling out the boule
as the most privileged group. The seminal position of the councillors at
the very top of the civic hierarchy is further reinforced by the fact that in
most cases they receive larger handouts than *any* other group of recipients.
To be sure, there are a few cases where they receive the same amount as
members of other groups, but, and that should be specifically noted, they
never receive *less* than members of any other group do. Another thing to

---

[64] Rogers (1991a) 70. The emphasis is his.
[65] Rogers (1991a) 72, where he adds that '[t]o the Ephesian aristocracy . . . which was more interested
in reproducing itself in the next generation at Ephesos than in the social mobility of cobblers,
wool-workers, and silversmiths, Salutaris' civic hierarchy no doubt seemed to represent the world
they imagined themselves to live in – and rule – very well indeed'.

note, and I have pointed this out before in my discussion of the hierarchisation of civic society in the previous chapter, is the very wide range of
social categories involved in the distributions. We find privileged groups
of citizens – *sitometroumenoi andres* (those on the list of grain receivers?),
ekklesiastai (those with a privileged position in the assembly?) – alongside
more institutionally defined groups such as the *gerousia* and the boule. We
also find professional and religious groups (teachers, rhetoricians, *Taureas-
tai*, priests), women and children of citizens, and sometimes even, at the
bottom of the hierarchy, freedmen and groups outside the citizenry: non-
citizen peasants (*paroikoi, katoikoi*), *metoikoi*, slaves. Clearly the ongoing
processes of '*ordo*-making' provided benefactors with a very wide range of
potential groups to choose from in 'composing' their ideal hierarchy, and
the many options were eagerly explored.[66]

This brings us to the question of the differences between the various
distributions. What such differences suggest is that the process of hierarchisation should certainly not be viewed as uniform across Asia Minor, and
that we always ought to be sensitive to the local socio-political context.
I will not, however, go on to discuss the precise circumstances of every
distribution in the table, as I did with the Salutaris distribution above. I
will not do so partly for reasons of space and partly because we are not
nearly as well informed about most of them as we are about Salutaris' foundation, but primarily because I wish to make a more general point. This
point relates not so much to detailed differences between the individual
representations of hierarchy as such as to *why* there should be such differences at all. What does their existence reveal about the social, political and
ideological context in which major acts of munificence were conceived,
proposed and put into effect? Earlier on I mentioned several factors that
might determine the idiosyncrasies of a specific distribution. These were
the benefactor's own predilections, perhaps heavily dependent on his or her
precise social and political position, the web of patronage relations in which
he/she was entangled, and the nature of the bargains struck with other elite
members and the demos in the background negotiations surrounding the
benefaction. It should be acknowledged that these were factors influenc-
ing the nature of every act of munificence, not just distributions, though
the differences between the various idealised hierarchies represented in the
latter offer us a convenient starting point. Though the first two factors
are by no means unimportant, I shall focus primarily on the third, the

---

[66] On the creativity displayed by benefactors in composing their distributive hierarchies see also van
Nijf (1997) Chapter 4, who introduces the concept of '*ordo*-making'.

influence of background negotiations with other individuals and groups in the community, since these are most important for an appreciation of the political context of euergetism, and hence for my argument.

In his book on the Salutaris foundation and in a seminal paper on the festival of Demosthenes at Oenoanda, Guy Rogers has specifically, and, to a large extent, convincingly, stressed the importance of the political processes surrounding major acts of euergetism.[67] And, though there has been some criticism, other ancient historians have tended to follow suit.[68] In particular, Rogers has pointed out the role played by the demos in determining the outcome of proposed acts of munificence. It is specifically this element of his analysis that I want to elaborate in the context of the general thesis on euergetism developed in this study. Though the *bouleutai* represented the effective ruling class of the cities of the Roman east, the rest of the population was by no means completely powerless politically. To begin with, the non-elite citizenry could simply rebel. This might cause serious trouble for the elite, and they did their utmost to avoid it. And, as is one of the main themes of this study, euergetism was in fact a crucial element in their strategy of conflict-avoidance. Secondly, however, and this is vital, euergetism was fundamentally a process of *exchange*. Generous elite members wanted something in return for their gifts. And the things they wanted – honours, prestige, and, with an eye to their role as members of the ruling elite, social stability and the legitimation of their elite position – could only be secured from the demos, the non-elite citizenry. Up to a point, this fact afforded the demos a measure of control over the behaviour of their elite superiors, at least when it came to munificence. The people could (and sometimes did)[69] simply refuse to bestow any honours on a benefactor. A politically shrewd benefactor would therefore allow some room for participation of the demos in the deliberations concerning the eventual outcome of his munificence, as Salutaris did at Ephesos, and Demosthenes at Oenoanda.[70] Fellow elite members, however, could not be ignored either. Euergetism was a field of intense competition between elite individuals for honour and prestige, and a potential benefactor would be very unwise to bypass the boule during the planning phase of his munificence. The boule would be sure to claim a role for itself, would aim to prevent the rise of political mavericks, would attempt to make sure that

---

[67] See Rogers (1991a) and (1991b).

[68] Criticism: van Bremen (1993); endorsement: van Nijf (1997), e.g. 194, and elsewhere; Zuiderhoek (2007).

[69] See below, pp. 108–9.

[70] See Rogers (1991a) 24–5 and *passim* on Salutaris, and (1991b) 93ff. on the foundation of Demosthenes.

one single individual did not gain too much prestige, and that some of the prestige gained would rub off on the council as a whole. Through the processes of deliberation taking place in the boule and the assembly after the benefaction had initially been proposed, other elite members and the non-elite citizenry would thus be able to influence both the nature and the shape of the eventual benefaction to their own advantage. However, the benefactors themselves also gained from the whole process. The devotion of large amounts of political time and energy to the benefactions of members of the ruling elite only served to underwrite the latter's crucially important position at the head of the civic hierarchy.[71] Thus context and meaning were added to their leading political role and to their generosity, by integrating both of these deeply into the social and political fabric of contemporary civic society.

If this model of background negotiations and participation of boule and demos in the political processes surrounding benefactions is true for most benefactions we know of from the Roman east (as I think it is), then an important conclusion follows. This is that virtually all benefactions we know of, recorded as they were on honorific or building inscriptions, represent cases in which the euergetist system had 'worked'. If the background negotiation model is broadly correct, it means that, in all these cases, the benefactor had got what he/she wanted in terms of prestige, legitimation and so forth. But it also means that the non-elite citizenry had been able to ensure, as far as was within its power, that the benefaction concerned would be such that they, as citizens, would gladly receive it, as befitting their status and preferences as members of a polis community. It implies that the ideas and ideologies concerning civic cohesion and civic hierarchy which we see represented in many acts of munificence, and which have been the subject of this chapter, by and large found broad acceptance among both elite benefactors and the non-elite recipients of their generosity. For, if any of the above conditions had not been fulfilled, the benefaction would never have made it through the negotiation process, and would never have reached the final stage of the honorific inscription. Ultimately, then, the thousands of honorific inscriptions for benefactors we have left from the Roman world constitute the surest indication we have for the success of the euergetist system in heading off social and political conflict. Precisely because they survive in such great numbers, however, the inscriptions are also our best evidence for the existence in the Greek cities of the Roman east of a constant necessity to invest in the prevention of such social conflicts.

---

[71] See van Nijf (1997) 118–19.

The system of exchange of benefactions for honours could never grind to a halt, on penalty of severe social disorder.

What were the potential sources of such disorder? We have discussed in much detail the vastly expanding wealth of the elite and the increasing oligarchisation of socio-political life, together creating huge disparities of wealth and power within the citizenry, as one such source. To a large extent, these tendencies might explain the sheer proliferation of euergetism in the second century AD, when its function of maintaining social cohesion within the citizenry was needed more than ever before. We have also briefly discussed the consequences, for an oligarchic and hierarchically structured society, of a demographic regime of harsh and unpredictable mortality, and the high degree of social mobility it generated. We have seen how the constant upward and downward movement of families through the hierarchy represented a threat to the very continuation of the hierarchy itself, which could best be averted by a constant, ritual re-affirmation of the civic hierarchy, something to which euergetism was ideally suited.[72] The preceding discussion, however, has provided us with yet another potential source of conflict. For the euergetist system did not always 'work'. Elite benefactors and non-elite citizens might have entirely different opinions as to what types of munificence best served the needs of the citizenry, and in which way citizenship entitlements might best be honoured. The chance survival of a small inscription from Ephesos teaches us that resolving such a conflict might sometimes even involve the intervention of an authority no less than the emperor himself. The text, a letter of Antoninus Pius to the Ephesians dated to AD 145, reads:

Titus Aelius Hadrianus [Antoninus] Augustus Imperator Caesar, son of the divine Hadrian, grandson of the divine Trajanus Parthicus, greatgrandson of the divine Nerva, *pontifex maximus*, tribune for the eighth time, imperator for the second, consul for the fourth, father of the fatherland, to the officials of Ephesos, the council and the people. Greetings.

I learned about the generosity that Vedius Antoninus [a wealthy Ephesian notable] shows towards you, but not so much from your letters as from his; for when he wished to secure assistance from me for the adornment of the buildings he had promised you, he informed me of the many large buildings he is adding to the city but that you are rather unappreciative of his efforts. I on my part agreed with every request that he made and was appreciative of the fact that he does not follow the customary pattern of those who discharge their civic responsibility with a view to gaining instant recognition by spending their resources on theatrical shows and distributions and prizes for the games; instead he prefers to show his

---

[72] I will return to this issue in more detail in the next chapter, see pp. 134–8.

generosity through ways in which he can anticipate an even grander future for the city . . .[73]

Clearly, in AD 145, the Ephesian demos held on to a somewhat different conception of the sort of benefactions that would fit the lifestyle of true citizens than did Vedius Antoninus the wealthy notable. Though, unsurprisingly, the epigraphic evidence is mostly silent on the topic, conflicts of this type may not have been particularly rare. Nor would they always have been particularly innocent. In fact, it may only have been the imperial intervention that caused the Ephesians finally, and belatedly, to acknowledge the generosity of Vedius, five years after the emperor's original letter was sent.[74] Evidently, the thin layer of *homonoia* that euergetism spread out over the social and political world of the eastern cities could be very brittle indeed.

CONCLUSION AND A DIGRESSION

In this chapter, I have sought to substantiate the claim that euergetism served as a social, political and ideological palliative designed to avert social conflict within the citizen body in an age when civic life in the Roman east was dominated by growing disparities of income within the citizenry (caused by a vast increase in elite wealth) and strong political oligarchisation. Analysing the main categories of benefactions we encounter in a large sample of gifts from Roman Asia Minor, I argued that, in various ways, they all served the glorification of the Greco-Roman civic ideal. More specifically, benefactions primarily served to underwrite the continued importance of citizenship and the social cohesion of the citizen body by granting all citizens, regardless of wealth or social position, access to those amenities deemed essential to civilised urban life. Thus, elite munificence helped to keep alive the civic ideology which put the unified status group of citizens at the centre of the definition of polis society, in the face of strong countervailing tendencies that led to increasing disparities of wealth and political power within the citizenry.

At the same time, euergetism reflected, and helped to propagate, a new hierarchical definition of the civic community. For, even though the citizen community remained of central ideological importance in the imperial

---

[73] *Syll.*[3] 850 = *I.Ephesos* (*IK* 11–17) 1491. Translation by Danker (1982) 69–70, slightly adapted. See also Reynolds (1988) 27 and most recently Steskal (2001) and Kalinowski (2002) for a diverging interpretation.

[74] See *I.Ephesos* (*IK* 11–17) 1492–3, two further letters by Antoninus Pius to the Ephesians, both dating to AD 149/50.

Greek cities, the old Classical ideal of the political equality of all citizens made little sense in the oligarchic political environment of the Roman east. Hence the civic community was ideologically reconceptualised as a hierarchy of status groups, headed by the bouleutic elite that effectively governed the city. Such a redefinition was in line with the actual trend in civic society towards increasing hierarchisation (*ordo*-making),[75] and, particularly in the area of festivals and distributions, benefactors contributed significantly to the propagation of the new ideal by continuously re-emphasising the importance of civic hierarchy. It is interesting to note that the hierarchies proposed in various distributions differ slightly in terms of their overall make-up. This leads to the conclusion that in each case a different bargain was struck between benefactor, boule and demos as to the proper definition of the society in which those involved thought they lived.

Euergetism's continuous re-affirmation of social hierarchy served still another purpose, however. The continuous, high rate of social mobility generated by the severe mortality regime of the Roman world presented a constant threat to the establishment of durable social hierarchies. In terms of the 'personnel' inhabiting the various 'sections' of the social order, society was in a constant state of flux. And who was to say that newcomers would always stick to the old ways and means? To keep this process of continuous change as changeless (in terms of maintaining the social and political order) as possible, a constant, unceasing re-affirmation of the hierarchical ideal to which society was expected to aspire was therefore a vital necessity. Here was a task that euergetism, being the preserve of the chief beneficiaries of the hierarchical system, could perform exceptionally well.

One element has been conspicuously absent from the analysis of benefactors' gifts presented in this chapter, and that is the role of the imperial *exemplum*. This absence is not without its reasons, and I shall give them here. Roman emperors were great public benefactors, as a casual glance at Suetonius' biographies or the *Scriptores Historiae Augustae*, or, for that matter, collections of published inscriptions from just about anywhere in the Roman world will confirm. They gave to the population of Rome (Juvenal's famous *panem et circenses*), to cities in Italy,[76] and to cities in the provinces.[77] And certainly, among local benefactors in the provinces, there is bound to have been some emulation of the emperor, or at least local benefactors and emperors often contributed the same sort of things, public

---

[75] For the term see van Nijf (1997).   [76] See Patterson (2003).
[77] Mitchell (1987); Boatwright (2000) on Hadrian.

buildings and festivals.[78] I do not think, however, that the imperial example was one of the *main driving forces* behind the proliferation of provincial munificence during the late first and second centuries AD. Euergetism as a phenomenon pre-dated the Roman emperors by several centuries: it was essentially an 'invention' of late Classical/Hellenistic Greek civic culture. It was practised by both local elites and Hellenistic kings, and, during late Republican times, easily blended in with the Roman traditions of electoral gift-giving and patronage. Euergetism had been very 'civic' in character from the outset, focusing, as it did in imperial times, on the citizenry, and consisting primarily of public building, games and festivals, and distributions. It would thus be more accurate to say that, with the onset of the Empire, Roman emperors modelled their behaviour as benefactors very much on the euergetism of Hellenistic elites and, particularly, Hellenistic kings (though of course Rome's own tradition of electoral public gifts and distributions was also a major influence). If the Roman imperial system had a major influence on the proliferation of public giving, as it surely did, then this was through the internal changes which the incorporation of the eastern cities into the imperial structure brought about in civic society, i.e. the growing oligarchisation of political life, and the increasing accumulation of wealth in the hands of tiny groups of rich families (see Chapter 4). Emperors, in fact, found themselves confronted with the same problem as the provincial oligarchies of rich citizens, only in even more acute form.[79] For how could emperors effectively reconcile the naked truth that they were the absolutist rulers of a military empire with the – legitimating – ideological fiction that they were merely *principes*, first citizens among a large community of (Roman) citizens? To some extent, the Roman division of society in distinct *ordines* took care of the job: some citizens were simply better than others. Greater virtue, however, had to show from actions to be believable, and hence good emperors, like good notables in the provincial cities, had to demonstrate their possession of the cardinal virtues of *philotimia, philopatria, liberalitas* and so forth by public displays of care for

---

[78] See Gordon (1990). Also, the emperor's name and/or image appeared on the buildings and during the festivals benefactors donated, and in the honorific inscriptions they received in return, but then the emperor was omnipresent in almost every other aspect of imperial public life (think of the coinage, the dating of documents and so forth). The references to the emperor in munificence simply show that euergetism conformed to the representational standards of Roman imperial public life, that is, it spoke the language of Roman power. This is a fascinating topic, worthy of investigation as such, but it does not, I think, provide a *sufficient* explanation for the peculiar proliferation of elite public generosity in the eastern provinces during the high Empire. For that, we have to look primarily to the effects incorporation into the Empire had on the internal socio-political dynamics of polis society.

[79] This point is developed somewhat further in Zuiderhoek (2007), esp. 207–13.

their fellow citizens. In this sense, emperors, senators and knights, and local notables, were simply all in the same boat. Hence, they sought similar ideological solutions: besides the reference to the virtues of the 'good leading citizen', characteristic of both imperial and local munificence, both emperors and local notables can also be seen to have employed the discourse of the family, with leading citizens being cast in the role of 'fathers' of their community,[80] and the emperor as the *pater patriae*, the father of all. Local elites could certainly capitalise to some extent on the fact that they did for their fellow citizens what the emperor did for all, but it was the reality of power, its increasingly unequal distribution within the citizen bodies of the provincial cities, and the social tensions this created, not imitation of imperial example, that primarily drove the proliferation of munificence in the high Empire.

---

[80] See Zuiderhoek (2008).

CHAPTER 6

Giving for a return: generosity and legitimation

What did benefactors receive in return for their generosity? Ever since the first publication of the French anthropologist Marcel Mauss's famous *Essai sur le don* in 1923–4, it has been a commonplace of anthropological studies of the gift that giving is always for a return, that it, in fact, constitutes a form of exchange.[1] This, however, places the ancient historian studying Greco-Roman public giving in a somewhat awkward position. For the main thesis of one of the most authoritative works ever published on the subject of euergetism is precisely that ancient benefactions did *not* require something in return. In his monumental study *Le pain et le cirque*, Paul Veyne is in fact strongly opposed to any social scientific explanation of euergetism (reciprocity, redistribution and so forth). Instead, Veyne argues that benefactions were chiefly a means for the elite to emphasise the social distance between themselves and their fellow citizens. According to Veyne, their generosity did not bring them any clear economic, social or political advantages. It was, in this sense, disinterested. Benefactors, Veyne argues, simply gave for the psychological satisfaction that could be derived from being generous, that is, for the pleasure of giving.[2]

How to resolve the potential conflict of interpretations here? My view is that the anthropologists have the better of it. Veyne, I think, has many interesting, original and worthwhile things to say on euergetism, yet we should part company with him on the so-called disinterested nature of ancient munificence. Benefactors, as I shall try to show in this chapter, had a strong and abiding interest. Others have also protested. In a long review of *Le pain et le cirque*, Jean Andreau, P. Schmitt and A. Schnapp criticised Veyne for ignoring the significant non-material rewards benefactors received in return for their gifts, the honour, status and prestige that could be acquired through making benefactions.[3] Recently, other scholars have

---

[1] For an English translation see Mauss (1967).   [2] Veyne (1976) 230, 237, 319.
[3] Andreau, Schmitt and Schnapp (1978) 317, 319.

joined in with this critique. Employing the concepts of 'symbolic capital' and 'symbolic exchange' developed by the French sociologist Pierre Bourdieu, both Richard Gordon and Onno van Nijf point out the non-material gains of status and prestige as an important rationale for euergetism.[4] Gordon argues that the language of piety, patriotism and 'duty towards one's community' that fills the honorific inscriptions effectively served to 'veil' the way in which euergetism underwrote and reinforced the elite's prestige, power, and control over their communities, by presenting it as disinterested generosity.[5] Van Nijf too stresses the role of honorific practices associated with euergetism in the fashioning of elite authority and identity. According to him, '[t]he exchanges between benefactors and cities were less disinterested than they may have seemed: honorific epigraphy was instrumental in the gradual process whereby the wealthy classes of the later Greek cities established their social superiority, and re-invented themselves as a ruling order of *honoratiores* . . .'[6]

I broadly sympathise with this approach. Indeed, much of my analysis is essentially carried out with just such a conceptualisation of euergetism as a system of exchange in mind. I have one important objection, however. Conceptualising euergetism as symbolic exchange does indeed usefully point out the significant non-material rewards elite benefactors derived from their gift-giving, yet, by doing so, as with describing the rewards in question as symbolic capital, we have performed little more than a labelling exercise. For what exactly *is* symbolic capital? It is often used as a synonym, or shorthand, for status or prestige. However, the explanation still remains irritatingly vague. For precisely *why* did the elite need that prestige, what did they do with it? Did their leading political role and their wealth not generate enough prestige already? More importantly still, why, out of all the possible options, did they pick euergetism as a means of acquiring prestige? In short, conceptualising munificence as symbolic exchange and prestige as symbolic capital can be no more than a first step in an explanation of euergetism. Something more is required if we really want to get to the heart of the phenomenon. On its own, this labelling exercise, however useful, fails to account, for instance, for the trends and patterns we can discern in the munificence of the wealthy (why did they give the things they gave?), nor does it reveal precisely *why* and *how* the accumulation of symbolic capital strengthened the position of the elite. In this chapter, therefore, I want to take the analysis a crucial step further. We shall look hard at the

---

[4] See Bourdieu (1977); Gordon (1990); van Nijf (1997) 111–20.
[5] Gordon (1990) 224–31, esp. 230.   [6] Van Nijf (1997) 119.

relation between euergetism and the legitimation of power and see whether my thesis that the social stability of the oligarchic political system in the eastern cities was largely predicated on the elite's role as civic benefactors truly stands up to the test.

HIERARCHY AND ITS JUSTIFICATION

The Roman Empire, as we saw earlier, was a vastly unequal society. The resources of a town councillor owning no more than the census minimum of HS 100,000 could provide hundreds of people with a year's bare subsistence.[7] Equestrian and senatorial fortunes often exceeded the wildest dreams of even the modestly wealthy local landowner.[8] At the same time, this apparently rigid economic hierarchy, which found its social and political expression in the top-down ranking of emperor, senators, knights, town councillors, citizens, freedmen and slaves,[9] was constantly challenged by countervailing social and demographic forces. Mortality was high and unpredictable, for rich and poor alike. High infant and childhood mortality in particular made it difficult for elite families to secure the long-term intergenerational continuity of wealth, power and prestige. Elite parents might survive all their offspring, which would cause their line to become extinct, or they might by chance end up with a relatively large number of children. This in turn might lead to impoverishment and consequent loss of elite status in the next generation, since the parents' fortune had to be divided equally among all surviving heirs. The continuously appearing gaps in the composition of elite groups had to be filled by socially mobile individuals coming from social levels just below the elite.[10] This continued mobility did not, however, undermine the existing hierarchy, since newcomers quickly (and probably to some extent forcibly) adopted the culture and mentality of the group to which they newly belonged, a phenomenon which one ancient historian has described as *imitatio domini*.[11] The net result was a continuous process of 'changeless change'.[12]

Hierarchies, however, are never self-evident, but have to be persuasively presented as such. Elites have to convince both themselves and those below

---

[7] See p. 4.   [8] For a list of examples of such fortunes see Duncan-Jones (1982) Appendix 7.

[9] Famously visualised in Géza Alföldy's pyramid model in his *Römische Sozialgeschichte*. See Alföldy (1975) 131.

[10] See p. 62, note 27 for references, and pp. 134–8 for further discussion.

[11] Pleket (1971) 245. See also Jongman (1991) 311: for social risers 'each successive step on the ladder required the support of those in higher positions . . . The need to conform was strong and social mobility could, therefore, not be a route to give effect to social dissent.'

[12] For this term see Jongman (1991) 281.

them that their domination is not arbitrary, but that the existing order is somehow the natural state of things.[13] The social hierarchy has to be shown to be morally justified in the sense that it accords with broadly shared beliefs about what is good and just.[14] Moreover, in order to retain stability in Roman society, where high social mobility continuously threatened to undermine the social order, it was not only paramount that newcomers were effectively socialised, but also that the hierarchy as it was perceived in its ideal form received continued expression and affirmation. Such naturalisation, expression and affirmation of the social order was often realised through communal activities with a decidedly ritualistic undertone, involving powerful evocative symbols in the form of various acts or artefacts with strong cultural and ideological connotations. In the Greek cities of the eastern Roman Empire, such activities and symbols were primarily associated with, and often even a product of, euergetism. As a channel for symbolic communication between socially unequal members of a community, euergetism, as we saw earlier, served to create and reinforce, rather than overcome, the hierarchical order of Greco-Roman society.[15] Thus we hit upon the central paradox of ancient munificence: a phenomenon which ostensibly seems to alleviate existing social inequalities by redistributing a (tiny) portion of elite wealth in fact served to perpetuate these same inequalities by means of a naturalisation of elite dominance. By playing a collective ideological game designed to underline the legitimacy of achieved position and the unity and harmony prevailing within the community, the participants tried to hide from view, or veil, to use Richard Gordon's powerful metaphor, the true relations of power.[16]

But how did it all work? How and to what extent could and did euergetism legitimate existing relations of power and inequality in the Greek cities of the Roman era? I will argue that it is primarily through close study of the honorific inscriptions which benefactors received in reward for munificence that we may hope to gain some insight into this process. The information the inscriptions yield should be interpreted within the dynamic context of continuity and change in civic social and political life in the post-Classical Greek cities. I shall focus on the way in which honorific inscriptions (as publicly displayed monuments, designed to sell the

---

[13] See Bourdieu (1977) 164: 'Every established order tends to produce . . . the naturalization of its own arbitrariness.' Quoted by Gordon (1990) 219.

[14] On this vital condition of political legitimacy see Beetham (1991) 16–18, discussed in more detail below.

[15] On euergetism's promotion of civic hierarchy, which paired up with its emphasis on the importance of citizenship, see Chapter 5, pp. 94–106.

[16] See Gordon (1990).

viewer a line) were used as a medium for the dissemination of powerful ideological fictions that served to justify and naturalise the existing social and political hierarchy. In a society that was still, however remotely, based on the ideal of the political equality of the citizen status group, the progressive oligarchisation of urban political life during the Hellenistic and Roman periods strongly demanded ideological justification. I will argue that the urban oligarchic families of the Greek cities of the Roman period used honorific epigraphy to present a picture of themselves as possessing a range of moral qualities and virtues that made them particularly fit to rule in comparison with their non-elite fellow citizens. What rendered this representation convincing to elite and non-elite citizens alike was the fact that the qualities the elite were thought to possess could actually be associated in many cases with classic social and political virtues of Greek polis society. The catch that made the fiction 'work' was not so much that the elite believed that they had a monopoly on these virtues – on the contrary, every good and therefore well-off citizen was thought to possess them – but that they believed that they possessed them in superior quantities compared to non-elite citizens. Hence the often-noted elaborate, or, if you will, inflated character of the rhetoric of Greek honorific epigraphy in the Roman era: the honorand could not simply be said to be good, he or she had to be presented as very, very good.

A MODEL OF LEGITIMATION

Marcel Mauss famously defined gift-exchange as a continuously re-enacted 'peace contract' between different social and/or ethnic groups in what he termed 'archaic' (i.e. pre-modern, non-western) societies.[17] With its stress on reciprocal exchange as a mechanism for the preservation of social order, Mauss's model would seem ideally suited to form the point of departure for any account of euergetism, which after all also involves the reciprocal exchange of gifts for honours. There is a drawback, however. The Maussian model, and its various offspring among anthropologists working in the substantivist tradition, was primarily developed to explain the maintenance of social stability in societies lacking formal institutions of government to which a monopoly on the use of violence could be entrusted.[18] The Greek city, however, did have such formal governmental institutions: council, assembly, magistrates, courts and so forth. This fact should truly be central to any analysis of euergetism. Preservation of social

---

[17] Mauss (1967) 151, 162–3, 277–9; Sahlins (1972) 171–83.   [18] See Mauss (1967); Sahlins (1972) 177–80.

stability was indeed a primary function of euergetism, but this preservation took on a very different shape than it did in Mauss's 'archaic societies'. It primarily concerned the prevention of conflicts arising *within* the civic institutional structure. That is, euergetism functioned to prevent, ease or overcome potential or actual social conflicts between elite and non-elite citizens resulting from increasing disparities of wealth and political power within the citizenry during the first two centuries AD. Such conflicts found their institutional expression mainly in clashes between boule and demos/assembly, which are quite often attested in the sources from the Roman east.[19] What euergetism did, and that is the central argument of this chapter, was to function as a medium for establishing the legitimacy of the oligarchic socio-political order that had arisen, and continued to develop towards even greater oligarchisation, within an institutional configuration still largely, if remotely, based on the Classical democratic polis. This was one of the ways in which euergetism served to prevent the social conflicts that were bound to arise frequently from such a politically schizophrenic situation.[20] The fact that the members of the most important political organ of the post-Classical Greek cities, the city council, were party to the exchange of gifts for honours is, I will argue below, crucial to an understanding of euergetism.

The oligarchisation of social and political life in the post-Classical Greek city, which fitted well the stark economic inequalities of the Roman world, has recently become the focus of some original new research. Scholars have studied the ways in which public rituals such as festivals and distributions became occasions for the representation of an ideal of civic hierarchy. Collective participation in such civic rituals and the idealised representations of social hierarchy they entailed are thought to have played a crucial part in 'naturalising' existing social, economic and political inequalities in civic society.[21] I want to argue, however, that the connection between euergetism and political legitimation was much more explicit than is often assumed. By stressing the symbolic and representational dimension of euergetism, recent research has moved on considerably from the social–psychological model of benefactions championed by Paul Veyne. What scholars have mostly not done, however, is to establish clearly and unequivocally the link between the symbols and representations generated by euergetism on

---

[19] See Chapter 4, pp. 66–70.
[20] The other way was through the repeated affirmation of the continued importance of the citizen status of non-elite individuals, and of the entitlements that this status entailed. See Chapter 5.
[21] See Gordon (1990); Rogers (1991a); van Nijf (1997) Chapter 5 and the analysis in the previous chapter at pp. 94–106.

the one hand, and the political legitimacy of oligarchic rule on the other. We may model euergetism as a form of symbolic exchange between social groups of unequal status, but our analysis should not stop short there. For what do we actually mean when we use the term 'symbolic'? It could be said to mean that public gifts brought benefactors social prestige, an intangible but essential form of 'capital' for anyone who aspires to high standing in the community – if we stick to the Bourdieu scheme for the moment. However, framing our analysis solely in these terms means neglecting one essential fact about euergetism at our peril, i.e. that the people who made public benefactions were at the same time also the people who constituted the governing elite of the city. This may seem something of a truism to anyone familiar with the history of the post-Classical Greek city, and yet it has not so far led to much research on the precise connections between euergetism and political legitimacy. This is all the more surprising since the simple observation we just made is, I think, at least suggestive of the existence of such a connection. Every political system needs legitimacy to remain stable and survive over longer periods of time, especially, we may add, an oligarchic form of rule that evolved in a society whose political culture was traditionally so dominated by ideals of *isonomia* and the political equality of citizens. In my view, it was above all the honorific practices associated with euergetism, and in particular their primary material products, the honorific inscriptions, that provided members of the social and political elite with a 'platform' on which to present themselves as the natural leaders of society.

Yet how did they do this? And what do I mean when I talk of 'the naturalisation of the social hierarchy' or 'legitimacy'? The political scientist David Beetham has defined political legitimacy in the following terms:

> The key to understanding the concept of legitimacy lies in the recognition that it is multi-dimensional in character. It embodies three distinct elements or levels, which are qualitatively different from one another. Power can be said to be legitimate to the extent that:
> (i) it conforms to established rules
> (ii) the rules can be justified by reference to beliefs shared by both dominant and subordinate, and
> (iii) there is evidence of consent by the subordinate to the particular power relation.[22]

Beetham develops his model of political legitimacy primarily in opposition to the Weberian definition, still common currency among social scientists,

---

[22] Beetham (1991) 15–16. I am grateful to Ed van der Vliet for referring me to this seminal study.

which focuses on people's beliefs about legitimacy instead of, as Beetham
would have it, on whether a given relationship of power can be 'justified
in terms' of people's beliefs.[23] In his model, therefore, the stress lies heavily
on the second element or level of legitimacy (rule (ii) above). As he writes,

[w]hen we seek to assess the legitimacy of a regime, a political system, or some
other power relation, one thing we are doing is assessing how far it can be justified
in terms of people's beliefs, how far it conforms to their values or standards, how far
it satisfies the normative expectations they have of it. We are making an assessment
of the degree of congruence, or lack of it, between a given system of power and
the beliefs, values and expectations that provide its justification.[24]

Thus there may be a law (or set of laws), formal or informal, written
or unwritten, that decrees that certain people govern and others are subjects. To make the political dominance of those who thus lawfully govern
truly legitimate, however, the law (or rule of power) needs to have a basis
in widely shared and deeply rooted beliefs about what constitutes good
and just behaviour, and under which circumstances unequal relationships
between people are right and proper. 'Qualified', i.e. politically free, subordinates, furthermore, must give expression to their conviction that the
rules governing the relations of power are backed up by the society's value
system by means of behaviour or actions clearly indicating their consent.
Finally, when the rules of power have their basis in deeply rooted beliefs
and value systems, the social hierarchy may come to be perceived of as 'the
natural state of things', as immutable by means of human action as the laws
governing the cosmos.[25] Thus legitimation may entail the naturalisation of
social inequality.[26]

Using the criteria developed by Beetham, I shall argue that euergetism
had an important part to play in securing the legitimacy of oligarchic
power in the Greek cities of the Roman period. About the first criterion,
the conformity of the power system to established rules, we can be fairly
short. As we saw, from the Hellenistic period onwards it became political
custom that, through the council, a minority of rich citizens effectively
governed the city. For Bithynia in Asia Minor, we can say that, by the

---

[23] Beetham (1991) 11.   [24] Beetham (1991) 11.

[25] See Beetham (1991) 58: 'Now it is possible to avoid such negative connotations [of power relations]
by simply removing the rules of power from the sphere of human agency and treating them as part
of the natural world, whose allocations, like the weather, are blind and beyond the possibility of
human control . . . Here, appeals to the idea of nature take the form much more of nature as "natural
order" or "natural law"'.

[26] To be sure, natural order is only one among several 'authoritative sources' from which legitimacy may
be derived; others are divine beings, science (external sources), 'tradition', or 'the people' (internal
sources). See Beetham (1991) 69–76.

Roman period, this informal oligarchisation acquired vestiges of formality first by means of the *lex Pompeia* and later by an edict of Augustus, both of which laid down constitutional rules for the functioning of the urban councils.[27] These rulings had the effect of more or less legally sanctioning the lifelong membership of the council that by the late Republic and early Empire had probably become the rule rather than the exception in most Greek cities.[28] The problem is that we do not know for certain whether other cities in the east were subject to constitutional arrangements similar to those existing in Bithynia, though there is some circumstantial evidence that this might have been the case at least from the first century AD onwards.[29]

As regards Beetham's second criterion, that 'the rules [of power] can be justified by reference to beliefs shared by both dominant and subordinate': the inscriptions awarded to generous members of the urban elite constituted, as publicly displayed honorific monuments, an ideally suited medium for aristocratic (self-)representation in terms of moral qualities and ethical virtues. I shall argue that the moral qualities and ethical virtues in question were both widespread and deeply rooted in the political tradition and political culture of the (post-)Classical Greek city. They were qualities, or character traits, of the good citizen, who was by definition also a rich citizen (whereas it was good to be philanthropic, patriotic, publicly generous and so forth, only the rich had the means to be all this, hence only the rich could show themselves to be good citizens. Not all rich men were good, but all good men were – usually – rich.)[30] Possession of abundant quantities of traditional civic virtues, as exemplified by their public benefactions, thus legitimated the rule of the – munificent – rich.

With reference to the third criterion of Beetham's model, that 'there [should be] evidence of consent by the subordinate to the particular power relation', I would argue that the honours awarded to benefactors, involving public acclamations in the assembly, crowning ceremonies, statues, inscriptions and so forth, can be interpreted as actions showing the consent of the subordinates (demos) to the rule of the rich but generous elite. It is here in particular that the Beetham model, when applied to the social

---

[27] Pliny *Ep.* 10.79.
[28] See Quass (1993) 382ff.; Pleket (1998) 205–6 and the discussion in Chapter 4 at pp. 60–2.
[29] Quass (1993) 384. See Wörrle (1988) 133 for evidence of lifelong membership of the boule in Lycia.
[30] See Finley (1985) 35–6: 'The judgement of antiquity about wealth was fundamentally unequivocal and uncomplicated. Wealth was necessary and it was good; it was an absolute requisite for the good life...'

processes of euergetism, displays its superiority over models of euergetism that focus solely on gift-exchange. For where such models rightly stress the active role of the non-elite citizenry by indicating that euergetism was a process of reciprocal exchange, the application of Beetham's criteria shows us that, in publicly awarding honours to elite benefactors, the non-elite citizenry were in fact participating actively in a political process of legitimation. Euergetism, therefore, was a highly politicised form of exchange, a process of legitimation of the oligarchic system in which both elite *and* mass were energetically engaged. This is of course a far cry from the stories of the depoliticised, passive mob and the death of polis-politics one tends to encounter in the older accounts of the post-Classical Greek city.[31] To resume, the legitimation of oligarchic rule by means of euergetism can thus be seen to meet the two most important criteria of the Beetham model: it was based on widespread and deeply rooted beliefs and values, and it entailed the frequent expression of consent by (politically free) subordinates.

All this may still sound rather abstract. Let us therefore turn to the honorific inscriptions themselves. When we do so, one of the first things to strike the eye is indeed the rich vocabulary of honour used to praise the virtues and moral qualities of the honorands. This vocabulary was widespread; we find it all over the Greek world of the Roman period, and it remained broadly consistent over a relatively long period. What we are confronted with, in fact, is a powerful honorific discourse, 'organised', as it were, around the notion of moral excellence. In most honorific inscriptions, the moral excellence of the honorands is illustrated by means of a wide variety of moral/ethical qualities or virtues that are ascribed to the honoured individuals. Such ascription might take several forms. The virtues might be mentioned in a straightforward manner: the honorand is then said to possess qualities such as φιλοτιμία (love of honour), φιλοδοξία (love of fame), φιλοπατρία (love of one's native city), μεγαλοπρέπεια (liberality), μεγαλοφροσύνη or μεγαλοψυχία ('greatness of mind/spirit', i.e. magnanimity, generosity). Alternatively, the virtuous character of the honorand might show from the manner in which he (or, less often, she) has performed certain duties or taken certain actions. He can then, for instance, be said to have acted σεμνῶς (in an august or stately manner), ἐνδόξως (honourably),

---

[31] See for instance Jones (1940), and most recently Runciman (1990). The continuing vitality of the assemblies in the Greek cities of the Roman period, as evident, for instance, from the writings of Plutarch (esp. *Prae. ger. reip.*) and Dio Chrysostom's orations also becomes easier to comprehend. The assembly, even more so than the theatre during shows or the agora, constituted *the* location where the non-elite citizenry could collectively give voice to their consent with the system of power.

ἐπιφανῶς (lit. 'shiningly', i.e. conspicuously, famously), λαμπρῶς (splendidly, illustriously). Often, also, one of the virtues mentioned above is used in adverbial form, i.e. someone can be said to have acted φιλοτίμως (ambitiously) or μεγαλοπρεπῶς (liberally, generously). Finally, virtues and qualities of character might be implied by certain honorific titles, such as σωτήρ (saviour), κτίστης (founder, mostly in the sense of restorer) or εὐεργέτης (benefactor).

All of the moral qualities just mentioned were in fact only aspects of the general ἀρετή (virtuousness) of the καλοὶ καὶ ἀγαθοὶ ἄνδρες (honourable and good men) who ruled the cities, and who showed their εὔνοια πρὸς τὸν δῆμον (goodwill towards the people) by holding public offices, performing liturgies and making public benefactions.[32] As Peter Brown has phrased it, virtues such as '*euergesia*, the urge to do good things for the city; and *megalopsychia*, a high-minded zest for open-handed gestures of largesse, were held to run in the blood of a notable'.[33] In its most elaborate form, the discourse appears in several long and complex honorific inscriptions from the imperial period, as a few examples will illustrate. C. Vibius Salutaris, the great benefactor from Ephesos who in AD 104 dedicated statues, images and money to Artemis and the city for the annual organisation of religious festivities, is praised as a man 'conspicuous by birth and personal worth' (γένει καὶ ἀξίᾳ διάσημος, line 15).[34] He is said to have been 'piously (εὐσεβῶν) making donations (φιλοτεί[μως])' and 'with generous dedications' to have 'honored the city in every way' (μεγαλοψύχο[ις δὲ] καθιερώσεσιν τὴν πόλιν κατὰ πᾶν τετε[ίμη]κεν, lines 19–22). Later on he is described as 'a man pious towards the gods, munificent to the city, to be honored with the most senior honors'(ἄνδρα ε]ὐσεβῆ [μὲν] πρὸς [τοὺς θεού]ς, εἰς δὲ τ[ὴν πόλιν φι]λότειμον, τε[τει[μῆσ]θαι τ[αῖς κρ]ατίσταις τιμαῖς, lines 84–6). Still later he is called 'an excellent citizen in all other respects [i.e., even leaving aside his foundation]', who had 'previously furnished numerous and extraordinary examples of his munificence' (τοῖς τε ἄλ[λο]ις πᾶσι[ν] [πολείτην ἄριστον καὶ πρό]τερον ἐν πολλ[ο]ῖς τῆς ἑαυ[τοῦ φιλοτειμίας πολλά τε καὶ οὐ]χ ὡς ἔτυχεν π[αρε]σχημένον [παραδείγματα εἰδώς, lines 338–41). Thus, the familiar ideological catchwords keep reappearing.

We find an even more baroque version of the same discourse in some inscriptions from Roman Lycia. The inscription in honour of Opramoas,

---

[32] For additional discussion of the honorific vocabulary in Greek inscriptions from the Hellenistic and Roman periods see Quass (1993) 19–79.
[33] Brown (1992) 83.
[34] For the Greek text and an English translation (quoted here) see Rogers (1991a) Appendix 1.

benefactor of a great number of Lycian cities, is a case in point. The entire text contains thirty-two honorific decrees from the Lycian League concerning Opramoas.³⁵ I quote here parts of the opening lines of only one of them:

> Since Opramoas, the son of Apollonios II and grandson of Kalliades, citizen of Rhodiapolis, a man of wide renown and magnanimity, endowed with all manner of virtues (ἀνὴρ] εὐφανέστατος καὶ μεγαλό[φρων καὶ πάσ]η ἀρετῆ κεκοσμημένος), whose ancestors were Lyciarchs and belonged to the first men in the province (πρωτευσάντων [ἐν τῷ ἔθνει) . . . and whose father Apollonios, son of Kalliades, is a man of dignity and magnanimity (ἀνδρὸς σεμνοῦ καὶ [μεγαλόφρο]νο[ς) . . . and since Opramoas himself from his earliest youth displayed a zeal for only the finest achievements and keeps exerting himself with good judgement, cultivation and all manner of virtues, trying to better the good deeds of his forebears (αὐτός τε Ὀπραμόας ἐκ πρώτης ἡλικίας ζηλωτὴς τῶν [κ]α[λ]λίστων ἐπιτηδευμάτων γενόμενο[ς] καὶ σωφροσύνην καὶ παιδείαν καὶ πᾶσαν [ἀ]ρετὴν ἀσκήσας, τοῖς προγονικοῖς ἀγα[θοῖ]ς ἁμιλλᾶται) . . .³⁶

Similar long-winding honorific formulae are employed in the inscription concerning the festival at Oenoanda founded by C. Iulius Demosthenes. Here, the benefactor is described as

> our most excellent citizen . . . , a man of the greatest distinction, outstanding in reputation, ancestry, and character not only in his home city but also in the province (ὁ κράτιστος πολείτης ἡμῶν . . . ἀνὴρ μεγαλοφρονέστατος πρωτεύων τῇ τε ἀξίᾳ καὶ τῷ γένει καὶ τῷ ἤθει οὐ μόνον τῆς πα[τρίδος] ἀλλὰ καὶ τοῦ ἔθνους, lines 49–50).

Similarly, later on, he is called 'a most distinguished man and first in the province'(ἀνὴρ ἐπισημότατος καὶ πρῶτος τῆς ἐπαρχε[ίας, line 103).³⁷ He is honoured

> for his continuous goodwill to the city and for his present patriotic zeal and his unsurpassed great-heartedness and for his devotion to the emperors (ἐπί τε τῇ διηνεκεῖ πρὸς τὴν πατρίδα εὐνοίᾳ καὶ τῇ νῦν φιλοτειμίᾳ καὶ ἀνυπερβλήτῳ μεγαλοψυχίᾳ καὶ τῇ πρὸς τοὺς Σεβαστοὺ[ς εὐσεβε]ίᾳ ἐπήνεσέν, lines 54–55).

As a final example I cite a long post-mortem honorific inscription from Kaunos in Caria.³⁸ Dating to the second century AD, the text probably formed part of the funerary monument of its honorand, a certain Agreophon. I quote:

---

³⁵ Along with thirty-eight letters from cities, Roman officials and the emperor Antoninus Pius.
³⁶ See Kokkinia (2000) no. 18, v A line 3–v B line 9. My translation is based on the German one of Kokkinia (2000) and the (at times incomplete) English translation of Danker (1982).
³⁷ See Wörrle (1988) 4–17. The translation is by Mitchell (1990).   ³⁸ Herrmann (1971) 36–9.

Ever since he was a boy and ephebe, Agreophon himself has shown his love of honour and, as an adult, he has continuously displayed his perfect and great-hearted disposition towards his native city (ὧν τε αὐτὸς Ἀγρεοφῶν ἀπὸ τῆς ἐν παισὶν καὶ ἐφήβοις ἡλικίας ἀρξάμενος φιλοτείμως κ<αὶ> ἐν ἀνδ[ρ]άσιν τέλειον καὶ μεγαλόψυχον ἐπλήρωσεν ἀεὶ τὴν εἰς τὴν πατρίδα διάθεσιν, lines 7–8).

There follows then a long list of all the offices Agreophon held and the benefactions he made. The list ends with a charming eulogy that can in fact serve as an ideal description of the attitude the good notable displayed towards his community:

On the whole, the purity of his soul and character outshone even the generosity assigned to him by fate [i.e. because he was rich, he could afford to be generous, but he was far more generous than expected]. He was decent and impartial while he was alive, respecting the elders as if they were his fathers and dealing with people of all ages in a kind and loving manner. He was just as a politician and fulfilled the public duties entrusted to him with integrity; envied for his wise judgement, he treated piously and lovingly the members of his household, was inimitable in his behaviour towards his friends and decent and humane towards his slaves.[39]

As I said earlier, what we encounter here in the many Greek honorific inscriptions from the Roman imperial period is a discourse of moral excellence originating in widespread and deep-rooted values and beliefs concerning the proper behaviour of the rich citizen towards his polis. Since, according to the inscriptions, the rich notables who made benefactions and ruled the cities embodied the virtues central to this discourse, it provided a justification for the (informal) 'rule of power' that the rich should govern. It may however be objected that, so far, I have only analysed epigraphic language. I have merely shown that a certain type of honorific vocabulary was widely used in inscriptions. Am I not misrepresenting things when I call this honorific vocabulary a discourse of moral excellence? Is what we have here not merely empty epigraphic rhetoric, a formulaic monumental language that has little or nothing to do with the Greek language actually spoken in the streets, squares and assemblies of the cities in the Roman east? In other words, are we really dealing here with what might be termed a 'living discourse'?

[39] *Ibid.* lines 15–18: Τὸ δὲ ὅλον λαμπροτέραν τῶν ἀπὸ τῆς τύχης φιλοτειμιῶν ἐπιδεικνύμενος τὴν τῆς ψυχῆς καὶ τῶν ἠθῶν φιλαγαθίαν ἐπιεικῆ καὶ ἰσότειμον τὸν ἑαυτοῦ παρεῖχεν βίον αἰδούμενος μὲν τοὺς πρεσβυτέρους ὡς πατέρας, φιλοστόργως δὲ καὶ φιλοκαλῶς προσφερόμενος πάσῃ ἡλικίᾳ, δίκαιος ἐμ πολιτείᾳ, ἁγνὸς καὶ περὶ τὰς δημοσίας πίστεις, ζηλωτὸς τῆς σωφροσύνης, εὐσεβὴς καὶ φιλόστοργος πρὸς τοὺς οἰκείους, ἀμείμητος πρὸς τοὺς φίλους, ἐπιεικὴς καὶ φιλάνθρωπος πρὸς τοὺς οἰκέτας.

This question leads us first to the issue of whether inscriptions were in fact read by anyone, and thus by implication reflected upon, and talked about. Were inscriptions actually put up to be read? It is difficult to give a straightforward answer to this question. First and foremost, at least from the point of view of the man in the street, inscriptions were (part of) public monuments; sometimes they were engraved so high up that they were hardly legible from street level. Often accompanied by statues of the honorand, often located at a spot closely associated with his or her benefaction, they had a strong symbolic and representational function.[40] This function, however, was in a sense merely additional to the highly ideologically charged language of the epigraphic text itself. And the content of inscriptions surely mattered greatly: epigraphic texts were often seen as the physical embodiments of decrees or decisions, even to the point of being taken down as a sign that the decree was no longer valid or had been overruled.[41] It has been suggested that, in antiquity, the stone decree was certainly not regarded merely as a publicly displayed copy, much less important than the original text filed in the public archive (a view often taken by modern historians).[42] On the contrary, the inscription itself, being at the same time text and artefact, message and monument, was given primacy. In the end, we have to treat inscriptions neither as solely documentary texts, which people read and talked about, nor completely as public monuments, that is, symbols, but – rather unusual from a modern perspective – as something in between.

Secondly, and much more importantly, however, we do actually have evidence that shows that the honorific vocabulary of the inscriptions constituted a living discourse, known to the majority of the inhabitants of the Greek cities, and used on important public occasions. Consider the following decree of the council and people of Kyme, which forms part of a long inscription in honour of the benefactor L. Vaccius Labeo that was set up somewhere between 2 BC and AD 14:

... therefore, with good fortune, the council and the people will decide: Labeo, who is worthy of all honours, should further be praised for his dignified way

---

[40] For instance, the ceremonies and festivities financed by C. Vibius Salutaris at Ephesos literally took place beneath the inscription recording his foundation, which was engraved on a wall in the theatre and somewhere on the Artemision. Thus congruence between text, location and rituals was established, with each element reinforcing the symbolic message of the others. See Rogers (1991a) 21–2. Similarly, Demosthenes of Oenoanda had his statue and the inscription recording his foundation placed near the food market he donated to the city, thus generating a 'Form dauerhafter Identifikation von Stifter und Monument' by creating an 'Ort gesteigerter persönlicher Repräsentation': see Wörrle (1988) 69.

[41] See Thomas (1992) 84–8 for examples and perceptive discussion.   [42] Thomas (1992) 86.

of life (τὸν βίον σεμνότατα), his love of fame (φιλοδοξίαν) and his attitude of liberality towards the city (τὰν μεγαλοδάπανον εἰς τὰν πόλιν διάθεσιν), and he should be held in the highest esteem and be most highly appreciated, and during all the agonistic festivals the city organises he should be invited to sit front seat in the theatre (εἰς προεδρίαν) and be crowned on the day of the libation, when the prayers are said, with the following words: 'The people crown Lucius Vaccius Labeo, son of Lucius, of the *tribus Aemilia*, friend of Kyme (φιλοκύμαιον), benefactor (εὐεργέταν), with a golden crown because of his virtue (ἀρετᾶς ἕνεκα) and his love of goodness (φιλ[ι]αγαθίας).' . . . And when he dies, he should be brought into the agora by the ephebes and the *neoi*, and be crowned by the city herald with the following words: 'The people crown Lucius Vaccius Labeo, son of Lucius, of the *tribus Aemilia*, friend of Kyme (φιλοκύμαιον), benefactor (εὐεργέταν), with a golden crown because of his virtue (ἀρετᾶς ἕν<ε>κα) and his goodwill (εὐνόας) towards the people.'[43]

Here we find that the honorific vocabulary recorded in inscriptions was hardly an empty monumental language. Rather, it formed part of a solemn discourse of praise and virtue, used during honorific rituals which were part of major public events (festivals, public burials) and which probably involved the larger part of the city's population. On both occasions when Labeo is crowned, the official performing the coronation speaks for the whole demos when uttering the honorific formulae, thus symbolically involving the entire community of citizens in the ritual. Prescribed public honours such as those for Labeo, however, still constituted quite solemn and ceremonial occasions. A looser and more spontaneous context in which the honorific vocabulary of inscriptions was used as a public discourse of praise is afforded by the so-called public acclamations of the demos. 'Is it not you', Dio Chrysostom told the assembly at Prusa early in the second century AD, 'who often praise us [i.e. the councillors, the urban elite] all day long, calling some "excellent" (ἀριστεῖς), others "Olympians" (Ὀλυμπίους), others "saviours" (σωτῆρας), others "nourishers" (τροφέας).'[44] As Louis Robert has shown, these honorific epithets that the people shouted from morning till night were precisely the ones that could (and can) be found in many honorific inscriptions lining the streets and squares of the cities in the Roman east.[45] The most striking portrayal, however, of the honorific rituals that constituted the real-life context of our epigraphic vocabulary of praise we find, perhaps ironically, in the work of a Christian critic. St John Chrysostom, preaching on the 'vainglory' still so feverishly sought

[43] *I.Kyme (IK 5)* 19 = *IGR* IV 1302.
[44] *Or.* 48.10. See Jones (1978) 113. On public acclamations in their late-antique form see particularly Roueché (1984).
[45] See Robert (1949), esp. 80–1, with additions in Robert (1960) 569–76.

after by the civic notables of his day, has left us the following graphic picture of the *philotimos*, the 'honour-loving man', making his grand entrée into the theatre of his city:

The theatre is filling up, and all the people are sitting aloft presenting a splendid sight and composed of numberless faces, so that many times the very rafters and roof above are hidden by human bodies. You can see neither tiles nor stones but all is men's bodies and faces. Then, as the benefactor who has brought them together enters in the sight of all, they stand up and as from a single mouth cry out. All with one voice call him protector and ruler of the city that they share in common, and stretch out their hands in salutation. Next, they liken him to the greatest of rivers, comparing his grand and lavish munificence to the copious waters of the Nile; and they call him the Nile of gifts. Others, flattering him still more and thinking the simile of the Nile too mean, reject rivers and seas; and they instance the Ocean (Ὠκεανέ) and say that he in his lavish gifts is what the Ocean is among the waters, and they leave not a word of praise unsaid . . . What next? The great man bows to the crowd and in this way shows his regard for them. Then he sits down amid the congratulations of his admiring peers, each of whom prays that he himself may attain to the same eminence and then die.[46]

In passages such as these, Christian writers like St John Chrysostom were shooting their arrows at what was by their time a well-established political culture with a long and distinguished pedigree. Indeed, the continuity of post-Classical Greek civic life into the later Empire, even if it was slowly, but in the end decisively, overtaken by a Christian world view proposing a radically different model of society, has been a central theme of recent scholarship on late antiquity.[47] Given this element of continuity, a text such as that of Chrysostom certainly 'donne beaucoup de vie à toutes nos inscriptions honorifiques de l'époque impériale'.[48] For centuries, in fact, the language used by the people in the public rituals of praise and the honorific vocabulary we find in the inscriptions formed a single discourse of moral excellence that underwrote the legitimacy of elite social and political dominance.

I have dwelt in some length on establishing whether our epigraphic vocabulary of praise actually constituted what I have called a 'living discourse'. This is because the contexts in which this discourse was used – the

---

[46] St John Chrysostom, *De inani gloria* 4–5. Translation by Laistner (1951) 87–8. See also Brown (1992) 83 and van Nijf (1997) 210. See Robert (1960) 570, note 4 on the use of the epithet Ὠκεανέ, which can also be found in some papyri, for instance *P. Oxy.* 1 (1898) 41 (referred to by Laistner (1951) 135, note 8), where the assembly greets the town councillor (?) Dioscoros with this cry. Robert (1960) 570ff. also adduces various passages from the homilies of St Basil. Here too the acclamations of the assembly crowd have found their way *verbatim* into the sermons of the church father, for instance the cry τροφεὺς καὶ εὐεργέτης.

[47] See Brown (2002).   [48] Robert (1960) 571, note 1.

crowning ceremonies of benefactors, the acclamations in the assembly, or the shouting of praise in the theatre during shows – clearly constituted situations in which the subordinates in the Greek city gave expression to their consent with the rules of power. As Beetham writes,

the consent of the subordinate makes its own distinctive contribution to the legitimacy of power, through the symbolic and normative force of actions which are conventionally recognised as expressing consent to the powerful, and, by implication, to the rules of power or constitutional system also . . . [S]uch actions *confer* legitimacy on the powerful, both through the public acknowledgement that is made of their position, and through the obligations that derive from that acknowledgement. To have this effect, they must be positive actions taking place in public, since inaction or privacy can have no legitimating force.[49]

Clearly, the public manifestations in the theatre, assembly or agora during which the non-elite citizenry gave voice to its approval of the generosity displayed by members of its ruling elite fit this definition well. By using, during these manifestations of praise for generous benefactors, *the same* honorific discourse members of the elite used in their self-representation in honorific inscriptions, the subordinate, but politically free, citizenry emphasised their consent with the oligarchic system. Thus, they conferred legitimacy on their ruling elite. In other words, here we have the third element required for political legitimacy in the Beetham model.

Let me take stock of the discussion so far. I have tried to show that a discourse centred on the notion of the moral excellence of members of the urban upper classes constituted one of the central characteristics of the political culture of the Greek cities in the Roman east. This discourse was used both as a semi-ritualistic language of praise during large public events in which both rulers and subordinates participated, and as an honorific vocabulary in the inscriptions set up for generous members of the ruling elite. I have argued that these public events can be interpreted as occasions when the subordinate demos expressed its consent with the oligarchic power system of the post-Classical Greek city. In addition, I have argued that the discourse of moral excellence used on those occasions and in the inscriptions was rooted deeply in notions about morally appropriate and virtuous behaviour of the citizen towards his polis community. The virtues that made up this discourse, I argued, more or less define the good citizen. I have, however, not yet substantiated these latter two claims. What we need to do next, therefore, is to bring to light, in outline at least, some of the *longue durée* ideological aspects of ancient Greek political culture.

---

[49] Beetham (1991) 150. The emphasis is his.

As a social category, the καλοὶ καὶ ἀγαθοὶ ἄνδρες that we encounter in the honorific inscriptions from the Roman imperial period certainly had a long history. From Homeric times right until the end of the Classical period, the ἀγαθός is the man 'who is held to be most effective in assuring the security, stability and well-being of the social unit, in war and in peace', to quote the definition of A. W. H. Adkins.[50] To properly fulfil this role, the ἀγαθός has to possess sufficient means, both materially and militarily. Without these he would be able neither to defend his *oikos* or polis nor to secure their material well-being. Consequently, the poor man can never become an ἀγαθός. The 'good man' attracts prestige because of his usefulness to the community. His resources alone allow him to purchase the weapons he needs on the battlefield, and to make material contributions to the community (relief in times of scarcity, liturgies and so on). A man without resources cannot be useful; hence he cannot be good. It was what you could do and did that defined who you were, but only *successful* action counted. To quote Adkins once more:

This [i.e. Greek culture] is both a results-culture, whose values are deeply influenced by the absolute demand that certain goals [such as defending the polis or securing its material well-being] be successfully attained, and a shame-culture, whose sanction, in addition to the disastrous nature of certain failures in themselves, is *overtly* 'what people will say'.[51]

Thus there was a strong emphasis on the usefulness to the community of individual wealth, and it was coupled with the notion that an individual's claim to moral superiority could only be substantiated through a successful contribution to the well-being of the community. It was this combination of moral requirements that actually provided the Greeks with an ideological solution to the problem of how to deal with economic inequalities in a politically egalitarian society. In a discussion of the rhetoric employed by elite litigants in the public law courts of that most egalitarian of poleis, fourth-century BC Athens, Josiah Ober shows how the 'solution' worked in practice:

[T]he speaker in court might ... attempt to demonstrate that certain of his elite attributes were valuable to the state. Especially important in this regard is the notion of *charis*. The wealthy man who contributed materially to the state in the correct spirit of generosity, patriotism and *philotimia* could request that the jury return the favor.[52]

---

[50] See Adkins (1972). The quote is from p. 60.   [51] Adkins (1972) 61. The emphasis is his.
[52] Ober (1989) 307.

Individual wealth was good if it was used for the benefit of the community. Anyone who used his wealth in such a way thereby testified to his moral excellence. He was an ἀγαθὸς πολίτης, a good citizen par excellence. Which ἰδιώτης, which κακός, which poor, ordinary citizen might dare challenge the ἀγαθὸς πολίτης's claim to prestige and, in many Greek cities if not quite in Athens, social and political dominance, when he had no means to show that he possessed the same high virtues himself?[53] Virtue showed from action, from public benefactions. To return once more to the fourth-century Athenian courts, here is the famous defence by an elite litigant suspected of trying to undermine democracy:

> I was trierarch five times; I fought in a sea battle four times; I made many contributions of money to the public finances; and I performed the other 'liturgies' in a manner not inferior to any other citizen. And I spent more money on these than I was required to do by the city, so that I might be thought more *agathos* by you [i.e. the citizen-jury], and if some misfortune should come upon me, I might *ameinon agōnizesthai* (fare better in court).[54]

The oligarchisation of civic politics from the Hellenistic period onwards led to an ever-stronger emphasis being placed on this particular element of Greek political ideology. While political power slowly became the prerogative of a small minority of rich citizens, the members of this elite increasingly felt the need to display their moral superiority by means of various kinds of public contributions. On them rested the burden of proof to show that they truly deserved their elevated position on account of their innate virtuousness. Again, it was deeds that counted. The more privileged the position of the governing elite became, the more individual members had to give evidence of their moral superiority, and they had to do so in hard cash. Aristotle, sharp observer that he was, clearly saw the price the rich few had to pay if they wished to hold on to their positions of power:

> The magistracies of the highest rank, which ought to be in the hands of the governing body, should have expensive duties attached to them, and then the people will not desire them and will take no offence at the privileges of their rulers when they see that they [i.e. the rulers] pay a heavy fine for their dignity. It is fitting also that the magistrates on entering office should offer magnificent sacrifices or erect some public edifice, and then the people who participate in the entertainment, and see the city decorated with votive offerings and buildings, will not desire an alteration in the government, and the notables will have memorials of their munificence.[55]

---

[53] See Adkins (1972) 64–5.   [54] Lysias 25.12. Translation by Adkins (1972) 121.
[55] *Pol.* 6.7. Translation by S. Everson in *Aristotle: the Politics and the Constitution of Athens* (Cambridge Texts in the History of Political Thought), Cambridge University Press, 1996.

Here, then, lies the origin of the system of public benefactions we call euergetism. The proliferation of benefactions and honorific inscriptions characteristic of political life in the post-Classical Greek city testifies more clearly than anything else to the pressing need of the members of its elite to acquire ideological legitimacy for their positions of power. The ideological 'model' developed in the earlier periods of Greek history as a solution to the problem of social and economic stratification in an egalitarian polis society proved to be eminently flexible. This 'model', centred on the notion of the rich man behaving as an ἀγαθὸς πολίτης, a φιλότιμος who showed his philanthropy, generosity and patriotism by using his individual resources for the benefit of the community, in fact became the core notion of the new, more hierarchical, political culture that took shape in the oligarchic post-Classical Greek city. It is in essence this ideology of the notable who owes his powerful position to his virtuous character as exemplified by his benefactions to the community that we encounter in the Greek honorific inscriptions from the Roman imperial period. In this same period, the oligarchisation of political life in the Greek city reached its final stage with what H. W. Pleket has described as the internal oligarchisation of the urban councils.[56] Increasingly, the councils became dominated by small groups of very rich, very influential families, the πρωτεύοντες, or *primores viri*, as Hadrian calls them in a letter to the city of Klazomenai.[57] These families alone among the urban upper classes possessed sufficient resources to make large benefactions frequently. More important in the present context, however, is the fact that their position at the very top of the urban status hierarchy provided them with a strong incentive often to display their moral excellence in the most grandiose fashion possible, and to have recorded, in an equally grandiose fashion, that they did so. As I wrote earlier, they had to show not only that they were good; they had to show that they were very, very good. Here, I think, lies part of the explanation for the elaborate character of much honorific rhetoric in Greek imperial inscriptions.

The discourse of moral excellence that formed such a central part of the honorific epigraphy and the public honorific rituals of the Greek cities in the Roman east was thus deeply rooted in Greek political ideology, its core theme of the ἀγαθός dating back to the earliest periods of Greek history. With this, I believe we have now also met the second and most important Beetham criterion for political legitimacy. That is, the 'rule of power' that the richer elite citizens should govern the city was justified by

[56] Pleket (1998) 208–10.   [57] *Dig.* 50.7.5.5.

a belief, shared by both rulers and subordinates, in the moral superiority of the members of this ruling elite. This moral superiority, defined in terms of age-old notions of morally just behaviour, found its expression in the benefactions made by the elite, and was emphasised by the subordinates in public rituals of praise. With these rituals, I argue, the subordinates gave expression to their consent to the power system (Beetham's third criterion). The honorific inscription, finally, proved an ideal medium for publicly advertising the virtuous and excellent character of the city's elite. Thus the legitimating fiction that, truly, the morally best men were governing the polity was kept vigorously alive on every street corner of the Roman east.

SOCIAL TURNOVER AND THE 'INDIVIDUALISM' OF HONORIFIC RHETORIC

From the foregoing discussion, several observations follow. The first is that, judged by the norms, values and beliefs of its participants, the power system prevailing in the Greek cities of the Roman imperial period was certainly perceived as legitimate. The second is that euergetism was central to the creation and maintenance of this sense of legitimacy. A third observation, however, may give us pause. It will perhaps have struck the reader of the previous section that the ideological rhetoric in the honorific inscriptions was primarily a discourse centring on the moral excellence of *the individual elite member and his or her family*. Yet, if my interpretation of this discourse is right, it served to provide legitimacy to *the oligarchic system of power in its entirety*. How should we explain this apparent discrepancy?

Earlier in this chapter, I stated in a rather general fashion that all political systems require legitimacy to remain stable over longer periods of time. A sceptic, however, might question whether legitimacy needed such clear and continuous articulation as I think it needed in the Greek cities of the Roman Empire. After all, the prevailing system of power – de facto oligarchy – had by Roman imperial times been common usage for several centuries, and to many of the inhabitants of the Roman east must have seemed as natural – and unchangeable – as the sunrise in the morning. A sceptic might indeed quote the following definition by J. G. A. Pocock of the so-called 'deferential society':

A deferential society in the classical – that is, eighteenth-century English and American – sense is usually conceived of as consisting of an elite and a nonelite, in which the nonelite regard the elite, without too much resentment, as being of a superior status and culture to their own, and consider elite leadership in political matters to be something normal and natural . . . Deference is expected to be spontaneously exhibited rather than enforced. A slave or serf is flogged into obedience, not deference, and the deferential man is frequently depicted as displaying deference as part of his otherwise free political behavior. *He defers to his superiors because he takes their superiority for granted, as part of the order of things.* It is often suggested that what makes him do so is *the conditioning effect of tradition* and that the deferential society is closely akin to another favorite conceptual tool of historical sociologists – the traditional society.[58]

In many ways, urban society in the Roman east seems compatible with this picture of the deferential society. But if that is so, what then was the purpose of the continuous reaffirmation of the legitimacy of existing power relations that I have argued for, given the 'conditioning effect of tradition' which should have made the demos naturally deferential towards the urban elite? Why was such reaffirmation at all necessary? And why, given the virtually limitless number of ways in which legitimacy might be expressed, did this reaffirmation assume the form of euergetism?

Pierre Bourdieu has emphasised the essential arbitrariness of any social hierarchy.[59] I would argue that in the Greek cities of the Roman east it was not the system of power as such that was considered arbitrary. Rather, the arbitrariness rested in the particular set of individuals inhabiting positions of power at any given time. That is why the legitimating ideology of virtue we have just analysed was so focused on *individual* character traits, on *individual* moral superiority. In trying to explain this 'individualism', we should not limit ourselves to the common sense observation that, naturally, the inscription was put up to honour an individual benefactor and his family. Rather, we should realise that it was *the individual* who had to prove that he was sufficiently virtuous to justify his position among the ruling elite of the city. This is not as strange as it might appear at first sight. A consideration of some of the demographic characteristics of the urban elite does provide a clue. As Jongman has recently written, '[w]e think of traditional society as a world where nothing ever changes, but the opposite is true: it is a world of fundamental uncertainty, mortal risks and extreme volatility'.[60] High and unpredictable mortality made it necessary for elite groups like the urban councillors continuously to recruit a certain number of new members from outside and below the circle of established elite families. A simple quantitative reconstruction might help us to appreciate the magnitude of the social turnover among local urban elites.

[58] Pocock (1976) 516. The emphasis is mine.   [59] Bourdieu (1977) 164.   [60] Jongman (2003) 121.

Urban councils in the Roman east frequently numbered a few hundred individuals, though totals varied. Oenoanda had a council of 500 members, Ephesos one of 450, while Thyatira seems to have had a council of at least 500 to 650 members. The council of Halicarnassos contained a hundred members, while at Cnidos, the total was just sixty.[61] As Jongman has shown in his analysis of the town council of Canusium in southern Italy, given prevailing levels of mortality, the customary annual intake of two ex-magistrates did not suffice to keep the Canusian council at the desired strength of one hundred members.[62] At Canusium, the problem was solved by accepting as council members a certain number of individuals of inferior social status.

In the analysis that follows, I adopt one of the fundamental assumptions underlying Jongman's demographic reconstruction of the council of Canusium, i.e. that 'the size of the ordo . . . equals the number of new entrants per year, multiplied by their average remaining life expectancy . . . given stable conditions'.[63] Following the established practice of ancient historians working on demographic problems, I take my data on age-specific life expectancies from so-called model life tables (mathematical models of age-specific mortality). Like Jongman, I employ Coale and Demeny model south.[64] Recent research on elite mortality in the Roman world has indicated that elite life expectancy at birth probably lay between twenty and thirty years, though in all likelihood it has to be located in the upper rather than the lower half of this range.[65] I shall therefore use life tables based on life expectancies at birth from twenty-five years onwards, with thirty-four as an absolute upper limit. Now if, for instance, the city of Oenoanda had followed prescribed Roman practice and only admitted to its council entrants aged thirty,[66] then given prevailing mortality levels it had to admit some sixteen to eighteen entrants per year to keep its council at a strength of 500 members.[67] Had it admitted, say, only ten new members annually,

---

[61] See Broughton (1938) 814 for references.   [62] Jongman (1991) 321–9.

[63] Jongman (1991) 321.   [64] Jongman (1991) 320; Coale and Demeny (1966).

[65] Scheidel (1999).   [66] See Pliny *Ep.* 10.79.

[67] The required number of entrants is calculated by dividing the size of the council (500 at Oenoanda) by the average remaining life expectancy at age thirty provided by the model life tables (e_0 = average life expectancy at birth; e_{30} = average life expectancy at age thirty). For Oenoanda, this gives the following results for the life tables selected:

   Coale and Demeny model south level 3 males (e_0 = 24.7; e_{30} = 28.1); annually required number of entrants: 17.8;

   Coale and Demeny model south level 5 males (e_0 = 29.3; e_{30} = 29.9); annually required number of entrants: 16.7;

   Coale and Demeny model south level 7 males (e_0 = 33.9; e_{30} = 31.6); annually required number of entrants: 15.8.

then its council (or bouleutic order) would only have numbered some 280 to 316 individuals. This difference between the preferred size of the boule and the achieved size if a lower number of new entrants was admitted than was necessary given prevailing mortality conditions we may term the 'mortality gap'. I should stress that these calculations carry no pretence of historical accuracy. They merely indicate the *possible* magnitude of the problem of social turnover under conditions of high mortality.

It seems unlikely however that all new recruits to the council came from very wealthy and established elite families. Naturally, they needed to be rich enough to carry the financial burden of office holding, but would that necessarily have been beyond the means of, say, owners of medium-sized estates or relatively well-to-do traders or manufacturers? My point is that, in most of the large city councils in the east, we should at all times expect to find in addition to the councillors from rich and established families a group of councillors who, like the *pedani* at Canusium, came from an inferior social background. They belonged to families that had until that time not been part of the *ordo*. In fact, we know that urban councils were internally stratified this way. In a letter to the city of Klazomenai, Hadrian draws a clear distinction between the *primores viri* and the *inferiores* in the urban council.[68] The *inferiores* should be exempt from making embassies to Rome, presumably because of their relative poverty. Pliny the Younger similarly differentiates between council members from wealthy and promi- nent families (*honesti*) and those from an inferior social background (*e plebe*), while arguing that it would be preferable if the latter were excluded from the council altogether.[69] In a celebrated passage from the *Digest*, the third-century jurist Callistratus admits, albeit grudgingly, that it will not do to deny council membership to 'those who are engaged in the trading and selling of foodstuffs' (*eos qui utensilia negotiantur et vendunt*). 'Yet', he continues, 'I believe it to be dishonourable for persons of this sort, who have been subject to the whippings [of the *aediles* in the marketplace], to be received into the *ordo*, and especially in those cities that have an abundance of honourable men (*honesti viri*). On the other hand, a needful shortage of the latter men requires even the former for municipal office, if they have the resources.'[70] Apparently, the problem of shortages of *honesti viri* was sufficiently widespread and persistent for its practical solution – admitting

---

[68] *Dig.* 50.7.5.5.   [69] *Ep.* 10.79.

[70] *Dig.* 50.2.12: *Inhonestum tamen puto esse huiusmodi personas flagellorum ictibus subiectas in ordinem recipi, et maxime in eis civitatibus, quae copiam virorum honestorum habeant: nam paucitas eorum, qui muneribus publicis fungi debeant, necessaria etiam hos ad dignitatem municipalem, si facultates habeant, invitat.* See Garnsey and Saller (1987) 115, whose translation I cite, for general comments.

wealthy but socially inferior citizens into the council – finally to receive legal sanctioning.[71]

But we also have to assume a greater stratification among the non-elite citizen population than is often envisaged. For if the lower echelons of the bouleutic order were the product of a social mobility necessitated by the desire to keep the *ordo* at a fixed numerical strength under conditions of high mortality, logic dictates that there should have existed a group of well-to-do non-elite citizens from which these new councillors could be recruited. Candidates abound in the sources: rich craftsmen, traders, manufacturers, owners of medium-sized estates, perhaps even professional men such as doctors, teachers and rhetoricians.

What I particularly want to stress now, however, is the extreme volatility that was characteristic of this entire urban social hierarchy. It was a volatility that worked primarily at the level of the individual; the social hierarchy as such remained intact. Its prime cause, as we saw, was the highly unpredictable nature of mortality. If, as a social and political system, the oligarchic order proved to be fairly durable, the particular configuration of individuals out of which it might consist at any given time was highly transient. Hierarchies were fragile, as one ancient historian has recently put it.[72] The consequent vulnerability of individual elite positions generated a strong need to emphasise their rightfulness and strongly predisposed members of the elite to produce durable symbols of their social power that might stand the test of time. Euergetism perfectly catered for both these needs. To new families within the *ordo*, it offered a chance to establish themselves by means of benefactions, while older families could emphasise their grandiosity through expenditure on a truly lavish scale. With luck, buildings, once donated, would still be there long after the donor's family had become extinct; so would honorific inscriptions recording benefactors' generosities. Indeed, it may have been precisely the lack of long term social and genetic continuity within an ever more oligarchic upper class that provided an important stimulus to the proliferation of honorific and funerary epigraphy in the Greek east during the imperial period. Honorific monuments, inscriptions and statues all served to provide a façade, or at least a sense, of continuity, precisely because such continuity was in reality often lacking.

The high demographic volatility within the confines of an essentially durable oligarchic social and political order also explains why the ideology

---

[71] For another, more detailed and striking, portrayal of the demographically induced social turnover among provincial urban elites see Tacoma (2006) on Roman Egypt.
[72] See Tacoma (2006).

we encounter in honorific inscriptions focuses primarily on the individual elite member and his or her family. Rather than the hierarchical order as such, which contemporaries probably took as more or less given, it was the position of the individual elite member and/or family *within* the hierarchy that was vulnerable, contested and therefore in need of legitimation. The individual notable was vulnerable primarily because mortality was harsh and unpredictable. What made his position also contested was the fact that, due to the same mortality regime, the appearance of new faces on the elite stage was hardly something exceptional in the experience of most citizens. Particularly the moderately well-to-do non-elite citizens who made up the middling group that served as a recruitment pool for additional council members would not have felt that there was much social distance between themselves and lower-ranking councillors. These citizens of moderate means, and especially the wealthier individuals among them, could easily imagine that they themselves might one day enter the ranks of the bouleutic order. The legitimating ideology of moral superiority devised to differentiate elite members from non-elite individuals is likely to have been targeted mainly at this category of citizens. After all, the greatest need to emphasise the qualities that marked out the true member of the urban elite arose precisely in confrontations with these potential competitors from below. As a group, the elite was forced to take in newcomers, but as individuals, elite members tried to differentiate themselves as sharply as possible from potential new recruits. Demographic volatility generated a continuous need for elite legitimation.

The focus on the individual elite member or family within the ruling oligarchy could also be carried onto the political plane. We should note that, whenever there was tension within the system, as when, during a grain shortage, a hungry mob attacked the house of Dio Chrysostom, or when the Ephesian crowd was unappreciative of the gifts of a local benefactor, it was not the oligarchic power system as such that was at issue.[73] Rather, the anger of the people was focused on certain *individual members of the elite* who had not done what was popularly expected of them. Dio was accused of hoarding grain instead of selling it cheaply, while Vedius Antoninus, the Ephesian benefactor, donated buildings instead of the shows, distributions and prize games the demos preferred. The oligarchic system worked, and was accepted, so long as the demos perceived that relations between elite and non-elite citizens were maintained in the proper way, and each party

---

[73] See Dio Chrys. *Or.* 46. Ephesian benefactor: *Syll.*³ 850, a letter of Antoninus Pius to Ephesos concerning the benefactions of Vedius Antoninus, see pp. 108–9 for the text.

did what was expected of it. Euergetism, in facilitating the legitimation of elite power in exchange for gifts, was an important way of structuring this relationship. However, as we saw in previous chapters, oligarchisation could and did become excessive during the first but primarily the second century AD, as disparities of wealth and political power within the citizenry increased at a rapid pace. It was to such excesses, which would of course often manifest themselves in the form of elite individuals neglecting the sort of behaviour towards the demos that was commonly expected of them, that the demos reacted, sometimes violently. And it was these excesses and the demos' reaction to them that created the increased need for the pacifying influence of euergetism at the time; not only because of its legitimating function, but also because of the way in which elite members used their gifts to underwrite the privileges inherent in the citizen status of the non-elite recipients.[74]

To sum up, then, the oligarchic system of power as such was probably never challenged in a basic sense, even though ordinary citizens did rebel against its growing excesses; we never hear of non-elite citizens striving actually to replace it with a more egalitarian system. On the contrary, when euergetism 'did its job' and elite–non-elite relations were maintained properly, the oligarchic system even received public approval in the rituals of praise we have analysed in the previous section. However, the demographic, social and political characteristics of urban society made it so that *individual* members of the elite and their families were vulnerable to continuous challenges from below. It was precisely this potential threat that the legitimating ideology of individual moral superiority was devised to ward off, by emphasising the truly essential difference in virtue between members of the upper class and their subordinates.

But how does the individual justification of position transform into the legitimation of the entire political system? How was the collective outcome of legitimation secured? As I argued in the previous section, the rhetorical discourse of elite self-representation contained a wide range of notions and moral precepts concerning the just behaviour of the rich man towards his community. As we saw, these notions and precepts had deep roots in the history of Greek political culture. They were widely shared among both the elite and the mass of ordinary citizens, as evidenced by the fact that they constituted a central element of the ritual language used during the festive, communal events when benefactors were publicly honoured. The language of elite self-representation in inscriptions was part of a living ideological

---

[74] See Chapter 5.

discourse of moral excellence, an excellence which, if demonstrated by elite individuals, would lead to harmonious and just relations between mass and elite, rich and poor. The fact that the honorific inscriptions advertising these elite moral qualities were displayed on every street corner of the Roman east only served to reinforce the central message of the discourse among all sections of the citizenry. Thus the self-representation of individual elite members contributed to the legitimation of the hierarchical social and political order as a whole.

SOCIAL CONTINUITY IN POWER

There is yet another aspect of elite self-representation in honorific inscriptions that can be understood better when interpreted against the background of harsh mortality and high social turnover in elite circles. This is the elite's claim of social continuity in power, which in inscriptions usually takes the form of a so-called 'ancestor clause', detailing and emphasising the achievements of the honorand's ancestors. Such clauses primarily served to draw attention to the supposed elite pedigree of the honorand and his family. Oligarchies by definition concentrate power in the hands of the few, the 'best men'. It will contribute greatly to their legitimacy if these few can show that their rule does not come out of the blue, but that their families have been part of the ruling class for a long time. In Greco-Roman society, descent from a leading family in itself already strongly qualified a person for positions of power. Moreover, part of successfully concentrating power in the hands of the few is to ensure that they remain broadly the same few, i.e., power has to be made hereditary.

Historians have indeed argued that, as part of the process of the oligarchisation of political life in the post-Classical Greek city, members of the urban council and their relatives increasingly became a socially closed circle, a hereditary ruling class of interrelated families. Social continuity and homogeneity within the bouleutic elite were maintained by the fact that council members sat for life and were able either to nominate their successors or to draw up the lists of candidates for magistracies (ex–office holders mostly automatically became boule members). Either procedure allowed them ample opportunity to privilege their own male offspring.[75]

Taken at face value, the sources seem to support the picture of a socially homogenous, de facto hereditary ruling class governing the cities of the

---

[75] See Jones (1940) 180–1; Magie (1950) 1 640–1 with 11 1504–5, notes 30 and 31; Pleket (1971) 235–6 and (1998) 205–6; Wörrle (1988) 133; Quass (1993) *passim*. Sons of councillors designated to succeed their fathers were called *patrobouloi* (*praetextati* in the western Empire), see Pleket (1971) 235.

Roman east. Dio Chrysostom, in many ways a very typical representative of the oligarchy of notables that dominated the Greek cities, declined the honours the Prusan assembly wished to bestow upon him because

I have here with you many honours already. In the first place those for my father, all those honours bestowed upon him for being a good citizen and for justly administering the city as long as he lived; then too, those for my mother, for whom you set up a statue as well as a shrine; furthermore, the honours bestowed upon my grandfathers and my other ancestors; and more than that, the honours possessed by my brothers and other kinsmen.[76]

C. P. Jones noted that '[t]his whole passage reveals how single families, through many branches and generations, maintained traditions of public generosity'.[77] Later on in the same speech, Dio states:

For even though I have been in many cities, I do not know better men than you [the Prusans]. Now I might speak at some length of individuals, were it not that, since virtually all are my kinsmen, I hesitate to praise them, even though I should be making to each a contribution, as it were, due in return for the honours paid to me.[78]

Again we may quote Jones: '[Dio's] words suggest a society in which interrelated families were accustomed to control local politics'.[79]

Truly overwhelming evidence for the seemingly closed and hereditary nature of the urban upper classes in the Roman east we find however not in the literary sources, but in the so-called ancestor clauses of the honorific inscriptions. A few examples will suffice to illustrate my point. In the long inscription for the Lycian benefactor Opramoas, it is repeatedly stressed that he was 'a man from a family distinguished among us, and [that he] descended from splendid and outstanding ancestors (προγόνων λαμπρῶν καὶ ἐπισήμων), who have made themselves conspicuous through their expenditures, their gifts and their magnanimity (μεγαλοφροσύνῃ), who were Lyciarchs and among the first in the province, and who were often honoured not just by their native cities, but also by the Lycian League for the benefactions they made towards their native cities and the province, and who were politically active in all Lycian cities'.[80] In the post-mortem honorific inscription for Agreophon from Kaunos, it is stated that, during the honorific ceremonies after Agreophon's death, the council and the people often reminded themselves of 'what his forefathers had already provided their native city with in terms of benefactions and the embassies

---

[76] *Or.* 44.3–4. [77] Jones (1978) 105. [78] *Or.* 44.5. [79] Jones (1978) 106.
[80] See Kokkinia (2000). Various versions of the ancestor clause appear throughout the text. I here quote II A, no. 6 lines 4–14.

which they took upon themselves'. The text goes on to list the achievements of Agreophon's father, who, during his career as *stephanephoros, prytanis,* ambassador to emperors and provincial governors, and *dekaprotos* had expended much private wealth for the good of the city.[81] At Ephesos, the *prytanis* Aurelia Iuliane describes herself as 'daughter, granddaughter, great-granddaughter and cousin of public secretaries, *prytaneis* and Asiarchs'.[82] In the same city, an honorific inscription for the Asiarch M. Aurelius Daphnus calls its honorand 'son of a secretary, grandson of secretaries, descendant of first secretaries, and great-grandson and descendant of single secretaries of the people'.[83] We encounter the glorification of ancestral achievement in its most explicit formulation in honorific monuments for deceased older children and young adults who belonged to the higher echelons of the urban elite. A good example is provided by the funerary honours for Nearchos IV, a junior member of a leading family from Boubon in Lycia, *c.* late second/early third century AD:

> The boule and demos of Boubon honoured with fitting honours Nearchos IV, great-great-grandson of Molesis, citizen of Boubon, kinsman of Lyciarchs, of parents and ancestors who were of first rank in the city (γονέων καὶ προγόνων πρωτευσάντων τῆς πατρίδος), and held the highest magistracies analogously to their family and status; a respectable and generous man, complete in all virtue and education, worthy of his parents and ancestors who have been priests of the *theoi Sebastoi* [deified *Augusti*], given banquets to everyone munificently and made distributions of money, who have contributed to [or ?supervised] the corn-dole assiduously, who have been *grammateus* [Secretary] beneficently and made distributions of money, who have been *gymnasiarchos* [President of the Gymnasium] and made provisions of olive-oil in the gymnasium assiduously and munificently, and who have held all the other magistracies assiduously and generously.[84]

Since the deceased child or adolescent had obviously died too young to accomplish much in terms of office holding or benefactions, the focus was deliberately on the achievements of his or her parents and ancestors.[85] Thus, these honorific decrees for *jeunes défunts* constitute a most explicit illustration of the ancient assumption that the prestige of achievement was passed on to one's descendants. They befit an oligarchic political culture and practice in which a relatively small number of elite families tried, often

---

[81] Herrmann (1971) 36–9, lines 5–8.   [82] *I.Ephesos* (*IK* 11–17) 1066.
[83] *I.Ephesos* (*IK* 11–17) 3070. On the secretarial offices in Ephesos see Schulte (1994).
[84] *RECAM* III 1. Translation by Milner and Hall.
[85] Save the reference to παιδεία, often found in honorific inscriptions for deceased junior members of the civic elite, see J. and L. Robert, *BE* (1973) 458. Accomplishments in schooling and 'Bildung' were apparently among the achievements one could credibly attribute to young-dead elite individuals.

unsuccessfully, to turn themselves into a hereditary ruling class.[86] If an adolescent son or daughter of an elite family died, a link was removed from the chain of wealth, power and prestige. Much familial investment (emotional, material, educational) turned out to have been wasted; but if the future had become more uncertain, at least the ties to the past could be firmly emphasised.

Not every honorific inscription has ancestor clauses as detailed or specific as the examples we have just seen. In many cases, the formulae employed are in fact quite concise; usually they are of what we might call the ἐκ προγόνων variety.[87] A text from Sebaste in Phrygia, for example, simply claims without adding any further details that its honorand came from a family of office holders and council members (ἐκ προγόνων ἀρχικὸν καὶ βουλευτὴν).[88] We also come across formulae such as 'ancestral benefactor of the city' (διὰ προγόνων εὐεργέτην τῆς πόλεως),[89] or, rather more tellingly, ἐκ προγόνων εὔνοιαν εἰς τὴν πόλιν, which literally means that the honorand inherited a favourable disposition towards the community from his ancestors.[90] As far as the texts themselves go, ancestor clauses of this last type form our most vital clue as to why so much emphasis was put on ancestral achievement in honorific inscriptions. After all, apart from making public benefactions, what better way was there for a notable to demonstrate that he truly possessed those seminal social and civic virtues which legitimated his position as part of the ruling elite than to show that he descended from a long line of equally virtuous ancestors? What better way was there to demonstrate that, to paraphrase Peter Brown, these very virtues actually 'ran in his blood'? The 'legitimating fiction' of social continuity in power, expressed in the form of ancestor clauses, is therefore intimately connected to the 'legitimating fiction' of vast moral superiority that we discussed in the previous section. We could say that, in fact, ancestor clauses and euergetism, and its associated discourse of moral excellence, formed part of a grand and overarching ideological 'argument'

---

[86] See in this context also the discussion of so-called 'consolation decrees' by Pleket (1994). More than in the inscription for Nearchos IV, in this type of decree for deceased older children and adolescents belonging to elite families stress is placed on the great loss their deaths mean to the family and the city. And indeed, the harsh demographic regime made living adult sons ready to follow in their fathers' footsteps in the council a relatively scarce commodity; a precious loss, therefore, even when viewed independently from the emotional horror of losing one's child. To be sure, some sons *did* succeed their fathers in office, but this happened much less often than historians tend to think.

[87] See Quass (1993) 47ff.   [88] *SEG* xxx (1980) 1489.   [89] See for instance *IGR* IV 410 (Pergamum).

[90] *IGR* IV 779 (Apamea). See also the honorific inscription for Aurelius Marcus, who in AD 237 donated a foundation to the town of Orcistus. In section B, lines 6–7 he is described as an ἀνὴρ ἐκ πρ[ογόνων] περὶ τὸν δῆμον φιλότείμως. See Buckler (1937) 4.

favouring – and legitimating – the rule of the few in the Greek cities of the Roman east.

Ideological rhetoric should however not be taken as a faithful portrayal of social reality. No matter how important the attested claims of elite social continuity were to the legitimation of the oligarchic power system, they cannot be used as unproblematic evidence for the supposedly closed, hereditary nature of the urban elite. In fact, it is precisely their constant repetition in countless honorific inscriptions (and literary sources) that should make us suspicious. If social continuity among the urban elites was indeed a historical reality, what then was the point of this continuous restatement of the obvious? As we all know now, given the prevailing regime of high and unpredictable mortality, it seems unrealistic to assume a high level of social and genetic continuity within the Empire's elites. My speculative calculations in the previous section together with the evidence for upward social mobility into the elite presented there indicate that the social turnover among local elites may indeed have been considerable. The suggestion of social continuity within elite circles was of major importance to the ruling oligarchy, because, like the discourse of elite moral excellence and the communal rituals of praise analysed earlier in this chapter, it contributed to the power system's appearance of legitimacy. It was precisely the fact that such continuity was in reality often lacking that must have provided the elite with a strong incentive publicly to emphasise it as often as possible. Their relative scarcity made long upper class ancestries very valuable assets in elite power games.[91] It was therefore extremely tempting for individual elite members to boast of possessing one, even if such a claim were manifestly untrue. Repeated often enough on the powerfully persuasive public monuments of self-representation we call honorific inscriptions, such a claim would sooner or later acquire the status of 'fact' and thus become an effective rhetorical tool.[92]

What will have made such fictions in general even more compelling is that, sometimes, they were actually true. Given the great variation of chances of survival around the mean, there were bound to be, at all times, some families whose successive members lived long lives and had the right

---

[91] In this sense, genealogical clauses in honorific inscriptions fulfilled the same function as the ancestor masks worn in Rome during the funerals of distinguished citizens, on which see Flower (1996): to suggest symbolically a continuity with the past that was often lacking in social and genetic terms.

[92] And we can only conclude that honorific inscriptions *must* have been persuasive, they *must* have successfully served their purpose of legitimating individual elite positions, and, at one remove, the oligarchic order as a whole, otherwise we would not have thousands of them left. It would have been pointless to continue erecting honorific inscriptions for several centuries if the benefits of doing so did not clearly outweigh the costs.

number of surviving offspring to be sufficient for replacement, but not so many as to cause the fragmentation of estates. Such families might remain part of the *ordo* for several generations, and therefore had far more time to accumulate wealth, power and prestige than families with a far shorter elite history. Hence the demographic 'lucky winners' often belonged to – and to a certain (but unknown) extent actually constituted – the highest echelons of the urban elite.[93] The epigraphically displayed claim of social continuity in power of such a family would thus be a rhetorically spiced-up but nevertheless more or less true reflection of its recent history. A case in point is the long genealogical inscription that once decorated the funerary monument of the Licinnii family from Oenoanda in Lycia.[94] Composed around AD 210, the genealogy meticulously records the names, offices and achievements of generations of men and women, starting more than 300 years ago with a Spartan, Cleander, who founded the nearby city of Kibyra. During the Principate, we see the family advance from local prominence in their cities to high federal offices in the Lycian League, and finally to the very pinnacle of the imperial aristocracy.[95] Other such families are known from the epigraphic evidence from Roman Asia Minor, and they represent the cream of the provincial urban elite. Possessing enormous resources, holding the highest civic, provincial and, frequently, imperial offices, making huge benefactions, they managed to retain their top position through a combination of demographic luck and clever strategies of marriage, adoption and succession. Other, lesser, elite families are likely to have tried to emulate their counterparts in the highest social stratum in terms of style, outlook and presentation, hence also in terms of epigraphic representation. Above I suggested that, as a medium, honorific inscriptions might have carried sufficient power of persuasion to render acceptable even dubious claims of social continuity in power. Still, families that had only recently entered the ranks of the urban elite will probably have been careful not to elaborate too much, so as not to make their claims stand out as too obviously fictitious. Up to a point, rhetorical fancy was part and parcel of the normal power game, but one should not push things; hence, perhaps, the frequent attestation in honorific inscriptions of the short, vague and rather unspecific ἐκ προγόνων formula. Only relatively few families managed to

---

[93] See Chapter 4, pp. 62–5.   [94] *IGR* III 500.
[95] See Jameson (1966), esp. 126; Hall, Milner and Coulton (1996). One member of the family, Ti. Claudius Dryantianus Antoninus (himself the son of another prominent scion of the Licinnii, the senator Claudius Claudius Agrippinus, *cos. c.* AD 151), married the daughter of Avidius Cassius, who revolted against the emperor Marcus Aurelius in AD 175. The (possible) involvement of one of their members in the rebellion does not however seem to have harmed the family's interests seriously.

remain part of the elite for a number of generations. As a consequence, long, elaborate and detailed ancestor clauses or genealogical notices are also comparatively rare in the epigraphic record.[96]

In addition, therefore, to the honorific rhetoric used both on inscriptions for generous members of the ruling elite and by the non-elite citizenry during public rituals of praise, the claim of social continuity in power also contributed to the legitimation of the oligarchic power system. However, unlike the honorific discourse of elite moral excellence, with its deep roots in Greek political culture, and the public manifestations of praise of the subordinate citizenry, it does not quite fit the categories of the Beetham model of legitimation. Nevertheless, it seemed too important and conspicuous an element of elite epigraphic self-representation to be left undiscussed, particularly when we take into consideration the effects of the harsh Roman mortality regime, in the context of which the claim of social continuity in power could sometimes acquire an awe-inspiring force.

LEGITIMATION OF OLIGARCHIC RULE IN A WIDER CONTEXT:
THE ABSENCE OF EXPLOITATION AND THE ENTITLEMENTS
OF CITIZENSHIP

Up to this point, we have mainly been concerned to show that the oligarchic system of power in the Greek cities of the Roman period was perceived as legitimate by its participants, elite *and* non-elite citizens. Our main aim has been to establish that euergetism was instrumental in creating and maintaining this sense, or element, of legitimacy. This partly explains the amazing proliferation of euergetism during the Roman period, when Greek civic life became ever more oligarchic, though in the context of an unchanging situation of high and unpredictable mortality and high social mobility. The result was a continuous and intense need to emphasise the rightfulness of elite position. Euergetism furnished an important means to this end: an honorific discourse that constantly underlined the legitimate character of the rule of the munificent rich.

---

[96] Note that, as always, we should take into account the distorting effects of transmission: we do not have all the texts that once existed, possibly we have only a fraction. Yet we may accidentally have more of a certain type of text than of another, while – who knows – in antiquity the numerical relation between the two types of text may have been quite the reverse from what it seems to us now. In other words, avoidance of the positivist fallacy means that we should be careful about establishing very direct links between patterns in our source material and past reality. Hence my arguments for correspondence between patterns in the epigraphic record and the social stratification of urban elites are necessarily quite tentative.

Now, however, we shall briefly turn our attention to a different, but equally important, question: not *if* but *why* the subordinate non-elite citizenry accepted the rule of the rich oligarchs as legitimate. After all, Greek city life during the Roman period was characterised by extreme, and increasing, disparities of wealth and power between citizens, and, as will have become clear in earlier chapters, elite benefactors were not very effective in remedying such gaps, nor was it their primary objective to do so. Munificence did not, on the whole, mollify existing economic disparities in urban society. Using the language of euergetism to force links with elite individuals by awarding them (as yet perhaps undeserved) honours might of course in the longer term prove beneficial to non-elite citizens. Van Nijf has suggested that such anticipatory honouring may have been a course of action frequently adopted by professional *collegia* in their dealings with members of the urban elite.[97] While here we have a likely reason why non-elite citizens might often address elite members in the language of euergetism, as a sole explanation for the acceptance of the legitimacy of oligarchic elite rule I find it unconvincing (van Nijf, to be sure, does not offer it as such). Something extra is required, I feel, to explain the phenomenon adequately. We need to widen our focus so that it includes not only urban society, but also the agrarian hinterland in which the city lay embedded. I suggest that, if we put the relations between mass and elite in urban society in the wider context of the economic structures of Roman agrarian society, a (tentative) explanation for the non-elite citizens' acceptance of the legitimacy of oligarchic rule can be formulated.

In a discussion of the relations between the aristocracy and the lower classes in eighteenth-century England, the British social historian E. P. Thompson observes the following:

> We have the paradox that the credibility of the gentry as paternalists arose from the high visibility of certain of their functions, and the low visibility of others. A great part of the gentry's appropriation of the labour value of 'the poor' was mediated by their tenantry, by trade or by taxation . . . The great gentry were defended by their bailiffs from their tenants, and by their coachmen from casual encounters. They met the lower sort of people mainly on their own terms, and when these were clients for their favours; in the formalities of the bench, or on calculated occasions of popular patronage.[98]

Thus the people on whose labours the fortunes of the eighteenth-century English gentry depended would encounter the latter only on highly ceremonial occasions, when the great lords might seem to be acting in their

---

[97] Van Nijf (1997) 111–13.   [98] Thompson (1991) 44–5.

interest (as local patrons and so forth). The direct exploitation of the agricultural labour of the poor tenants was co-ordinated not by the lords themselves, but by the bailiffs overseeing their estates. Hence, from the perspective of the tenants, the link between the 'appropriation of their labour value' and the gentry was at best only very indirect. My argument is that a situation somewhat different in structure, but quite similar in outcome, prevailed in the Roman world.

Unlike their counterparts in eighteenth-century England, the elite landowners of the Roman Empire lived in cities, where they constituted the social and political upper class. The bulk of the income of urban councillors derived from estates they owned in the territory of their cities or elsewhere. There, tenants or, less often in the provinces, slaves, overseen by bailiffs or other personnel of the absentee owner, worked hard to produce the surplus that provided the basis of the owner's income. As a result – and this is the point I want to make here – there generally existed only few, if any, personal relations of economic exploitation between the urban elite and the urban lower classes. The economic activities of the non-elite citizenry, whether they were poor day-labourers or members of the so-called *plebs media*, i.e. self-employed shop owners, petty traders and manufacturers and so forth, did not constitute the basis for the bulk of the income of the urban elite. The burden of exploitation was carried by the rural poor.[99] I admit that the picture is to some extent complicated by the fact that a minority of tenants may have been city-based, while some members of the elite derived part of their income from ownership of urban property (apartments, workshops),[100] but I think that, by and large, the argument stands. Consequently, therefore, the majority of the non-elite citizenry in the cities of the Roman world encountered members of the urban elite primarily as magistrates and benefactors, or as customers for the goods and services non-elite citizens produced, but not as employers, bosses, or in any way as direct controllers of their labour.[101] The social inequality between rich councillors and ordinary urban inhabitants may have been great, but the latter were not likely to interpret this as a direct consequence of their exploitation by the rich, since such exploitation did for the most part not exist. On the contrary, everywhere they looked around them in

---

[99] And even for them, the link with the urban elite may have seemed tenuous at best, since, like eighteenth-century English tenants, Roman tenants were also primarily confronted with their landlord's personnel, not with the landowner himself.

[100] On elite investment in urban property see Garnsey (1976).

[101] Though, occasionally, some members of the elite did supply capital to traders and manufacturers, by indirect means, i.e. as patrons to their freedmen.

their cities, poorer citizens would be reminded, not of exploitation, but of the unfailing public generosity of their social and political elite, and of the great service the latter rendered their city by governing it as magistrates and councillors. Statues and inscriptions honouring individuals from leading elite families for their generosity and brilliant performance in office were on display everywhere. And if these did not suffice to drive the point home, there were the constantly recurring festivals, games, banquets, handouts, distributions and so forth, all financed by members of the urban elite, which would confirm the notion of a benign, generous and 'natural-born' ruling class, a blessing to the city.

Once we become conscious of the true nature of the relations between the urban elite and the non-elite urban citizenry, and in particular of the relative absence of an element of economic exploitation in this relationship, it becomes much easier to understand why the urban lower classes were prepared to accept as legitimate the elite's claim to social and political dominance. We can see why the non-elite citizenry themselves were prepared to confer legitimacy on the elite by affirming the latter's moral excellence, and hence their fitness to rule, during public manifestations of acclaim for generous elite members. As far as we know, the inhabitants of the cities in the Roman east seem by and large to have accepted the oligarchic order as the natural state of things. I suggest that the virtual absence of direct economic exploitation of the non-elite urban citizenry by the urban elite contributed significantly to the continuation of this attitude among the mass of urban inhabitants during the greater part of Roman imperial history.

I should add one important qualification to this argument, however. For even if the absence of an exploitative relationship between elite and non-elite citizens will have facilitated the latter's acceptance of the elite's claim to legitimacy, the actual bestowal of legitimacy itself did of course take place in the context of elite gift-giving. In other words, absence of exploitation may have been a necessary condition for the legitimation of oligarchic rule in the cities, but it was by no means a sufficient one. For, as we saw, it was euergetism that made possible this very process of legitimation, and this meant that the elite had to give, and keep on giving incessantly, to ensure the legitimation of their political position. Why then were these elite gifts so important to the non-elite citizens? No doubt the gifts made civic life somewhat more comfortable in material terms. However, on the whole, as we saw, euergetism did very little to increase the actual standard of living of the ordinary population, nor was it intended to do so. The explanation must rather be framed in political and ideological terms. We saw, after all, that the increasing oligarchisation of civic life, and the concomitant rising income-gap within the citizenry caused by a sustained rise in elite wealth during the early Empire, had the potential to erode the very basis of polis society. That is, these developments put in danger the very notion, let alone the political reality, of the special position accorded to the non-elite members of the citizenry on the basis of their citizen status. For if political power and wealth were almost exclusively concentrated in the hands of a few grand families at the very top of the social hierarchy, what then would be the essential difference between a poor citizen and, say, a metic or a non-citizen tenant in the countryside? To prevent the potential social conflicts that might (and frequently did) arise out of this situation, to maintain social stability and a harmonious functioning of the polity, the ideal of the citizen community and the entitlements inherent in citizenship needed somehow to be acknowledged and find public recognition. This is precisely what the elite tried to do, and what the non-elite citizenry expected elite citizens to do, by means of their gift-giving to the citizen community. This, as we saw in the previous chapter, was an element virtually all the elite gifts had in common: they were directed at citizens, either the entire community or a subsection of it, and entailed recognition of the privileged status of citizens by making it possible for them to live the sort of life a citizen should live. Hence elite munificence continuously underlined the fact that, no matter how poor, wretched and low-status a citizen was, because of his citizenship he was still a member of a viable political community, a polis, and that this made him better – morally, socially, politically – than those who were not. It was on this vitally important function of elite gift-giving that the bestowal by the demos of legitimacy on the oligarchy of rich, munificent citizens who ruled them was ultimately predicated.

CONCLUSION

Every social and political order needs to affirm its legitimacy by reference to (1) its laws (or rules of power) and (2) the values and beliefs justifying the particular distribution of power and inequality among its members, and (3) through the public expression of consent with the system by politically free subordinates. However 'set' or established the regime is, or appears to be, the three elements just mentioned are vital to the long-term preservation of the system's legitimacy. We have seen that, in the Greek cities of the Roman east, euergetism provided the oligarchic political system with the two most important requirements of this model of legitimation. The exchange of gifts for honours between the ruling elite and the non-elite citizenry generated an elaborate discourse of praise, centred on the notion of elite moral excellence, which was rooted deeply in ancient Greek ideas of good and just behaviour of the rich man towards his community. According to these ideas, the morally excellent rich man was someone who used (part of) his wealth for the benefit of the whole community. Such men might justifiably claim, and were accorded, social and political influence. Publicly generous members of the *ordo* used the discourse based on this notion of the good rich to portray themselves in honorific inscriptions as the ideal, i.e. natural-born, leaders of society. At the same time, the discourse provided the non-elite citizenry with a rhetoric that could be used in the public manifestations of praise for generous elite members. Because during such manifestations citizens consciously made use of a discourse that emphasised the fitness to rule of the good rich, these manifestations do in fact constitute a public expression of the subordinates' consent to the system of power.

By the time of the high Roman Empire, the oligarchic system of the Greek cities had basically become the accepted order of society. No disaffected non-elite group ever tried to replace it with a different, perhaps more egalitarian, political system. Yet the extremes to which oligarchisation developed during the second century certainly put a lot of pressure on polis society. The many thousands of surviving honorific inscriptions, the countless attested festivals and public manifestations, and the great amounts of time and political energy invested in (major) benefactions all testify to the intensity and ubiquitousness of the need for political legitimation. To explain the intensity of legitimation through euergetism as visible in our sources, I argued that, in addition to the reality of an unprecedented accumulation of wealth and power in the hands of the elite discussed in earlier chapters, we should also consider the factor of demography. For the inner social workings of the oligarchic order were characterised by a great demographic volatility. Due to high and unpredictable mortality, urban elites were inherently unstable groups: a high degree of social mobility was necessary to keep their numbers intact. The consequent social differentiation of both the elite and the non-elite citizenry generated a strong need for individual elite members and their families to emphasise the rightfulness and naturalness of their position. This was particularly true for lesser elite families because of the relative lack of social distance between them and the (potentially upwardly mobile) upper echelons of the non-elite citizenry. Thus we can account for the individualist character of the discourse of elite moral superiority as we encounter it in inscriptions, and the continuing intensity and proliferation of euergetic activity. Since in their attempts to justify their own position individual elite families employed a rhetoric centred on the notion that the good – that is, generous – rich were entitled to rule, their epigraphically displayed self-representations contributed to the legitimation of the oligarchic system as a whole.

Linked to the issue of high and unpredictable mortality, but less easy to integrate within the Beetham model, is another claim that we encounter in honorific inscriptions. This claim too served to justify elite position. It is the claim of social continuity in power, which in most inscriptions takes the form of ancestor clauses that (either very briefly or in elaborate form) list the achievements of ancestors of the honorand, i.e. offices held and benefactions made. The primary aim of these clauses was to emphasise that the honorand was not a 'new man', since previous generations of his family had already belonged to the urban elite. I argued that such claims contributed to the legitimation of the political power held by elite families, since in Greco-Roman society it was generally assumed that descent from a family of office holders was an important qualification for office. Furthermore, the best way to underline that the virtues of public generosity and civic patriotism (i.e. the moral excellence required of elite members) actually ran in your blood was to show that you descended from a line of virtuous office holders and benefactors yourself. Yet I also argued that we cannot use ancestor clauses as unproblematic evidence for the supposedly closed, hereditary nature of the ruling classes in the Greek cities. The social turnover generated by severe and unpredictable mortality was simply too high to allow for much social and genetic continuity in elite circles. It was precisely its relative rarity that made social continuity in power such a valuable asset in elite power games, and that explains why we encounter it so often in honorific inscriptions. Given the nature of the mortality regime, many such claims will have been rhetorical fictions. This may explain why many ancestor clauses we encounter are rather vague, and do not mention specific individuals holding specific offices or making specific benefactions. That such fictions were nevertheless accepted may be because of (a) the fact that competitive elite struggles were partly carried out on the rhetorical plane, (b) the powerfully persuasive character of honorific inscriptions, and (c) the fact that, in the case of some families, the claims were actually true. Families that through a combination of demographic luck and clever succession strategies managed to remain part of the elite for several generations would indeed have a distinguished pedigree to display. They would also have sufficient resources to do so on a lavish scale, due to the competitive advantage of having more time available to accumulate wealth, power and prestige than first-generation elite families. Such successful families, however, were relatively rare: a lottery has many losers, and only a few winners.

Here we have a potential explanation for the relative scarcity of elaborate and detailed ancestor clauses in our epigraphic material.

Finally, after establishing that the urban elite's claim to rule was accepted as, and affirmed to be, legitimate by the urban non-elite citizenry, I considered the question why this should be so. I suggested that we might find the answer if we place the urban oligarchic system in a wider context of social, economic, and political relations between the urban landowning elite on the one hand and the urban and rural lower classes on the other. If we do this we can see that, since the bulk of the income of the urban elite derived from its landed possessions, a relation of direct economic exploitation existed only between the elite and the rural lower classes. The urban non-elite citizenry was on the whole free from such exploitation by the urban elite. Consequently, the urban non-elite citizenry primarily encountered elite members as magistrates, as customers for goods and services, and, above all, as benefactors. The absence of exploitative relations between mass and elite in the cities provided elite members with ample scope to use the medium of euergetism to present a benign image of themselves as the natural leaders, saviours and benefactors of the community. More importantly still, euergetism also afforded the elite the opportunity to emphasise, by means of their gifts, the continuing value of the citizen status of their non-elite beneficiaries. This was highly important at a time when growing oligarchisation and income disparities within the citizenry put increasing pressure on the very notion and functioning of polis society. Hence the acceptance and legitimation by the non-elite citizenry of the oligarchic order, even of the development towards ever-greater oligarchic exclusiveness, was predicated on these two things: the absence of elite exploitation, and the elite's continuing public acknowledgement, by means of their gifts, of the citizen status of the non-elite members of the community. These two elements allowed the non-elite citizenry to accept and confirm the benign image the elite presented of itself, and they did so by consenting to the oligarchic system and conferring legitimacy on the rule of the rich elite families that dominated their cities.

The decline of civic munificence

During the course of this study we have primarily discussed the unprecedented rise in the number of civic benefactions during the second century
AD, and the reasons that may lie behind this trend. We saw that, in a context of increasing oligarchisation and growing disparities of wealth within
the citizenry (due to a rapid, vast and sustained rise of elite incomes),
euergetism tended to underwrite the continuing importance of the citizen
status of the non-elite members of the civic community, and the entitlements this status entailed. At the same time, analysis of the honorific
discourse found in inscriptions, and of the public rituals of praise in which
the non-elite citizenry expressed their gratitude to generous elite members,
reveals that euergetism contributed in important ways to the legitimation
of the oligarchic political system in the cities.

While discussing all this, however, we have mainly been talking about
roughly the left half of Fig. 1.2 (see Chapter 1, p. 18), the graph that gave us
the chronology of the rise and decline of euergetism in Roman Asia Minor.
It is however in the right half of that same graph that we are confronted
with a trend that is in many ways as fascinating as the second-century boom
in munificence, and that is the sharp decline in the number of recorded
benefactions from the 220s AD onwards. How to account for this seemingly
fundamental change?

Like the rise in the number of benefactions visible in the left half of
Fig. 1.2, the decline we see in the graph's right half cannot simply be
attributed to a change in epigraphic fashion. For, once again, there is a
close correspondence between the slope of the curve and the chronological
patterns exhibited by the other archaeological data series mentioned during
the discussion in Chapter 1.[1] Dated shipwrecks, public buildings, meat
consumption as evidenced by animal bones, lead and copper pollution in
the Greenland ice cap, all these series show a marked decline in the third

---

[1] See Chapter 1, notes 35 and 36.

century AD.[2] Clearly, therefore, something fundamental was happening to Roman economy and society during that century. Jongman has suggested tentatively that the catastrophic mortality caused by the smallpox epidemics during the reign of Marcus Aurelius and after may have been the cause that triggered all this change.[3] Though the precise connections are still unclear, I would suggest that a sharp decline in the number of actual producers, caused by the epidemics, may have represented a very real threat to elite incomes and the government's tax base. The answer of both the central government and elite landowners, increased control over and increased exploitation of rural (and urban?) producers, so familiar to us from the later Empire, may have prevented the population from ever retaining its pre-smallpox level. Also, it may have prevented the diminished number of rural producers from truly profiting from the increased availability of land. Consequently, and unlike the late medieval peasants in Western Europe after the Black Death, they were unable to raise their standard of living.[4]

What does all this have to do with the decline of euergetism during the third century? Perhaps, in the case of civic munificence, the possible connection with the Antonine plague was not very direct. After all, the clear drop in the number of recorded benefactions during the reign of Marcus Aurelius visible in Fig. 1.3 (see Chapter 1, p. 19) is followed by an impressive recovery during the early Severan period.[5] Still, the third century saw a changed Empire, where a reduced number of rural producers made elite incomes less secure, and where the central government increasingly tried to control provincial civic life 'from the ground up', limiting the room for manoeuvre of local elites.[6] Under these novel conditions, would the full-blown participation in civic life in the form of office holding, liturgies and benefactions that we know so well from the first and second centuries still be as rewarding for the elite in terms of prestige as it used to be? Prestige aside, would it still be affordable, especially for the not-so-rich middle and lower ranks of the bouleutic elite?[7] Would a salaried post in the continuously expanding central government apparatus not bring more economic security, and perhaps constitute a new and far more attractive

---

[2] *Ibid.*   [3] Jongman (2006). See also Duncan-Jones (1996).   [4] Jongman (2006).

[5] When benefactions consisted mostly of donations of festivals, though (see Appendix 3), a cheaper form of munificence than donating large public buildings, which was very much *en vogue* during the second century AD.

[6] Mitchell (1993) 232–4 points to the increasing presence of central government officials concerned with matters of taxation in Asia Minor during the third century as visible in the epigraphic record. Note also Eich (2005), who finds that increasing administrative centralisation was one of the prime characteristics of the third-century Empire.

[7] Jones (1940) 190 comments that 'in the third century we find cities hunting in the highways and byways to fill their magistracies'.

source of symbolic capital? And for those who did not succeed in joining the imperial bureaucracy? Was it not wiser and more economical for them to withdraw to their landed estates?

All this is highly speculative, and these questions are no more than hypotheses which should be explored at some other place and time. What does seem fairly clear, however, is this. If euergetism represented a political–cultural reaction to the increasing disparities of wealth and political power within the citizenry caused by local landowning elites becoming ever richer and turning into ruling oligarchies, then the third-century decline of euergetism meant either that these tendencies stopped, or that political culture changed, or both. The most likely answer, I think, is: (a bit of) both. Third-century cities were probably as oligarchic as ever – perhaps even more so than before. However, the trend of growing rural populations and rising rents that had made the urban elites of large landowners ever richer during the first and second centuries AD had ground to a halt, checked by the Antonine plague. Instead, the decline in the number of rural producers probably made elite incomes increasingly insecure, hence the need for increased exploitation. Due to such factors, and with the maintenance of stable social relations in the cities becoming less of a priority due to the increasing, Empire-wide, centralisation of power manifest in the growing attempts at direct, central government control and exploitation of local communities, euergetism simply lost much of its rationale, and hence much of its traditional appeal.

Political culture, however, also underwent a slow but profound change, and the main culprit here was Christianity. Peter Brown has recently argued in favour of what he calls 'a revolution in the social imagination' of ancient cities 'that accompanied the rise and establishment of the Christian Church in the Roman Empire . . . between the years 300 and 600 of the Common Era'.[8] In Brown's view, this revolution encompassed a shift from a pagan, civic, model of society to a Judeo-Christian, more comprehensive, model that emphasised primarily the vital relations of charity between the rich and poor. Commenting on the role of public benefactors in the pagan, civic, model of society, Brown writes:

[T]he community these civic benefactors, the *euergetai*, addressed and helped to define through their generosity was, first and foremost, thought of as a 'civic' community. It was always the city that was, in the first instance, the recipient of gifts, or, if not the city, the civic community, the *dēmos* or the *populus*, of the city. It was never the poor. What one can call a 'civic' model of society prevailed. The

---

[8] Brown (2002) 1.

rich thought of themselves as the 'fellow citizens' of a distinctive community – *their* city. It was their city they were expected to love . . . The *euergetēs* showed his 'love of his city' by lavishing gifts upon it so as to increase the glory of its urban fabric and the comfort and overall vigor of its citizens. These gifts were directed either to the city as a whole . . . or to a clearly designated core of 'citizens,' a *dēmos*, a *populus* or *plebs*. This core of citizens was thought of, ideally, as persons who were descended from citizens and who had long resided in the city.[9]

I think the picture Brown sketches here of the Greco-Roman cities during the first two centuries AD, and of the role of civic benefactors within them, is fundamentally correct, and it will be apparent that I have drawn much inspiration from his brief sketch for the argument developed in this study. Brown continues:

'Love of the poor,' therefore, did not grow naturally out of the ideals of public beneficence . . . It could only come to the fore as a meaningful public virtue when the ancient, 'civic' sense of the community was weakened. In the period of late antiquity, then, Christian and Jewish charity was not simply one accustomed form of generosity among others, practiced with greater zeal than previously but not otherwise remarkable. It was a new departure. It gained a symbolic weight far out of proportion to its actual extent and efficacy. It was frequently presented as a challenge to the classical, pagan image of a 'civic' community. For it threw open the horizons of society . . . This more comprehensive community was presented now as frankly divided between the rich and the poor, with the rich having a duty to support the poor . . . Their relation to the poor acted . . . as a symbolic clamp. It bracketed and held in place an entire society.[10]

As we saw, Brown dates this shift from a pagan model of society focused on citizens to a Christian all-embracing one with special emphasis on the destitute poor to the period 300–600 AD. As we saw in Fig. 1.2, however, the demise of euergetism in Asia Minor started already from the 220s AD onwards. Does such clear evidence of the manifest third-century decline of euergetism, the social phenomenon so centrally important to Brown's (and my own) 'civic' model of society, not give us reason to assume that the shift in the social imagination he posits started about half a century or more earlier? Did the fundamental change in political culture Brown tries to trace already start to make itself felt roughly halfway through the third century? It is agreed among historians that, despite the persecutions under Decius and Valerian, Christian communities grew significantly during the third century. Also, an episcopal hierarchy started to emerge, with bishops becoming ever more influential figures in many cities. Would they and their communities already during the third century have been able to confront

---

[9] Brown (2002) 4–5. The emphasis is his.   [10] Brown (2002) 5–6.

broader, pagan civic society with a potent rival socio-ideological model along the lines proposed by Brown? The idea is suggestive, especially when, as seems realistic, we interpret the third-century decline of euergetism as a clear indication for the weakening of the civic model of society, and accept that the vigorous intellectual creativity displayed by third-century Christian writers like Tertullian and Cyprian represented only the tip of an iceberg, with far more ideological activity going on underneath.

Again, however, all this is hypothetical, and must remain speculation until further research provides some empirical grounding. But it offers us at least some suggestions for a possible explanation of the remarkable decline of the tradition of civic munificence in the Roman east during the third century, and its failure ever to revive completely.

By now, it will be clear that, during the course of the first but primarily the second century AD, the gains the local urban elites of the Roman east made both in terms of material wealth and socio-political power increased significantly. At the same time, however, we witness a similarly significant increase in their willingness to invest part of this wealth and political influence in the long-term preservation of the entire social order. That investment, as we have seen, took the form of munificence, and the central ideological message of this munificence concerned the continuing vitality and importance of the citizen community, of the 'civic model' that the urban communities of the Roman east saw as constituting the basis of their social order. Despite all the efforts of benefactors, however, the threat of social disruption and conflict never entirely disappeared; it kept brewing underneath the surface of civic life, and occasionally it erupted. Yet, we have thousands of honorific inscriptions left from the high Empire, and these are but a mere fraction of all those that once existed. Once we realise that almost every single one of them represents the conclusion to a successful 'transaction', a successful bargain struck between elite benefactor, other elite members and the non-elite citizenry, it turns out that, in fact, euergetism must have been pretty successful at keeping the peace. One conclusion should be that, as socio-political systems, the cities in fact 'worked' during the first two centuries AD. By and large, they functioned properly, both in terms of their internal political dynamics and in terms of their function as cogs in the wheel of the larger imperial system. In that sense, euergetism can be said to have made a significant contribution to the stable functioning of the (eastern) Roman Empire during the first and second centuries AD. However, as the decline of civic munificence in Roman Asia Minor during the third century indicates, the peace did not last forever. The civic model of society probably never entirely disappeared;

at least, it did not do so until very late antiquity. Ironically, perhaps, one of the liveliest ancient evocations of the civic spirit of euergetism comes in fact from a fourth-century author, the famous rhetorician Libanius, in a eulogy on the council of Antioch as it functioned in the recent past. 'First let us look at the council', he says, 'since the whole structure of the city is based upon it as upon a root'.

[T]hese men [i.e. the councillors] inherited their ancestral property by their good fortune, and spent it freely through their generosity, and through their industry they acquired many possessions; and just as the foundations of their wealth were blameless, they used it with all magnificence for the liturgies, avoiding poverty through their prudence, taking greater pleasure in spending for the benefit of the city than others take in amassing wealth, meeting expenses so lavishly that there was fear lest they be brought to indigence, and making their outlays in varied forms, sometimes supporting the populace in times of need and wiping out the failures of the soil through their gifts, and always enriching the whole city through the enjoyment of baths and pleasures of spectacles . . . and by their magnificent generosity turning into occasions for spending money the immunities granted to them by the laws, spending their own wealth more lavishly than men who had never yet borne a liturgy . . . As though they had some god as a surety that whatever they lay out, double gain will come from Good Fortune, they spend lavishly on horse races and gymnastic contests, some according to their means, others more than is suitable for their means . . .[11]

With his great skill, Libanius drew on all the age-old *topoi* of Greek honorific rhetoric to paint this wonderful picture of his native city's elite, and up to a point, he sounds convincing. In the world around him, however, emperors were issuing decree after decree in a desperate but ultimately unsuccessful attempt to force local elite members to stay on the council and to continue to carry the burden of liturgies and benefactions. Meanwhile, the Christian church, with its novel and very different ideas about the structure of the social order, and the imperial bureaucracy, ever expanding, and taking over many of the functions previously carried out by the local elites, were in the process of transforming the Roman Empire to its very core. Times were changing.

---

[11] Libanius *Or.* 11 (In praise of Antioch) 133–7. Translation by G. Downey, 'Libanius' *Antiochikos*: Oration 11 in Praise of Antioch', *Proceedings of the American Philosophical Society* 103.5 (1959), 652–86, at 667, slightly adapted.

List of source references for the benefactions assembled in the database

NB: For a description of this database and its properties see Chapter 1, pp. 16–17. If a source is listed more than once, this means that it contained information on more than one benefaction. I have added this list with the sole purpose of providing the reader with the source references to the benefactions contained in the database. It is therefore but a crude summary of the actual database. For a key to the abbreviations employed here see the abbreviations list.

A CONTRIBUTIONS TOWARDS PUBLIC BUILDING

Agoras

Balland (1981) no. 67; Balland (1981) no. 67; *IGR* III 66 = *I.Prusias ad Hypium* (*IK* 27) 20; *I.Prusias ad Hypium* (*IK* 27) 9; Wörrle (1988) = *SEG* XXXVIII 1462; *IGR* IV 860 = *I.Laod. Lyk.* (*IK* 49) 82; *I.Stratonikeia* (*IK* 21–2) 229a; *BCH* XVII (1993) 279; *I.Ephesos* (*IK* 11–17) 3004; *I.Ephesos* (*IK* 11–17) 3008; *IGR* IV 636; *I.Side* (*IK* 44) 155; *I.Tralleis* (*IK* 36.1) 77; *I.Tralleis* (*IK* 36.1) 145; *I. Arykanda* (*IK* 48) 41.

Aqueducts

IGR III 804; *IGR* III 811; *BCH* XII (1888) 85 no. 10 = *I.Stratonikeia* (*IK* 21–2) 293; *I.Prusias ad Hypium* (*IK* 27) 20 ; *I.Ephesos* (*IK* 11–17) 435.

Arches

I.Perge (*IK* 54) 56.

Baths/gymnasia

I.Iasos (*IK* 28) 260; *CIG* 2782; *SEG* IV 263 = *I.Stratonikeia* (*IK* 21–2) 15; Balland (1981) no. 67; *I.Keramos* (*IK* 30) 26; *IGR* III 833 and *Mon. Ant.* XXIII (1914–16) 174–5; Balland (1981) no. 69 = *AE* (1981) 834; *TAM* II 193; *TAM* II 361; *IGR* III 739 = Kokkinia (2000); *IGR* IV 257 = *I.Assos* (*IK* 4) 16–17; *I.Keramos* (*IK* 30) 19; *IGR* III 739 = Kokkinia (2000); *I.Sestos* (*IK* 19) 29, 1592; *IGR* IV 881; *IGR* IV 946, 938 with Robert, *Ét. Épigr.* 128–50; *IGR* III 739 = Kokkinia (2000); *BCH* XI (1887) 379 with Robert, *Ét. An.* 549 no. 8; *IGR* IV 555; *SEG* XXVI (1976/77) 1474; *IG* XII.3 326; *AM* XXI (1896) 261; *AE* (1974) 618 = *TAM* V 758; *SEG* XXVII (1977) 842 = *AE* (1981) 782; *IGR* IV 1378; *IGR* IV 1763 = *I.Ephesos* (*IK* 11–17) 3249; *PAS* III (1884–5) no. 426; *CIL* III 7146 = *I.Tralleis* (*IK* 36.1) 148; *I.Ephesos* (*IK* 11–17) 443; *REG* XIX (1906) 245–8 = Laum II 102; *I.Iasos* (*IK* 28) 247; Philostratos *VS* II, 26, p. 613; *IGR* III 833 and *Mon. Ant.* XXIII (1914–16) 174–5; *TAM* II 15; *REG* VI (1893) 187; *I.Prusias ad Hypium* (*IK* 27) 42; Balland (1981) no. 67; *I.Ephesos* (*IK* 11–17) 438; *BCH* XI (1887) 213 no. 2 = *I.Iasos* (*IK* 28) 122; *I.Perge* (*IK* 54) 36–9; *Term. Stud.* 77–81 = Lanck. II no. 6; *FE* II, 66 = *I.Ephesos* (*IK* 11–17) 3066; *IGR* III 115; *IGR* III 206; *I.Perge* (*IK* 54) 193; *I.Perge* (*IK* 54) 61; Judeich 70, nos. 6–7; *I.Stratonikeia* (*IK* 21–2) 281; *I.Ephesos* (*IK* 11–17) 672, 3080; *I.Ephesos* (*IK* 11–17) 427; Robert, *Ét. An.* 339; Balland (1981) no. 67; *IGR* IV 501; *I.Ephesos* (*IK* 11–17) 453; *SEG* XIX (1963) 830; *IGR* III 66 = *I.Prusias ad Hypium* (*IK* 27) 20; *AE* (1906) 177–8 = A. von Gerkan and F. Krischen, *Thermen und Palaestren* (Berlin: Schoetz, 1928) 164–6, no. 339; *IGR* IV 1302 = *I.Kyme* (*IK* 5) 19; *I.Perge* (*IK* 54) 193; *I.Ephesos* (*IK* 11–17) 500; Balland (1981) no. 67.

Governmental structures

Lanck. II no. 184 = *Mon. Ant.* XXIII (1914–16) 205–6; *CIL* III 6873; *I. Ephesos* (*IK* 11–17) 404; *I.Ephesos* (*IK* 11–17) 460; W. M. Ramsay, *Cities and bishoprics of Phrygia* (Oxford: Clarendon Press, 1895–7) 223; Judeich 72, no. 9; *IGR* IV 555; *I.Perge* (*IK* 54) 58; *AM* XXXV (1910) 383; *IGR* IV 504–5; *I.Selge* (*IK* 37) 17; *IGR* IV 1637; *I.Ephesos* (*IK* 11–17) 14; *BCH* I (1877) 55 = Laum II 98 = *I.Tralleis* (*IK* 36.1) 146; *I.Ephesos* (*IK* 11–17) 987.

Libraries

I.Ephesos (*IK* 11–17) 5101, also 5113; *I.Ephesos* (*IK* 11–17) 3009.

Macelli

IGR III 351; *IGR* III 828.

Miscellaneous

I.Perge (*IK* 54) 195, cf. also 196; *I.Laod. Lyk.* (*IK* 49) 24; *IGR* III 639, 642; LW
1591; *I.Ephesos* (*IK* 11–17) 3015; *I.Side* (*IK* 44) 104; *I.Selge* (*IK* 37) 62; *BCH* I
(1877) 55 = Laum II 98 = *I.Tralleis* (*IK* 36.1) 146; *BCH* I (1877) 55 = Laum
II 98 = *I.Tralleis* (*IK* 36.1) 146; *I.Ephesos* (*IK* 11–17) 690; *I.Ephesos* (*IK* 11–17)
626; *I.Iasos* (*IK* 28) 102; *IGR* IV 1222–3; *I.Side* (*IK* 44) 104; *I.Ephesos* (*IK*
11–17) 721; *I.Tralleis* (*IK* 36.1) 145; *I.Ephesos* (*IK* 11–17) 3013; *I.Stratonikeia*
(*IK* 21–2) 267; *AM* VIII (1883) 71; *BCH* V (1881) 99; *I.Ephesos* (*IK* 11–17) 449;
I.Ephesos (*IK* 11–17) 3086; *I.Tralleis* (*IK* 36.1) 164; *I.Ephesos* (*IK* 11–17) 518;
I.Ephesos (*IK* 11–17), 506; *I.Ephesos* (*IK* 11–17) 857; *I.Ephesos* (*IK* 11–17) 509;
BCH XXVIII (1904) 30 = *I.Stratonikeia* (*IK* 21–2) 144; *BCH* I (1877) 55 =
Laum II 98 = *I.Tralleis* (*IK* 36.1) 146; *I.Perge* (*IK* 54) 65; *I.Perge* (*IK* 54) 60;
I.Ephesos (*IK* 11–17) 3852; *I.Ephesos* (*IK* 11–17) 444; *I.Ephesos* (*IK* 11–17) 445;
I.Stratonikeia (*IK* 21–2) 522; *I.Hadrianoi u. Hadrianeia* (*IK* 33) 47; *I.Side*
(*IK* 44) 104.

Nymphaea

I.Ephesos (*IK* 11–17) 424a; *I.Ephesos* (*IK* 11–17) 424.

Odeia

I.Ephesos (*IK* 11–17) 1491; *I.Selge* (*IK* 37) 17; *I.Hadrianoi u. Hadrianeia* (*IK*
33) 46.

Religious structures

I.Selge (*IK* 37) 17; *I.Iasos* (*IK* 28) 257; *BCH* V (1881) 39 = *I.Mylasa* (*IK* 34–5)
337; *JHS* 28 (1908) 190; *BCH* V (1881) 185–9 no. 10 = *I.Stratonikeia* (*IK*
21–2) 690–1; *JRS* XIV (1924) 177; *IGR* III 684; *IGR* IV 624; *IGR* IV 1304 =
TAM V 903; *I.Ephesos* (*IK* 11–17) 434; *BCH* X (1886) 216; *Milet* I 6.95ff.;
Balland (1981) no. 67; *IGR* III 158; *FE* IV.1 23; *SEG* II 732; LW 313; LW
589; LW 590–1, 1587; *IG* XII.3 326; *I.Ephesos* (*IK* 11–17) 3233; *I.Ephesos* (*IK*
11–17) 3239a; *I.Stratonikeia* (*IK* 21–2) 200; *IGR* III 716; LW 314–18; *REG*

XIX (1906) 231–43 = Laum II 102; *R. Ph.* XI (1937) 334ff.; *I.Stratonikeia* (*IK* 21–2) 281; *FE* II 42; *IGR* III 868; *IGR* III 556; Lanck. II no. 201; Balland (1981) no. 67; *I.Hadrianoi u. Hadrianeia* (*IK* 33) 130; *IGR* III 962; *BCH* XI (1887) 389 no. 6 = *I.Stratonikeia* (*IK* 21–2) 207; *I.Lampsakos* (*IK* 6) 11; *I.Hadrianoi u. Hadrianeia* (*IK* 33) 135; *I.Smyrna* (*IK* 23–4) 753; *I.Ephesos* (*IK* 11–17) 690; *I.Ephesos* (*IK* 11–17) 1210; W. M. Ramsay, *Cities and bishoprics of Phrygia* (Oxford: Clarendon Press, 1895–7) 334–5; *IGR* IV 1533 = *I.Erythrae u. Klazomenai* (*IK* 1–2) 132; *IGR* III 933; *IGR* III 831; W. M. Ramsay, *Cities and bishoprics of Phrygia* (Oxford: Clarendon Press, 1895–7) 333; *JHS* XXXVIII (1918) 138; *IGR* III 342; Lanck. II no. 75 = *TAM* III 17; *IGR* III 732, 733 = *TAM* II 906, 910. Cf. also *BE* (1969) 551; *SEG* XXXIX 1823; *CIG* 4316h = *I.Arykanda* (*IK* 48) 108; *I.Side* (*IK* 44) 104; *IGR* III 739 = Kokkinia (2000); *I.Ephesos* (*IK* 11–17) 429; *IGR* III 833 and *Mon. Ant.* XXIII (1914–16) 174ff.; *IGR* III 739 = Kokkinia (2000); *IGR* III 833 and *Mon. Ant.* XXIII (1914–16) 174ff.; *IGR* III 739 = Kokkinia (2000); *JRS* 16 (1926) 94; *IGR* III 739 = Kokkinia (2000); *I.Kyzikos* (*IK* 26) 35; Lanck. II no. 250 = *I.Selge* (*IK* 37) 17; *IGR* III 90; *BCH* XII (1888) 85 no. 10 = *I.Stratonikeia* (*IK* 21–2) 293; *I.Anazerbos* (*IK* 56) 21; *IGR* III 366; *IGR* III 365; Lanck. II no. 83 = *TAM* III 19; *IGR* III 364; *SEG* II (1924) 724; *I.Ephesos* (*IK* 11–17) 3865a; *I.Ephesos* (*IK* 11–17) 4105.

Stadiums

IGR IV 845 = *I.Laod. Lyk.* (*IK* 49) 15. Cf. also *ibid.* 83; *CIG* 4437; *JÖAI* 15 (1912) Beiblatt 181–2.

Stoas

IGR III 739 = Kokkinia (2000); *I.Perge* (*IK* 54) 193; *I.Stratonikeia* (*IK* 21–2) 267; *MAMA* IV 309; *BCH* XXVIII (1904) 24 no. 3 = *I.Stratonikeia* (*IK* 21–2) 226; *IGR* IV 1422 = Robert, *Ét. An.* 134–6 = *I.Smyrna* (*IK* 23–4) 424; *I.Keramos* (*IK* 30) 14; *I.Smyrna* (*IK* 23–4) 424; *Philostratos VS* II, 23, p. 605; *IGR* IV 1306 = *TAM* V 1244; *IGR* IV 712; *TAM* II 179; Laum II 98 = *I.Tralleis* (*IK* 36.1) 146; *IGR* III 704; *IGR* III 739 = Kokkinia (2000); *I.Ilion* (*IK* 3) 157; *REG* VI (1893) 187; *IGR* IV 256 = *I.Assos* (*IK* 4) 15; Balland (1981) no. 67; *IGR* IV 159; *TAM* II 178; *IGR* IV 208 = *I.Ilion* (*IK* 3) 90; *IGR* IV 447; Laum II 92 = *IGR* IV 1572; cf. *SEG* XLIV (1994) 1686; H. Swoboda, J. Keil, F. Knoll, *Denkmäler aus Lykaonien, Pamphylien und Isaurien* (Vienna, 1935) 73 no. 147; *I.Ephesos* (*IK* 11–17) 3419; *IGR* IV 640; *FE* III 5 = *I.Ephesos* (*IK* 11–17) 3005; *SEG* I (1923) 444 = *I.Ilion* (*IK* 3) 152; *I.Prusa ad Olymp.* (*IK* 39)

8; *BCH* xliv (1920) 87–9 no. 19 = *I.Stratonikeia* (*IK* 21–2) 684; *I.Tralleis* (*IK* 36.1) 147; *MAMA* iv 139; *I.Ephesos* (*IK* 11–17) 3001; *I.Stratonikeia* (*IK* 21–2) 530; *IGR* iv 1189 ; *I.Iasos* (*IK* 28) 251; *I.Ephesos* (*IK* 11–17) 3421; *TAM* ii 18; *I.Arykanda* (*IK* 48) 29; *I.Ephesos* (*IK* 11–17) 430.

Theatres

Reynolds (1991) Appendix c; *I.Ephesos* (*IK* 11–17) 2038; *IGR* iv 1632; *I.Side* (*IK* 44) 141; *I.Side* (*IK* 44) 142; *I.Side* (*IK* 44) 145; *I.Side* (*IK* 44) 146; *I.Side* (*IK* 44) 147; Reynolds (1991) Appendix b; Reynolds (1991) Appendix a; *I.Ephesos* (*IK* 11–17) 2033; *IGR* iii 1474; *I.Side* (*IK* 44) 148; *I.Ephesos* (*IK* 11–17) 2039; *CIG* 2782; *FE* ii 37, 61; Aphrodisias & Rome doc. 36; *I.Arykanda* (*IK* 48) 38; *I.Side* (*IK* 44) 140; *CIL* iii 231 = *IGR* iii 803; *IGR* iii 704; *IGR* iii 739 = Kokkinia (2000); *IGR* iii 739 = Kokkinia (2000); *TAM* ii 550–1; *IGR* iii 679 = *TAM* ii 578; *TAM* ii 736; *BCH* xliv (1920) 96 = *I.Stratonikeia* (*IK* 21–2) 662; *TAM* ii 420; *TAM* ii 408.

Unidentified structures

I.Kios (*IK* 29) 15; *I.Prusias ad Hypium* (*IK* 27) 29; *FE* ii 61 = *I.Ephesos* (*IK* 11–17) 2061 ii; *FE* iii 66 = *I.Ephesos* (*IK* 11–17) 3066; *I.Ephesos* (*IK* 11–17) 565; Lanck. ii no. 249 = *I.Selge* (*IK* 37) 18; *I.Side* (*IK* 44) 162; *I.Adramytteion* (*IK* 51) 6; *I.Smyrna* (*IK* 23–4) 641; *IGR* iii 407; *TAM* ii 147; *I.Ephesos* (*IK* 11–17) 446; *JÖAI* xxvii (1933) Beiblatt 100; *IGR* iii 739 = Kokkinia (2000); *I.Ephesos* (*IK* 11–17) 449; *I.Iasos* (*IK* 28) 255; *IGR* iii 344–5.

B DISTRIBUTIONS

I.Stratonikeia (*IK* 21–2) 662; *Mus. Iznik (Nikaia)* (*IK* 9) 61; *Mus. Iznik (Nikaia)* (*IK* 9) 62; *I.Ephesos* (*IK* 11–17) 690; *I.Ephesos* (*IK* 11–17) 644a; *I.Ephesos* (*IK* 11–17) 2061 ii; *I.Stratonikeia* (*IK* 21–2) 237; Robert, *Ét. An.* 343ff., no. 4; *I.Tralleis* (*IK* 36.1) 90; *I.Tralleis* (*IK* 36.1) 75; *I.Magnesia am Sipylos* (*IK* 8) 34; *IGR* iv 454; *IGR* iv 216 = *I.Ilion* (*IK* 3) 121; *I.Stratonikeia* (*IK* 21–2) 205; *SEG* xxxviii (1988) 1462 = Wörrle (1988) 4–17; *I.Prusias ad Hypium* (*IK* 27) 18, cf. also 19; *SEG* xix (1963) 835; *I.Prusias ad Hypium* (*IK* 27) 17; *I.Stratonikeia* (*IK* 21–2) 1028; Balland (1981) no. 67; *I.Stratonikeia* (*IK* 21–2) 527; *I.Ephesos* (*IK* 11–17) 644; *IGR* iii 493; *I.Ephesos* (*IK* 11–17) 618; *I.Histria* 57; *IGR* iv 1429; *I.Selge* (*IK* 37) 17; *BCH* xxviii (1904) 27 = Laum ii 133; *BCH* xiv (1890) 233–4, no. 6 = *Laum* ii 132; *CIG* 3094 = Laum ii 93; *PAS* i 98–9, no. 5 = *I.Tralleis* (*IK* 36.1) 66; Laum ii 96 = *I.Tralleis* (*IK* 36.1)

220; *I.Tralleis* (*IK* 36.1) 145 = Laum II 95; Laum II 71 = *TAM* v 1197; *REG* vi (1893) 177, no. 11 = Laum II 122 = *I.Iasos* (*IK* 28) 87; *SEG* xxvii (1977) 938; *SEG* xxiv (1984) 1175; *IGR* III 739 = Kokkinia (2000); *CIG* 4336 = Laum II 169; *FE* iv 1 23; *IGR* III 492 = Laum II 164; Laum II 60.3; Laum II 60.4; *IGR* iv 1222 = de Hoz 22.9; Laum II 11; *IGR* iv 1127; LW 496 = *R. Ph.* 1 (1927) 122 = Laum II 116; *MAMA* III 50; *CIG* III 4332 = Laum II 140; *CIG* 2836b = Laum II 109; *CIG* 2817 = Laum II 106; *CIG* 2817 = Laum II 106; *CIG* 2774 = Laum II 104; *TAM* II 145 = Laum II 136; *REG* xix (1906) 208, no. 86 = Laum II 115; *REG* vi (1893) 149ff. = Laum II 124; *BCH* ix (1885) 76, no. 6 = Laum II 112; *I.Ephesos* (*IK* 11–17) 26; Laum II 41; Laum II 60.2; Laum II 83; *TAM* II 188–90 = Laum II 144; *CIL* III 6998; Laum II 72 = *IGR* iv 1168 = *TAM* v 828; Balland (1981) no. 66; Laum II 94 = *TAM* v 939; *REG* vi (1893) 177, no. 12 = Laum II 123 = *I.Iasos* (*IK* 28) 114; *IGR* III 422; Laum II 100; Laum II 73a; LW 1351 = Laum II 138a; *CIG* 3417 = Laum II 85; *IGR* iv 1629 = Laum II 84; *BCH* xiv (1890) 611, no. 6 = Laum II 113; *I.Side* (*IK* 44) 103; *I.Stratonikeia* (*IK* 21–2) 172; *I.Lampsakos* (*IK* 6) 12; *I.Ephesos* (*IK* 11–17) 3016; *I.Ephesos* (*IK* 11–17) 3017; *I.Ephesos* (*IK* 11–17) 3018; *I.Ephesos* (*IK* 11–17) 932; *I.Ephesos* (*IK* 11–17) 3014; *I.Iasos* (*IK* 28) 84; *I.Stratonikeia* (*IK* 21–2) 1325a; *I.Stratonikeia* (*IK* 21–2) 199; *I.Stratonikeia* (*IK* 21–2) 192; *I.Prusias ad Hypium* (*IK* 27) 50; *IGR* III 800–2; *I.Ephesos* (*IK* 11–17) 661; *I.Ephesos* (*IK* 11–17) 3015; *IGR* iv 860 = *I.Laod. Lyk.* (*IK* 49) 82.

C FESTIVALS

IGR III 115; *I.Smyrna* (*IK* 23–4) 637; Balland (1981) 69 = *AE* (1981) 834; Laum II 101 = Aphrodisias & Rome doc. 59; *SEG* xxxviii (1988) 1462 = Wörrle (1988) 4–17; Laum II 195; Laum II 194; Laum II 148; *JHS* lvii (1937) 1–10; *I.Ephesos* (*IK* 11–17) 27; *TAM* II 671; LW 1336 = Laum II 143a = *TAM* II 910; *IGR* iv 337; *IGR* iv 336; Laum II 166; *CIG* 2741 = *OGIS* 509 = Laum II 103 = Aphrodisias & Rome doc. 57; *TAM* II 578–9 = Laum II 139; Laum II 170; Laum II 171. 4 = *TAM* III 176; Laum II 152; *TAM* II 24, 29 = Laum II 145; Laum II 157; *TAM* II 301, 302–6; Lanck. II 251 = Laum II 168; *BCH* xvi (1892) 433, nos. 64, 65 = Laum II 160; *CIG* III 4380h = Laum II 161; *BCH* xvi (1892) 445, no. 95 = Laum II 142; *CIG* 4369 = Laum II 167; Laum II 138; *IGR* III 497/8 = Laum II 165; Lanck. II 193; *CIG* III 4352 = Laum II 149; Laum II 171.2 = *TAM* III 182; *BCH* xvi (1892) 444, no. 94 = Laum II 140; *Digest* 50, 12, 10 (Modestinus); Laum II 153; Laum II 155; Laum II 154; Laum II 146; *IGR* III 360; Laum II 171.1 = *TAM* III 154; *TAM* III 180; *TAM* III 141; *TAM* III 144; Laum II 10; *I.Perge* (*IK* 54) 77; *TAM* III 170; *BCH* ix (1885) 125 = Laum II 130; *I.Iasos* (*IK* 28) 99;

I.Smyrna (*IK* 23–4) 653; *I.Ephesos* (*IK* 11–17) 3070; *I.Ephesos* (*IK* 11–17) 2061
11; *I.Stratonikeia* (*IK* 21–2) 303; *I.Side* (*IK* 44) 111, cf. also 112; *Mus. Iznik
(Nikaia)* (*IK* 9) 60; *I.Ephesos* (*IK* 11–17) 859a; *I.Selge* (*IK* 37) 20; *TAM* III
145; Heberdey (1923) 198–9; *TAM* III 148; *TAM* III 151; *TAM* III 188; *TAM*
III 178; Heberdey (1923) 198–9; *CIG* 2741 = *OGIS* 509 = Laum II 103 =
Aphrodisias & Rome doc. 57; Lanck. II 201; *I.Ephesos* (*IK* 11–17) 721; *IGR*
IV 1632; *I.Stratonikeia* (*IK* 21–2) 199; *I.Parion* (*IK* 25) 11; *IGR* III 492.

D MISCELLANEOUS

I.Keramos (*IK* 30) 14; *IGR* IV 316; *JHS* LVII (1937) 1–10; *BCH* IX (1885) 339,
no. 22 = Laum II 118. See also Laum II 119; Lanck. I 175ff., nos. 58–61 =
Laum II 150. Cf. also *IGR* III 800–2; *IGR* IV 915 = *I.Kibyra* (*IK* 60) 41; *FE*
III 66 = *I.Ephesos* (*IK* 11–17) 3066; Lanck. II 11; *I.Magnesia* 131, no. 188 =
Laum II 127; Laum II 80 = *IGR* IV 1342 = *I.Magnesia am Sipylos* (*IK* 8) 20;
BCH IX (1885) 127 = Laum II 131; *SEG* VI (1932) 647; Laum II 60.1; Laum
II 60.5; Lanck. I 175ff., nos. 58–61 = Laum II 150. Cf. also *IGR* III 800–2;
I.Assos (*IK* 4) 28; Judeich 293; Judeich 195; Judeich 133; Judeich 227 = Laum
II 184; *AM* XVI (1891) 146 = Laum II 193; Laum II 35; Judeich 209; Judeich
278; *CIG* 3754 = Laum II 202; Laum II 37; Laum II 38; *TAM* II 188–90 =
Laum II 144; Robert, *Ét. An.* 305f. = LW 1006 = Laum II 197; *SEG* XIII
(1956) no. 258; *TAM* II 188–90 = Laum II 144; *SEG* VI (1932) 674; Laum
II 98 = *I.Tralleis* (*IK* 36.1) 146; Laum II 73 = *TAM* V 925; Laum II 75 =
I.Ephesos (*IK* 11–17) 3216; Judeich 153; *IGR* IV 1632 = de Hoz 151, no. 3.79;
Judeich 342; Laum II 185; *IGR* IV 788 = Laum II 177; *I.Ephesos* (*IK* 11–17)
26; LW 1603; *CIG* 2927 = *I.Tralleis* (*IK* 36.1) 80; *I.Prusias ad Hypium* (*IK*
27) 6; *I.Ephesos* (*IK* 11–17) 702; *I.Stratonikeia* (*IK* 21–2) 205; *CIG* 2930 =
I.Tralleis (*IK* 36.1) 77; *I.Stratonikeia* (*IK* 21–2) 229a ; Robert, *Ét. An.* 339;
I.Ephesos (*IK* 11–17) 22; *BCH* XVI (1892) 425; *IGR* IV 941; *I.Assos* (*IK* 4) 25;
I.Stratonikeia (*IK* 21–2) 203; *BCH* XI (1887) 379–83, no. 2 = *I.Stratonikeia*
(*IK* 21–2) 203; *TAM* II 671; *CIG* 2930 = *I.Tralleis* (*IK* 36.1) 77; *I.Ephesos*
(*IK* 11–17) 3016; *I.Ephesos* (*IK* 11–17) 3071; *I.Rhod. Per.* (*IK* 38) 110; *TAM* II
291; Laum II 77 = *I.Ephesos* (*IK* 11–17) 5113; *I.Stratonikeia* (*IK* 21–2) 172.

Capital sums for foundations in the Roman east
(c. I–III AD)

NB: All sums are in denarii.

Sum	Town	Reference
500,000	Philadelphia	Laum II 86 = *IGR* IV 1632
420,000	Sillyon	Lanck. I 58–61; *IGR* III 800–2; Laum II 150
400,000	Kibyra	*IGR* IV 915 = *I.Kibyra* (*IK* 60) 42
300,000	Sillyon	Lanck. I 58–61; *IGR* III 800–2; Laum II 150
300,000	Selge	*I.Selge* (*IK* 37) 17
264,179	Aphrodisias	*REG* XIX (1906) 231–2
165,500	Termessos	Laum II 169 = Lanck. II 123 = *CIG* 4366
122,000	Aphrodisias	*REG* XIX (1906) 231–2
120,000	Aphrodisias	*OGIS* 509; *CIG* 2759
110,000	Lycian koinon, Oenoanda	Laum II 164; *IGR* III 492
105,000	Aphrodisias	*CIG* 2782
100,000	Pergamum	*IGR* IV 316
70,000	Pergamum	*IGR* IV 337
61,000	Cadyanda	*TAM* II 671
55,000	Rhodiapolis	Laum II 143; *IGR* III 739
50,000	Philadelphia	Laum II 86 = *IGR* IV 1632
50,000	Philadelphia	Laum II 86 = *IGR* IV 1632
50,000	Nacoleia	*MAMA* V 202; *CIL* III 6998 II[1]
31,839	Aphrodisias	*OGIS* 509 = *CIG* 2759 = Aphrodisias & Rome doc. 57
30,500	Sagalassus	Lanck. II 201
30,000	–	*Dig.* 50.12.10 (Modestinus)
30,000	Xanthos	*TAM* II 291
25,000	Tlos	*TAM* II 578–9[2]
25,000	Melos	Laum II 51
25,000	Ephesos	Laum II 77
21,500	Ephesos	*I.Ephesos* (*IK* 11–17) 27
20,000	Synaus	LW 1006; Robert, *Ét. An.* 305–6, no. 2; Laum II 197[3]
20,000	Rhodos	Laum II 41; *JÖAI* VII (1904) p. 92

Sum	Town	Reference
19,000	Apameia Celaenae	*IGR* IV 788; Laum II 177. Cf. also *IGR* IV 787, 789–90
18,500	Tenos	*IG* XII 5 946 = Laum II 60
15,000	Apameia Celaenae	*IGR* IV 788; Laum II 177
15,000	Rhodiapolis	LW 1336 = Laum II 143a
12,600	Aphrodisias	Laum II 101 = Aphrodisias & Rome doc. 59
12,500	Tlos	*SEG* XXVII (1977) 938
11,000	Aphrodisias	LW 1603
10,500	Sparta	Laum II 10
10,000	Philadelphia	Laum II 86 = *IGR* IV 1632
10,000	Tenos	*IG* XII 5 946 = Laum II 60
10,000	Chios	*R.Ph.* XI (1937) 334ff.
10,000	Ephesos	*FE* III 66
10,000+	Magnesia at Sipylus	*IGR* IV 1342
8,000	Gytheion	*SEG* XIII (1956) 258
8,000	Ephesos	*FE* IV.1 23
7,209	Hierapolis	Judeich 153
7,000	Nysa	*BCH* XIV (1890) 233 = Laum II 132[4]
6,500	Thyatira	*IGR* IV 1222
6,000	Tenos	*IG* XII 5 946 = Laum II 60
6,000	Aphrodisias	*BCH* XIV (1890) 611
5,000	Tenos	*IG* XII 5 946 = Laum II 60
5,000	Tenos	*IG* XII 5 946 = Laum II 60
5,000	Aphrodisias	*CIG* 2836b
5,000	Iasos	*REG* VI (1893) 156ff.
4,450	Oenoanda	Wörrle (1988) = *SEG* XXXVIII (1988) 1462
4,000	Attaleia	*SEG* VI (1932) 647
3,333	Tralles	*PAS* I 108
3,000	Laodiceia	*AM* XVI (1891) 146
3,000	Miletos	*SEG* XXXIV (1984) 1175
3,000	Hierapolis	Judeich 227
2,545	Aphrodisias	*CIG* 2817
2,500	Philadelphia	Laum II 85
2,500	Hierapolis	Laum II 185
2,500	Nicaea	Laum II 202
2,370	Aphrodisias	*CIG* 2774 = LW 1609a
1,670	Aphrodisias	*BCH* IX (1885) 76
1,500	Philadelphia	Laum II 85
1,500	Philadelphia	Laum II 84
1,500	Orcistus	Buckler (1937) 1ff.
1,500	Aphrodisias	*CIG* 2817
1,500	Perge	*SEG* VI (1932) 674
1,500	Deriopos	Laum II 35
1,300	Philadelphia	Laum II 84
1,200	Hierapolis	Laum II 185
1,200	Elaeusa Sebaste	*MAMA* III 50

Sum	Town	Reference
1,000	Orcistus	Buckler (1937)
1,000	Hierapolis	Judeich 195
1,000	Teos	Laum II 93
500	Ephesos	*CIG* 3028 = Laum II 75
300	Hierapolis	Judeich 209
300	Hierapolis	Judeich 278
300	Hierapolis	Judeich 293
200	Hierapolis	Judeich 342
150	Hierapolis	Judeich 342
150	Hierapolis	Judeich 133
140	Philippi	Laum II 38
120	Philippi	Laum II 37

Notes

1 The inscription records HS 200,000, but for reasons of uniformity I give the equivalent in denarii.

2 The inscriptions state that the donor, Opramoas of Rhodiapolis, gave lands yielding a yearly revenue of 1,250 denarii to Tlos. Assuming 5 per cent annual return on landed property, the estates would have represented a capital value of 25,000 denarii. Note that strictly speaking we are not dealing with a cash-based foundation here. Since, however, the inscriptions allow us to make an estimate of the value of the land donated, and since we are primarily concerned with the size and value of foundation capitals here, inclusion seems justified.

3 In addition to the foundation for the eternal *stephanephorate* based on the cash fund of 20,000 denarii donated by Demosthenes and his wife Ammion together with their children, the parents also donated land to the city, value alas unknown.

4 The reading is a bit uncertain here, but probably ζ (7,000) is meant, rather than ζ' (7), not 700 as Laum II 132 translates, since, if that were the case, the text would have read ψ'.

Public buildings, distributions, and games and festivals per century (N = 399)

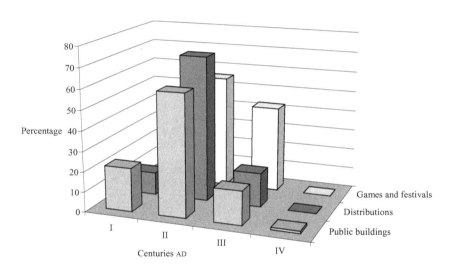

Bibliography

Abbott, F. F. and A. C. Johnson (1926) *Municipal administration in the Roman Empire*. Princeton: Princeton University Press.

Adkins, A. W. H. (1972) *Moral values and political behaviour in ancient Greece: from Homer to the end of the fifth century*. London: Chatto & Windus.

Alcock, S. E. (2007) 'The eastern Mediterranean' in: W. Scheidel, I. Morris and R. Saller (eds.) *The Cambridge economic history of the Greco-Roman world*. Cambridge University Press, 671–97.

Alföldy, G. (1975) *Römische Sozialgeschichte*. Wiesbaden: Steiner.

Anderson, J. C., Jr. (1997) *Roman architecture and society*. Baltimore and London: Johns Hopkins University Press.

Andreau, J. (1974) *Les affaires de monsieur Iucundus* (Collection de l'École française de Rome 19). Rome: École française de Rome.

(1977) 'Fondations privées et rapports sociaux en Italie romaine (Iᵉʳ–IIIᵉ s. ap. J.-C.)', *Ktema* 2: 157–209.

Andreau, J., P. Schmitt and A. Schnapp (1978) 'Paul Veyne et l'évergétisme', *Annales ESC* 33: 307–25.

Balland, A. (1981) *Inscriptions d'époque impériale du Létôon* (Fouilles de Xanthos 7). Paris: Klincksieck.

Beetham, D. (1991) *The legitimation of power*. Basingstoke: Macmillan.

Boatwright, M. T. (2000) *Hadrian and the cities of the Roman Empire*. Princeton University Press.

Boëthius, A. and J. B. Ward-Perkins (1970) *Etruscan and Roman architecture*. Harmondsworth: Penguin.

Bogaert, R. (1968) *Banques et banquiers dans les cités grecques*. Leiden: Sythoff.

Bolkestein, H. (1967) *Wohltätigkeit und Armenpflege im vorchristlichen Altertum*. Groningen: Bouma.

Boulanger, A. (1923) *Aelius Aristide et la sophistique dans la province d'Asie au IIe siècle de notre ère*. Paris: De Boccard.

Bourdieu, P. (1977) *Outline of a theory of practice*. Cambridge University Press.

Bremen, R. van (1993), review of Rogers (1991a), *Journal of Roman Studies* 83: 245–6.

(1994) 'A family from Sillyon', *Zeitschrift für Papyrologie und Epigraphik* 104: 43–56.

(1996) *The limits of participation: women and civic life in the Greek east in the Hellenistic and Roman periods*. Amsterdam: Gieben.

Broughton, T. R. S. (1938) 'Roman Asia Minor' in: T. Frank (ed.) *An economic survey of ancient Rome* IV. Baltimore: Johns Hopkins University Press, 499–918.

Brown, P. (1992) *Power and persuasion in late antiquity: towards a Christian empire*. Madison: University of Wisconsin Press.

(2002) *Poverty and leadership in the later Roman Empire*. Hanover and London: Brandeis University Press.

Buckler, W. (1937) 'A charitable foundation of AD 237', *Journal of Hellenic Studies* 57: 1–10.

Burkert, W. (1985) *Greek religion: archaic and classical*. Oxford: Blackwell.

(1987) 'Die antike Stadt als Festgemeinschaft' in: P. Hugger, W. Burkert and E. Lichtenhahn (eds.) *Stadt und Fest: zu Geschichte und Gegenwart europäischer Festkultur*. Unterägi: W&H and Stuttgart: Metzler, 25–44.

Callataÿ, F. de (2005) 'The Graeco-Roman economy in the super long-run: lead, copper and shipwrecks', *Journal of Roman Archaeology* 18: 361–72.

Cipolla, C. M. (1994) *Before the Industrial Revolution: European society and economy 1000–1700*. New York and London: Norton.

Clark, C. and M. Haswell (1970) *The economics of subsistence agriculture*. London: Macmillan.

Coale, A. J. and P. Demeny (1966) *Regional model life tables and stable populations*. Princeton: Princeton University Press.

Corbier, M. (1991) 'City, territory and taxation' in: J. Rich and A. Wallace-Hadrill (eds.) *City and country in the ancient world*. London and New York: Routledge, 211–39.

Cornell, T. J. and J. Matthews (1982) *Atlas of the Roman world*. Oxford: Phaidon.

Coulton, J. J. (1987) 'Opramoas and the Anonymous Benefactor', *Journal of Hellenic Studies* 107: 171–8.

Curchin, L. A. (1986) 'Non-slave labour in Roman Spain', *Gérion* 4: 177–87.

Danker, F. W. (1982) *Benefactor: epigraphic study of a Graeco-Roman and New Testament semantic field*. St Louis: Clayton.

Darnton, R. (1984) 'A bourgeois puts his world in order: the city as text' in: R. Darnton, *The great cat massacre and other episodes in French cultural history*. Harmondsworth: Penguin, 105–40.

Dmitriev, S. (2005) *City government in Hellenistic and Roman Asia Minor*. Oxford University Press.

Duncan-Jones, R. P. (1963) 'Wealth and munificence in Roman Africa', *Papers of the British School at Rome* 31: 159–77.

(1982) *The economy of the Roman Empire: quantitative studies*. Cambridge University Press.

(1990) *Structure and scale in the Roman economy*. Cambridge University Press.

(1996) 'The impact of the Antonine plague', *Journal of Roman Archaeology* 9: 108–36.

Eck, W. (1997) 'Der Euergetismus im Funktionszusammenhang der kaiserzeitlichen Städte' in: M. Christol and O. Masson (eds.) *Actes du Xe congrès international d'épigraphique grecque et latine*. Paris: Université de Paris-Sorbonne, 305–31.

Eich, P. (2005) *Zur Metamorphose des politischen Systems in der römischen Kaiserzeit: die Entstehung einer 'personalen Bürokratie' im langen dritten Jahrhundert*. Berlin: Akademie.

Erdkamp, P. (2002) 'A starving mob has no respect: urban markets and food riots in the Roman world, 100 BC–400 AD' in: L. de Blois and J. Rich (eds.) *The transformation of economic life under the Roman Empire: proceedings of the second workshop of the international network Impact of Empire (Roman Empire, c. 200 BC–AD 476), Nottingham, July 4–7, 2001*. Amsterdam: Gieben, 93–115.

Fagan, G. G. (1999) *Bathing in public in the Roman world*. Ann Arbor: University of Michigan Press.

Farrington, A. (1987) 'Imperial bath buildings in south-west Asia Minor' in: S. Macready and F. H. Thompson (eds.) *Roman architecture in the Greek world* (The Society of Antiquaries of London, Occasional papers (new series) X). London: Thames & Hudson, 50–9.

(1995) *The Roman baths of Lycia: an architectural study*. Ankara: British Institute of Archaeology at Ankara.

Finley, M. I. (1985) *The ancient economy*. Harmondsworth: Penguin.

Flower, H. I. (1996) *Ancestor masks and aristocratic power in Roman culture*. Oxford University Press.

Frier, B. W. (2000) 'Demography' in: A. K. Bowman, P. Garnsey and D. Rathbone (eds.) *The Cambridge ancient history*, 2nd edn, XI. *The High Empire, AD 70–192*. Cambridge University Press, 787–816.

(2001) 'More is worse: some observations on the population of the Roman Empire' in: W. Scheidel (ed.) *Debating Roman demography*. Leiden: Brill, 139–59.

Garnsey, P. (1976) 'Urban property investment' in: M. I. Finley (ed.) *Studies in Roman property*. Cambridge University Press, 123–36.

(1988) *Famine and food supply in the Graeco-Roman world: responses to risk and crisis*. Cambridge University Press.

(1991) 'The generosity of Veyne', *Journal of Roman Studies* 81: 164–8.

Garnsey, P. and R. Saller (1987) *The Roman Empire: economy, society and culture*. London: Duckworth.

Gauthier, Ph. (1985) *Les cités grecques et leurs bienfaiteurs (IVe–Ier siècle avant J.-C.): contribution à l'histoire des institutions*. Paris: De Boccard.

Goldhill, S. (ed.) (2001) *Being Greek under Rome: cultural identity, the Second Sophistic and the development of Empire*. Cambridge University Press.

Gordon, R. (1990) 'The veil of power: emperors, sacrificers and benefactors' in: M. Beard and J. North (eds.) *Pagan priests*. London: Duckworth, 199–231.

Halfmann, H. (1979) *Die Senatoren aus dem östlichen Teil des Imperium Romanum bis zum Ende des 2. Jh. n. Chr*. Göttingen: Vandenhoeck & Ruprecht.

Hall, A. S., N. P. Milner and J. J. Coulton (1996) 'The mausoleum of Licinnia Flavilla and Flavianus Diogenes of Oinoanda: epigraphy and architecture', *Anatolian Studies* 46: 111–14.

Hands, A. R. (1968) *Charities and social aid in Greece and Rome*. Ithaca: Cornell University Press.

Hanfmann, G. M. A. (1975) *From Croesus to Constantine: the cities of western Asia Minor and their arts in Greek and Roman times*. Ann Arbor: Michigan University Press.

Herrmann, P. (1971) 'Zwei Inschriften von Kaunos und Baba Dag', *Opuscula Atheniensia* 10: 36–40.

Hopkins, K. (1980) 'Taxes and trade in the Roman Empire (200 BC–AD 400)', *Journal of Roman Studies* 70: 101–25.

  (1983) *Death and renewal: sociological studies in Roman history* II. Cambridge University Press.

  (2002) 'Rome, taxes, rents and trade' in: W. Scheidel and S. Von Reden (eds.) *The ancient economy*. New York: Routledge, 190–230.

Jameson, S. (1966) 'Two Lycian families', *Anatolian Studies* 16: 124–37.

Johnston, D. (1985) 'Munificence and *municipia*: bequests to towns in classical Roman law', *Journal of Roman Studies* 75: 105–25.

Jones, A. H. M. (1940) *The Greek city from Alexander to Justinian*. Oxford: Clarendon Press.

Jones, C. P. (1978) *The Roman world of Dio Chrysostom*. Cambridge, Mass. and London: Harvard University Press.

  (2006) 'A letter of Hadrian to Naryka (Eastern Locris)', *Journal of Roman Archaeology* 19: 151–62.

Jongman, W. M. (1991) *The economy and society of Pompeii*. Amsterdam: Gieben.

  (2000) 'Hunger and power: theories, models and methods in Roman economic history' in: A. C. V. M. Bongenaar (ed.) *Interdependency of institutions and private entrepreneurs* (MOS Studies 2). Istanbul: Nederlands Instituut voor het Nabije Oosten, 259–84.

  (2002a) 'The Roman economy: from cities to Empire' in: L. De Blois and J. Rich (eds.) *The transformation of economic life under the Roman Empire: proceedings of the second workshop of the international network Impact of Empire (Roman Empire, c. 200 BC–AD 476), Nottingham, July 4–7, 2001*. Amsterdam: Gieben, 28–47.

  (2002b) 'Beneficial symbols: *alimenta* and the infantilization of the Roman citizen' in: W. M. Jongman and M. Kleijwegt (eds.) *After the past: essays in ancient history in honour of H. W. Pleket*. Leiden: Brill, 47–80.

  (2003) 'A golden age: death, money supply and social succession in the Roman Empire' in: E. LoCascio (ed.) *Credito e moneta nel mondo romano. Atti degli Incontri capresi di storia dell'economia antica (Capri 12–14 ottobre 2000)*. Bari: Edipuglia, 181–96.

  (2006) 'The rise and fall of the Roman economy: population, rents and entitlement' in: P. Bang, M. Ikeguchi and H. Ziche (eds.) *Ancient economies and modern methodologies: archaeology, comparative history, models and institutions.* Bari: Edipuglia, 237–54.

(2007) 'The early Roman empire: consumption' in: W. Scheidel, I. Morris and R. Saller (eds.) *The Cambridge economic history of the Greco-Roman world.* Cambridge University Press, 592–618.

Jouffroy, H. (1986) *La construction publique en Italie et dans l'Afrique romaine.* Strasbourg: AECR.

Kalinowski, A. (2002) 'The Vedii Antonini: aspects of patronage and benefaction in second-century Ephesos', *Phoenix* 56: 109–49.

King, A. (1999) 'Diet in the Roman world: a regional inter-site comparison of mammal bones', *Journal of Roman Archaeology* 12: 168–202.

Kokkinia, Ch. (2000) *Die Opramoas-Inschrift von Rhodiapolis: Euergetismus und soziale Elite in Lykien.* Bonn: Habelt.

Laistner, M. L. W. (1951) *Christianity and pagan culture in the later Roman Empire.* Ithaca: Cornell University Press.

Lanckoronski, K., G. Niemann and E. Petersen (1890–2) *Städte Pamphyliens und Pisidiens,* 2 vols. Paris: Firmin-Didot and Vienna: F. Tempsky.

Lane Fox, R. (1986) *Pagans and Christians.* Harmondsworth: Penguin.

Laum, B. (1914) *Stiftungen in der griechischen und römischen Antike: ein Beitrag zur antiken Kulturgeschichte,* 2 vols. Leipzig and Berlin: Teubner.

Lewis, N. (1974) *Greek historical documents. The Roman Principate: 27 BC–285 AD.* Toronto: Hakkert.

Liebenam, W. (1900) *Städteverwaltung im römischen Kaiserreiche.* Leipzig: Duncker & Humblot.

Ligt, L. de (1993) *Fairs and markets in the Roman Empire: economic and social aspects of periodic trade in a pre-industrial society.* Amsterdam: Gieben.

Lomas, K. and T. J. Cornell (eds.) (2003) *'Bread and circuses': euergetism and municipal patronage in Roman Italy.* London: Routledge.

MacMullen, R. (1974) *Roman social relations 50 BC to AD 284.* New Haven and London: Yale University Press.

(1982) 'The epigraphic habit in the Roman Empire', *American Journal of Philology* 103: 233–46.

(1988) *Corruption and the decline of Rome.* New Haven and London: Yale University Press.

Magie, D. (1950) *Roman rule in Asia Minor to the end of the third century after Christ,* 2 vols. Princeton: Princeton University Press.

Marrou, H.-I. (1948) *Histoire de l'éducation dans l'Antiquité.* Paris: Seuil.

Matthews, J. F. (1984) 'The tax-law of Palmyra: evidence for economic history in a city of the Roman east', *Journal of Roman Studies* 74: 157–80.

Mauss, M. (1967) *The gift: forms and functions of exchange in archaic societies.* New York: Norton.

McLean, B. H. (2002) *An introduction to Greek epigraphy of the Hellenistic and Roman periods from Alexander the Great down to the reign of Constantine (323 BC–AD 337).* Ann Arbor: University of Michigan Press.

Meyer, E. A. (1990) 'Explaining the epigraphic habit in the Roman Empire: the evidence of epitaphs', *Journal of Roman Studies* 80: 74–96.

Migeotte, L. (1997) 'L'Évergétisme des citoyens aux périodes classique et hellénistique' in: M. Christol and O. Masson (eds.) *Actes du xe congrès international d'épigraphique grecque et latine.* Paris: Université de Paris-Sorbonne, 183–96.

Millar, F. (1993) 'The Greek city in the Roman period' in: M. H. Hansen (ed.) *The ancient Greek city-state.* Copenhagen: Royal Danish Academy of Sciences and Letters, 232–60.

Mitchell, S. (1987) 'Imperial building in the eastern Roman provinces', *Harvard Studies in Classical Philology* 91: 332–64.

   (1990) 'Festivals, games and civic life in Roman Asia Minor', *Journal of Roman Studies* 80: 183–93.

   (1993) *Anatolia: land, men, and gods in Asia Minor* I. *The Celts and the impact of Roman rule.* Oxford University Press.

Mrozek, S. (1987) *Les distributions d'argent et de nourriture dans les villes italiennes du Haut-Empire romain.* Brussels: Latomus.

Muir, E. (1981) *Civic ritual in Renaissance Venice.* Princeton: Princeton University Press.

Neugebauer, O. and H. B. van Hoesen (1959) *Greek horoscopes.* Philadelphia: American Philosophical Society.

Nijf, O. M. van (1997) *The civic world of professional associations in the Roman east.* Amsterdam: Gieben.

   (2001) 'Local heroes: athletics, festivals and elite self-fashioning in the Roman East' in: S. Goldhill (ed.), 306–34.

   (2003) 'Athletics, *andreia* and the *askêsis*-culture in the Roman east' in: R. M. Rosen and I. Sluiter (eds.) Andreia: *studies in manliness and courage in classical antiquity.* Leiden: Brill, 263–86.

Ober, J. (1989) *Mass and elite in democratic Athens: rhetoric, ideology and the power of the people.* Princeton: Princeton University Press.

Parrish, D. (ed.) (2001) *Urbanism in western Asia Minor: new studies on Aphrodisias, Ephesos, Hierapolis, Pergamon, Perge and Xanthos* (*JRA* Suppl. 45). Portsmouth, RI: Journal of Roman Archaeology.

Patterson, J. R. (2003) 'The emperor and the cities of Italy' in: Lomas and Cornell (2003), 89–104.

Pera, R. (1984) *Homonoia sulle monete da Augusto agli Antonini.* Genoa: Il Melangolo.

Pleket, H. W. (1971) 'Sociale stratificatie en sociale mobiliteit in de Romeinse Keizertijd', *Tijdschrift voor Geschiedenis* 84: 215–51.

   (1994) 'Troostdecreten: een maatschappelijk verschijnsel' in: H. F. J. Horstmanshoff (ed.) *Pijn en balsem, troost en smart: pijnbeleving en pijnbestrijding in de Oudheid.* Rotterdam: Erasmus, 147–56, 224.

   (1998) 'Political culture and political practice in the cities of Asia Minor in the Roman Empire' in: W. Schuller (ed.) *Politische Theorie und Praxis im Altertum.* Darmstadt: Wissenschaftliche Buchgesellschaft, 204–16.

Pocock, J. G. A. (1976) 'The classical theory of deference', *The American Historical Review* 81: 516–23.

Price, S. R. F. (1984) *Rituals and power: the Roman imperial cult in Asia Minor.* Cambridge University Press.

Quass, F. (1993) *Die Honoratiorenschicht in den Städten des griechischen Ostens: Untersuchungen zur politischen und sozialen Entwicklung in hellenistischer und römischer Zeit.* Stuttgart: Steiner.

Reynolds, J. M. (1988) 'Cities' in: D. Braund (ed.) *The administration of the Roman Empire, 241 BC–AD 193.* Exeter: University of Exeter, 15–51.

(1991) 'Epigraphic evidence for the construction of the theatre: 1st c. BC to mid 3rd c. AD' in: R. R. R. Smith and Kenan T. Erim (eds.) *Aphrodisias Papers 2: the theatre, a sculptor's workshop, philosophers, and coin-types. Including the papers given at the Third International Aphrodisias Colloquium held at New York University on 7 and 8 April, 1989 (JRA* Suppl. 2). Ann Arbor: Journal of Roman Archaeology, 15–28.

(1996) 'Honouring benefactors at Aphrodisias: a new inscription' in: Ch. Roueché and R. R. R. Smith (eds.) *Aphrodisias Papers 3: the setting and quarries, mythological and other sculptural decoration, architectural development, Portico of Tiberius, and Tetrapylon (JRA* Suppl. 20). Ann Arbor: *Journal of Roman Archaeology*, 121–6.

Rhodes, P. J. and D. M. Lewis (1997) *The decrees of the Greek states.* Oxford University Press.

Robert, L. (1949) 'Sur une monnaie de Synnada: Τροφεύς', *Hellenica* 7: 74–81.

(1960) 'Tome VII: Τροφεύς et Ἀριστεύς', *Hellenica* 11/12: 569–76.

(1966) *Documents de l'Asie Mineure méridionale.* Paris: Minard.

Rogers, G. M. (1991a) *The sacred identity of Ephesos: foundation myths of a Roman city.* London and New York: Routledge.

(1991b) 'Demosthenes of Oenoanda and models of euergetism', *Journal of Roman Studies* 81: 91–100.

Rossum, J. A. van (1988) 'De gerousia in de Griekse steden van het Romeinse Rijk'. Unpublished PhD thesis, Leiden University.

Rostovtzeff, M. (1926) *The social and economic history of the Roman Empire.* Oxford: The Clarendon Press.

Roueché, Ch. (1984) 'Acclamations in the later Roman Empire: new evidence from Aphrodisias', *Journal of Roman Studies* 74: 181–99.

Runciman, W. G. (1990) 'Doomed to extinction: the polis as an evolutionary dead-end' in: O. Murray and S. R. F. Price (eds.) *The Greek city from Homer to Alexander.* Oxford University Press, 347–67.

Sahlins, M. (1972) *Stone age economics.* Chicago: Aldine-Atherton.

Saller, R. (1994) *Patriarchy, property and death in the Roman family.* Cambridge University Press.

Salmeri, G. (2000) 'Dio, Rome, and the civic life of Asia Minor' in: S. Swain (ed.) *Dio Chrysostom: politics, letters and philosophy.* Oxford University Press, 53–92.

Sartre, M. (1991) *L'Orient romain: provinces et sociétés provinciales en Méditerranée orientale d'Auguste aux Sévères (31 avant J.-C.–235 après J.-C.)*. Paris: Seuil.

Scheidel, W. (1999) 'Emperors, aristocrats and the Grim Reaper: towards a demographic profile of the Roman élite', *Classical Quarterly* 49: 254–81.

(2001a) *Debating Roman demography*. Leiden: Brill.

(2001b) 'Progress and problems in Roman demography' in: Scheidel (2001a), 1–81.

Schuler, Ch. (1998) *Ländliche Siedlungen und Gemeinden im hellenistischen und römischen Kleinasien*. Munich: Beck.

Schulte, C. (1994) *Die Grammateis von Ephesos: Schreiberamt und Sozialstruktur in einer Provinzhaubtstadt des römischen Kaiserreiches*. Stuttgart: Steiner.

Schwarz, H. (2001) *Soll oder Haben? Die Finanzwirtschaft kleinasiatischer Städte in der römischen Kaiserzeit am Beispiel von Bithynien, Lykien und Ephesos (29 v. Chr.–284 n. Chr.)*. Bonn: Habelt.

Sen, A. (1982) *Poverty and famines: an essay on entitlement and deprivation*. Oxford University Press.

Sherwin-White, A. N. (1966) *The letters of Pliny: a historical and social commentary*. Oxford: Clarendon Press.

Smallwood, E. M. (1967) *Documents illustrating the Principates of Gaius, Claudius and Nero*. Cambridge University Press.

Stahl, M. (1978) *Imperiale Herrschaft und provinziale Stadt: Strukturprobleme der römischen Reichsorganisation im 1.-3. Jh. der Kaiserzeit*. Göttingen: Vandenhoeck & Ruprecht.

Ste. Croix, G. E. M. de (1981) *The class struggle in the ancient Greek world: from the Archaic age to the Arab conquest*. London: Duckworth.

Steskal, M. (2001) 'Zu den Stiftungen des M. Claudius P. Vedius Antoninus Phaedrus Sabinianus und ihrem Echo in Ephesos', *Tyche* 16: 177–88.

Strubbe, J. H. M. (1987) 'The sitonia in the cities of Asia Minor under the Principate (I)', *Epigraphica Anatolica* 10: 45–82.

(1989) 'The sitonia in the cities of Asia Minor under the Principate (II)', *Epigraphica Anatolica* 13: 97–122.

Swain, S. (1996) *Hellenism and empire: language, classicism, and power in the Greek world, AD 50–250*. Oxford: Clarendon Press.

Tacoma, L. E. (2006) *Fragile hierarchies: the urban elites of third century Roman Egypt*. Leiden: Brill.

Tarn, W. W. and G. T. Griffith (1952) *Hellenistic civilisation*. London: Arnold.

Thomas, E. and C. Witschel (1992) 'Constructing reconstruction: claim and reality of Roman rebuilding inscriptions from the Latin west', *Papers of the British School at Rome* 40: 135–78.

Thomas, R. (1992) *Literacy and orality in ancient Greece*. Cambridge University Press.

Thompson, E. P. (1971) 'The moral economy of the English crowd in the eighteenth century', *Past and Present* 50: 76–136.

(1991) *Customs in common: studies in traditional popular culture*. London: Merlin Press.

Veyne, P. (1976) *Le pain et le cirque: sociologie historique d'un pluralisme politique.* Paris: Seuil.

(1990) *Bread and circuses: historical sociology and political pluralism*, trans. B. Pearce. London: Viking.

Ward-Perkins, J. B. (1947) 'The Italian element in late Roman and early medieval architecture', *Proceedings of the British Academy* 33: 1–31.

Wilson, A. (2002) 'Machines, power and the ancient economy', *Journal of Roman Studies* 92: 1–32.

Wörrle, M. (1975) 'Zwei neue Inschriften aus Myra zur Verwaltung Lykiens in der Kaiserzeit' in: J. Borchhardt (ed.) *Myra: eine Lykische Metropole in antiker und byzantinischer Zeit.* Berlin: Gebr. Mann Verlag, 254–300.

(1988) *Stadt und Fest im kaiserzeitlichen Kleinasien.* Munich: Beck.

Yegül, F. K. (1975) 'The bath-gymnasium complex in Asia Minor during the Roman era'. Unpublished PhD thesis, Harvard University.

(1982) 'A study in architectural iconography: *Kaisersaal* and the imperial cult', *The Art Bulletin* 64.1: 7–31.

(1986) *The bath-gymnasium complex at Sardis.* Cambridge, Mass. and London: Harvard University Press.

(1991) 'Roman architecture in the Greek World', *Journal of Roman Archaeology* 4: 345–55.

(2000) 'Memory, metaphor, and meaning in the cities of Asia Minor' in: E. Fentress (ed.) *Romanization and the city: creation, transformation, and failure. Proceedings of a conference held at the American Academy in Rome to celebrate the 50th anniversary of the excavations at Cosa, 14–16 May, 1998 (JRA* Suppl. 38). Portsmouth, RI: Journal of Roman Archaeology, 133–53.

Zuiderhoek, A. (2005) 'The icing on the cake: benefactors, economics, and public building in Roman Asia Minor' in: S. Mitchell and C. Katsari (eds.) *Patterns in the economy of Roman Asia Minor.* Swansea: The Classical Press of Wales, 167–86.

(2007) 'The ambiguity of munificence', *Historia* 55: 196–213.

(2008) 'Feeding the citizens: municipal grain funds and civic benefactors in the Roman east' in: R. Alston and O. M. van Nijf (eds.) *Groningen–Royal Holloway studies on the Greek city after the Classical Age* I. *Feeding the ancient Greek city.* Leuven: Peeters, 159–80.

(forthcoming) 'Oligarchs and benefactors: elite demography and euergetism in the Greek east of the Roman Empire' in: R. Alston and O. M. van Nijf (eds.) *Groningen–Royal Holloway studies on the Greek city after the Classical Age* II. *Political culture in the post-Classical city.* Leuven: Peeters.

Index

CPSIA information can be obtained
at www.ICGtesting.com
Printed in the USA
LVHW010910290721
693967LV00008B/365

9 781108 994033